The Sullivan Saga: Memories of an Overseas Childhood

The Sullivan Saga:

Memories of an Overseas Childhood

M. H. Sullivan

Romagnoli Publications

Copyright © 2023 by Maureen H. Sullivan

All rights reserved. No part of this publication may be reproduced, stored, or transmitted in any form or by any means, electronic, mechanical, photocopying, recording, scanning, or otherwise without written permission from the copyright owner. It is illegal to copy this book, post it to a website, or distribute it by any other means without prior permission of the copyright owner.

This book was printed in the United States of America.

First Edition

ISBN-13: 978-1-891486-26-5 (hardcover)

ISBN-13: 978-1-891486-13-5 (paperback)

ISBN-13: 978-1-891486-11-1 (ebook)

Cover designed by Lisa M. Romagnoli

Romagnoli Publications
Manchester, NH, USA

email: romagnoli.publications@gmail.com

website: www.romagnoli-publications.com

For my daughters:
Lisa & Beth

The whole object of travel is not to set foot on foreign land; it is at last to set foot on one's own country as a foreign land.

~ G.K. Chesterton.

Table of Contents

Chapter 1 Prologue: Return of the Native 1
    Fall 1968, Freshman, University of Montana, Missoula, MT....... 1

Chapter 2 From Maryland to Korea, September, 1957 ... 5
    The Move 5
    The Sullivan Family, circa 1957

Chapter 3 Seoul, South Korea (1957 - 1962) 10
    Moving to Seoul 10
    First House: Shin Dang-Dong
    (Near the East Gate) 1957 – 1958 12
    Playing at Shin Dang-Dong 14
    First Christmas at Shin Dang-Dong 17
    Shin Dang-Dong and the Slicky boys 19
    First School: Seoul Foreign School
    (1957-1958) 21
    Singing Protestant Songs 21
    Mike & Denny Find a Bomb 22
    Catholic School - Sacred Heart Academy
    (1958 - 1959) 23
    Second House: Itaewon (1958 - 1959) 25
    Third House: Life on Yongsan Army Garrison, South Post
    (1959–1962) 27
    Our Pets: Cats, Dogs, Chickens & a Duck 28
    South Post: Living on a Military Base 29
    My Mother's Activities in Korea 33
    OEC Picnic at King's Tomb 34

Chapter 4 Intermission—Our Home Leaves 37
    Home Leave of 1959 37
    Home Leave of 1962 39
    Saying Farewell to the Relatives 44

Chapter 5   Taipei, Taiwan (1962 – 1964) 47
   Grass Mountain – Yangminshan 48
   The Neighborhood 49
   The Plum Club 50
   Exploring Grass Mountain 50
   Formosa, "Snake Island" 53
   Our House on Grass Mountain 54
   Stealing Tangerines 55
   The Difference between Firecrackers and Bombs 56
   Neighborhood Activities 58
   Halloween and the Taiwanese Children 59
   Earthquakes 60
   The Great Alaskan Earthquake of 1964 61
   Typhoon & Floods 62
   The City of Taipei 62
   Denny at 16 63
   My Mother's Parties 64
   Our Pets in Taiwan 66
   Preteens in Taipei 67
   World Events 68
   Becoming a Teenager 69

Chapter 6   Manila, Philippine Islands (1964 – 1966) 71
   The Sullivan Kids, circa 1964 71
   Our Mid-Tour Move to the Philippines 72
   The Beatles in Hong Kong 74
   Choosing a Catholic Girls School 76
   The Move to Manila 77
   Our House at 26 Cambridge Circle, Forbes Park Estates,
   Makati, a Suburb of Manila 78
   Mike and the LaSalle School for Boys 80
   The American School in Manila 81
   Being a Teenager in Manila 83

Life in the Philippines...84
Gabe, Our Driver 85
Christmas in a Christian Country 86
Easter in the Philippines...87
Beaches in the Philippines..88
Visit to Corregidor 89
Pagsanjan Falls 90
Going to the PX and Commissary..92
Pets in the Philippines 93
Home Leave of 1965..94
Jamie's Birthday and the Round Table......................................95
Next Post: Bangkok, Thailand 97

Chapter 7   Bangkok, Thailand (1966 – 1967).................. 99
The Sullivan Kids, circa 1966 99
Welcome to Bangkok, Part 1 – May, 1966 to May, 1967.........100
The Erawan Hotel..100
The House in Bangkabua 101
The Thai Neighborhood..105
The Spoon Incident 106
Pets in Bangkok: The Monkey 107
Tropical Pests 112
Family Lingo..113
Summer School at ISB..113
ISB, International School of Bangkok.....................................115
Bangkok, "Teen Heaven" 116
The Teen Club...117
Settling in to Thailand 119
Holidays at Pattaya Beach 120
Judy Harper...121
Easter, 1967 – Air America to Vientiane, Laos......................122
Seeing Thailand – Trips Outside Bangkok 124

**Chapter 8   Intermission – Home Leave -
June to Dec., 1967** **126**
    The Long Home Leave 126

Chapter 9   Hawaii (Aug. – Dec., 1967) **131**
    The Sullivan Kids, circa August, 1967 131
    Home in Hawaii 132
    Kalani High School 132
    Jerry at Kaimuki Middle School 133
    The "Little Kids" go to the Catholic School 133
    Our House at 3741 Lurline Drive, Wilhelmina Rise, Kaimuki. 134
    The Red Sox World Series 1967 136
    Sunday Breakfast or Dinner at Makapu'u 139
    The New Paperboy 141
    Pets in Hawaii 141
    The Genius Kid Down the Block 142
    The BB Gun Incident 143
    Penny, the Nanny 144
    Winter Surf at Waimea 144
    Return to Bangkok 147

Chapter 10   Bangkok, Thailand (1967 - 1968) **149**
    The Sullivan Kids, circa 1967 149
    Welcome (Back) to Bangkok – Dec. 1967 to Dec. 1968 150
    Our Bangsue house 151
    Life in Bangkok, The Second Time Around 152
    Mike's Car Accident April, 1968 153
    Senior Skip Day 155

Chapter 11   Addis Ababa, Ethiopia (1968 – 1972) **157**
    The Sullivan Kids, circa 1968 157
    Surprise Move to Africa 158
    Addis Ababa, Ethiopia, located on the Ethiopian Highlands,
    altitude 8000 ft. above sea level 160

Our First House near the Airport.. 161
Owning Horses in Addis 162
Our Second Addis House 164
Field Mice 168
Family Pets in Ethiopia... 170
My First Visit to Ethiopia.. 171
The Kingdom of Ethiopia.. 172
Summer of 1969 in Addis 176
Shopping at the Mercato... 177
Camping at Lake Langano 178
Arage 182
Moonwalk – Apollo 11, July 20, 1969 183
Hippos in Lake Langano... 184
Dating in Addis... 185

Chapter 12   Home Leave – Summer of 1970 191
Hawaii Reunion Summer of 1970 191
Trip through Asia.. 192
Nairobi, Kenya.. 194
My Father and the Army Ants.. 195

Chapter 13   Addis Ababa, Ethiopia (1970 – 1972) 197
The Sullivan Kids, circa 1970 197
Addis, Fall of 1970... 198
Trips around Ethiopia 198
Plays, Addis Style... 200
Turkey Soup.. 203
My 20th Birthday.. 204
My Last Family Trip... 205
Back to the States 205
A Death in the Family.. 206

Chapter 14 Epilogue 209
Fall of 1972, Boston University, Senior Year 209
The End of a Chapter; Not the End of the Story 211

Aftermath: Our lives and fortunes, 1972 – 2010 212
In Memoriam 216

Chapter 15   Appendix:
My Mother's Christmas Letters **217**

Christmas 1958 218
Christmas 1960 221
Christmas 1962 226
Christmas 1963 229
Christmas 1964 233
Christmas 1965 237
Christmas 1966 243
Christmas 1967 249
Christmas 1968 254
Christmas 1969 258
Christmas 1970 264
Christmas 1971 270
Christmas 1972 277
About the Author: M.H. Sullivan 283

Chapter 1   Prologue: Return of the Native

Fall 1968, Freshman, University of Montana, Missoula, MT

It was overcast, cold, and spitting rain and snowflakes on the streets of Missoula as I stared down from my dorm room on the 10th floor of Jesse Hall. Jesse Hall was the freshmen women's dorm at the University of Montana. This was 1968 and I was a freshman, 17 years old, away from home for the first time. Three months before, I had been living in Bangkok, Thailand. It had been the end of June, 90-plus degrees, sunny, and the air was so humid you could watch the droplets of moisture forming on your skin as you baked in the tropical sun.

I sighed as I glanced down at the postcard in my hand. It was an invitation from the university inviting me to a foreign exchange student meeting. How very welcoming, you might say.   Except that I wasn't a foreign exchange student. I was as American as my roommate, Karen, who was born and raised in Big Sandy, Montana. In fact, I think I could even be considered MORE American because I was born in Washington, D.C., our nation's capital. What could be more American than that?

But the doubt was there, too. Was I American enough? Sure, my mother's family had been in America since at least the French & Indian War and before. Her grandparents carted 13 children across the country in a covered wagon and settled them in the Dakotas and Nebraska.   My father was third-generation Irish-American.

His grandparents had escaped Ireland's Potato Famine along with thousands of other hungry immigrants. They faced discrimination and the challenges of surviving in the tenements of South Boston and the mill cities of western Massachusetts. How American was that?

So if my heritage was so unassailably American, why was I standing there with an invitation to a meeting of foreign exchange students in my hand? I flipped the card over; and yes, it was definitely addressed to me: Maureen H. Sullivan. No mistake had been made there.

I could call them up and let them know that I didn't belong at the foreign exchange student meeting. It was an honest mistake; I bore no hard feelings. They saw "Bangkok, Thailand" in my parents' address and naturally assumed.

But as I looked back over the previous ten years I wasn't certain that I didn't belong at the foreign exchange student meeting. After all, when people ask me, "Where are you from?" I invariably hesitated, not really knowing what to say. Should it be "Bangkok, Thailand" because that's where my parents were living? Should I say "Washington, D.C." because that's where I was born, or perhaps "Rockville, Maryland" because that was my hometown before we went overseas? Or even "Honolulu, Hawaii" because my parents bought a house there in 1959 and that was considered my "official" home residence even though the longest we'd ever lived in the house was five months?

It's a problem for kids like me – overseas brats, third-culture kids, American dependents of diplomats or the U.S. military – to have this problem with the semantics of the otherwise simple question "Where are you from?" The intent of the question is to place you in some context, to begin to know you. Like everyone else, I have my "elevator speech" of who I am: " I was born in Washington, D.C. My father works for the State Department and I was raised overseas in Korea, Taiwan, the Philippines, Thailand, and Ethiopia."

That answers the question but it is apparently quite intimidating and is generally received with one giant step back. People don't know what to make of me or of my background. They wonder if I am bragging? Or is my family rich? At any rate, all that world travel and exotic experience isn't conducive to creating comfort in my peers or a sense of camaraderie. Like an alien, I have discovered I am a stranger in my own country.

There is a term for this type of alienation – culture shock. Usually it refers to what an American experiences when they are plunked down in a foreign country and they have to quickly learn to fend for themselves. But, kids like me experience culture shock in reverse, for us it happens when we come "home" to the States. And it is sometimes worse because it is totally unexpected.

We were nominally "Americans", after all. In fact, I had traveled more miles across the United States than most of my peers. When my family came home on our "home leave" every two or three years, my parents made it a point to take us to visit the National Parks, to Disneyland, to the San Diego zoo, to the Empire State Building, or to the World's Fair. We'd seen much of our country, spoke the language, and felt an affection and pride for America that I realized much later, was based on seeing our country from a gauzy top-down global viewpoint. It turns out that it wasn't the same kind of affection and pride that my fellow homegrown Americans felt for the place they had always lived.

We may have known our country, but we were like those German spies in old World War II movies where they can't answer the folksy questions about the Chicago Cubs. Ah ha! It proved they aren't one of us! And it's true. We don't feel the reassuring security of being "from someplace" where people know your name, your family and your history. Instead we have a different set of skills – mobile skills, if you will. We know how to maneuver in new places, to learn our way around, to feel at ease in discomforting situations, to entertain ourselves and to be OK with ambiguity. Good skills, to be sure, but they don't make you many friends.

I used to think that if only I could explain what it was really like to be raised overseas, then maybe people would understand how alike we are in so many ways. After all, I was raised in an American family. I went to English-speaking schools. I learned to ride a bicycle, dressed up in costume and went trick-or-treating at Halloween, took dance classes, played sports, listened to rock music, went to dances, watched movies, did homework, and experienced just about everything kids my age did back in the States. Sure, it was different. We could only trick-or-treat at the homes of other Americans, our music was usually six months behind the times, and newly released movies didn't reach us sometimes for a year. And, oh yeah, our neighbors spoke a foreign language. We were often exposed to abject poverty and there were dozens of vaccinations we had to get each year against diseases we couldn't even pronounce. But we were kids and kids are pretty much the same everywhere. Really.

We were The Sullivans, a family of seven children — six boys and me, the only girl. I used to find it a little embarrassing when people pointed out my only-ness to me. What was it like to be the only girl with all those brothers? They had asked.

The answer is that there were positives and negatives to being the only girl, surrounded by six brothers. The positives were that I never had to wear hand-me-down clothes, and usually, I had my own bedroom. Rarely did I have a toy or game that my brothers wanted so I didn't have to fight to protect my stuff. I was lucky that in simply being the only girl, I didn't have to vie for position or attention and could opt out of any can't-win battle by resorting to tears.

The negatives were mostly in not having a sister to share "girl stuff" with and sometimes being sidelined from "boy games" when my brothers didn't absolutely need another player. I used to rail against the unfairness of missing out simply because I was "a girl" (I once stubbornly sat on home plate to protest not being allowed to play). After all, how could gender be the basis for being included or not? I wondered. I was lucky to come of age in the late 1960's when I wasn't the only female wondering what was wrong with that picture. Still, being left out meant a certain amount of solitariness, which may have been a positive where maturity is concerned, but felt like a lonely negative at the time.

What was living overseas really like? For me, it all began in Rockville, Maryland.

Chapter 2 From Maryland to Korea, September, 1957

The Move

I was six years old, nearly seven, and entering the second grade when my family left the United States for Korea in September of 1957.

I don't remember being asked at the time how I felt about moving overseas. No one thinks to ask the six year old. My mother, four brothers and I moved because of my father's career. He worked for the U.S. State Department and living overseas was part of his job description.

Home in Rockville, Maryland

It had also been his dream to travel and live in foreign lands, so he felt lucky and excited in 1956 when he received his first overseas assignment to Seoul, South Korea. It was three years after the Korean War and my father saw it as a huge opportunity.

My mother had a bit of the wanderlust, too. She had met my father in 1944 at the University of Colorado where she was a student and he was enrolled in the Navy's language school studying Mandarin Chinese. I'm sure that appealed to her since, as the story goes, when she was a preschooler back in Omaha, she tried to dig a hole to China in her backyard.

She couldn't wait to join my father in Korea and as soon as they allowed families to go, there was no question but that we'd be on the next available flight.

I was too young to question my life and ask if it was "normal". What kid does? But looking back, I admit that my world view was a bit distorted at the time. For instance, I had no idea that Korea was a separate country or for that matter, what the word "foreign" meant. Children are very accepting travelers; which is probably the best kind.

Leaving America in 1957 was like going on a grand expedition into the unknown. It took a lot of careful planning and organizing and a certain amount of bravado.

There were immunizations and physicals to be had, passports to acquire, and lots and lots of packing. My poor mother had to do it all alone since my father was already in Korea. Well, if you can call having five children under the age of 10 "alone". It's quite a picture imagining her packing up our house in Rockville, Maryland. She was pregnant with my brother, Jamie, surrounded by the rest of us, her five other children ranging in age from the oldest, Denny, who was ten, down to Pat, who had just turned two on July 4th. I have to guess that total naiveté was at the root of her bravery.

What I remember most about the trip were the long flights and that the stewardesses thought it would be "so sweet" if I helped them give out the Chiclets chewing gum to the other passengers. These were unpressurized propeller planes and they used to give out gum to help passengers relieve some of the inner ear discomfort during take-offs and landings.

I loved at least one thing about the Pan Am Pacific Clipper jets that flew us across the Pacific: they had beds that folded down from the ceiling like railway sleepers. My mother would tuck three of us under a blanket and we slept pretty much all the way from Anchorage, Alaska, through the island hopping fuel stops at Wake Island and Guam and Okinawa until finally, nineteen hours later, we arrived in Tokyo. My father met us at the airport and then we spent the next day or two trying to acclimate to the massive time difference before continuing on the last leg to our new home in Seoul.

Jerry, Maureen, Mike, Denny, 1957

Denny

Mike

Reeny

The Sullivan Family, circa 1957

When we arrived in Seoul, South Korea, in September of 1957, there were five children in my family:

> *Dennis (Denny), age 10*
>
> *Michael (Mikey), age 8*
>
> *[me] Maureen (Reeny), age 6*
>
> *Robert (Jerry), age 4*
>
> *Patrick (Patty), age 2.*
>
> *James (Jamie), my fifth brother, was born September 19th, just ten days after we arrived.*
>
> *Christopher (Ku), my sixth and youngest brother, was born in the military hospital on Yongsan military base in January of 1960.*

Jerry

Jamie

Patty

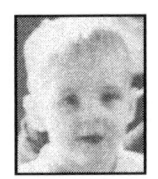

Chris (Ku)

Memories of an Overseas Childhood 9

Chapter 3 Seoul, South Korea (1957 - 1962)

Moving to Seoul

My father had been living in Korea for a year when we — my mother, four brothers and I — arrived. He had been sent by the U.S. State Department to Seoul in 1956 to work for the Office of the Economic Coordinator (OEC) in Korea. OEC was an agency of the ICA (International Cooperation Administration). It was also the precursor of the U.S. Operations Mission (USOM), which later morphed into USAID (U.S. Agency for International Development), the State Department's foreign aid organization, which still exists and operates around the world in developing countries today. My father also worked for the C.I.A. and its precursor agency, the O.S.S. (Office of Strategic Services), but none of us children were aware of that aspect of his work until we read about it in his obituary many years later.

At the time, not only wasn't I aware of my father's job but I don't remember wondering why we were going overseas. That makes sense. I was six years old and my focus was a little more immediate: that of adjusting to first grade at St. Mary's School in Rockville, Maryland, a quiet suburb of Washington, D.C. It was not an easy task for a very shy, left-handed girl having to deal with nuns who felt it was their duty to try to change me into an extroverted right-handed child.

It's actually a tribute to my stubbornness, or perhaps my inability to rise to the occasion, that the introverted left-hander won out. I use the term "won" very loosely. Left-handers never learn to write properly and I don't think I ever received higher than a "C" in Handwriting in all my elementary school years. I also remained shy and introverted until late in my high school and early college years. As any truly shy person knows, you never really grow out of it, so much as you learn ways to accommodate it and shield it from others. In that way it's like any other handicap, because underneath it all, I'm still self-conscious and tongue-tied on occasion and I don't think I'll ever feel comfortable walking into a room full of strangers. The difference now is that I have learned how to do it and can even fool that room full of strangers into believing that I don't mind. Even so, I can't help but wish the nuns had won that long-ago battle. Parts of my life would have been so much less stressful.

Dad at work in Korea

Korea, to a six year old, is not the same Korea that my parents experienced. I don't pretend to describe what they saw; I can only describe how I viewed it and I'm aware that what I describe may very well be wrong. It is, after all, the view of a very young child and memory is a fragile vessel.

For example, I didn't know, for the longest time, that Korea was a different country. I guess I thought it was just another state located somewhere in the far, far west. I also didn't "get" that the squiggly marks on Korean signs were of another language, one that other people could read and understand, even though I couldn't. It's just as well that I didn't know. After all, I had just finished a year of learning to read about Dick and Jane, and felt pretty full of myself over my awesome command of the ABC's. It might have been discouraging to discover at so tender an age that there was yet much I didn't know about the world.

First House: Shin Dang-Dong (Near the East Gate) 1957 – 1958

We moved into a Japanese-style house in the Shin Dang-Dong section of Seoul. I'm sure I would feel differently about life overseas if we had immediately moved onto the military base and its quasi-American lifestyle. We did move on base a few years later, to a ranch-style house on South Post, and to this day, it's my notion of what it would have been like to have been raised in a neighborhood in America. Still, I'm glad that our first experience overseas was living off base, often described as living "on the local economy", and among the Korean people.

The house we rented that first year was a Japanese-style house in a walled compound that we shared with our Japanese landlady. By "Japanese-style house", I mean that it had tatami floors (woven straw mat) and rice paper sliding doors between rooms.

We left our shoes at the front door, a habit most of us haven't outgrown even now. The house was exotic and wonderful. I can't imagine how many of those rice paper doors were re-papered in our year of living in the house – but with six children under the age of 10, and a total of 60 little fingers that loved the feeling (not to mention the soft popping sound) of poking through that soft paper – well, all I can say is that my folks probably should have bought stock in rice paper futures.

Tatami floors

We arrived in the fall of 1957 with cool days just beginning and a cold winter on the horizon; but we didn't have to worry. The house was heated with radiant heat that rose up from below the first floor. The upper floor where we all slept was unheated, so in the winter months we spent most of the daylight hours on the first floor of the house. My younger brother, Jerry, and I would climb under the carpeting in the living room to revel in the warmth emanating from the floors beneath.

Jerry & Dad at Shin Dang-Dong house, Korea, 1958

"Radiant heat" sounds very modern; so let me explain that the heat for the house was created by little coal fires kept burning at the ends of tunnels that ran under the first floor of the house. These tunnels, we later discovered, also harbored colonies of rats during the rest of the year and I have vivid (and sad to say, enjoyable) memories of accompanying the servants on the daily rounds of drowning cages of rats each morning. The cages would be set out in the evening using rice as bait, and the next morning we would walk around and inspect the little thieves trapped in the cages. The servant would then take each cage and submerge it in a large earthen vat of water. To be honest, I don't recall being horrified by the drowning. The rats were pretty nasty looking creatures.

Another touch of the exotic was the bathtub on the first floor of the house (there was no bathroom upstairs). It was a Japanese "Ofuro" bathtub.

These tubs are deep enough for total immersion up to the neck and are twice as large as the average American bathtub and are designed for sitting and soaking in, not unlike the hot tubs of today. Of course, back then we didn't have hot running water, so the servants

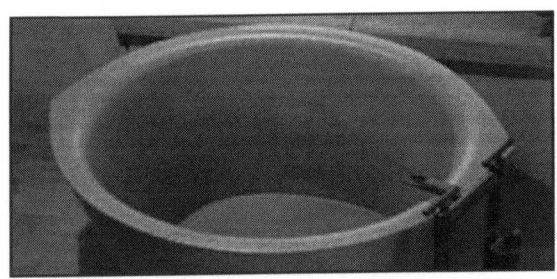

Ofuro bathtub

had to heat water on the stove in the kitchen and painstakingly carry it to the bathroom to fill the tub. Needless to say, the water didn't go to waste and we all bathed in the same water.

Playing at Shin Dang-Dong

In Korea in the late 1950's we had no TV entertainment, not that there was that much back in the States either. In fact, we didn't own a television set while we were living in Korea. We did have a television five years later when we moved to Taiwan, but even then, there was only one or two shows in English per night. I vaguely recall weekly episodes of *Rawhide* and *Combat*, which might partially explain why foreigners have such skewed views of America and Americans.

In Korea, though, we did have the Armed Forces radio station on base that played old radio shows in the evening that I could pick up with my little transistor radio. I had an earphone (stereophonic reception was still in the future) that I hid under my pillow at night so I could listen to the shows after I went to bed. I got to know all the old radio shows that my grandparents probably listened to – *The Great Gildersleeve, Gunsmoke, Johnny Dollar, Groucho Marx, Jack Benny, My Little Margie,* and many more. Later on, when I would talk about these shows I found I had more in common with people 20 or 40 years older than myself than I did with kids my own age.

This lack of entertainment technology meant we were left to our own devices and imaginations. This is one area where a large family really comes into its own, because we were very good at entertaining ourselves. We played board games, elaborate war games with large sets of two-inch plastic soldiers or cowboys-and-Indians complete with white, brown and black horses. I didn't care much for the soldier games, but I did have a thing for the horses in the cowboys-and-Indians sets. Sometimes I would steal all the horses and create huge herds of wild stallions. I also played with my dolls and stuffed animals while my brothers played with their cap pistols and toy rifles, but most of all, we developed great imaginations and we always had playmates in each other to play with.

One of our favorite group activities was building "forts." We built them outside if the weather cooperated, with whatever materials were available – pieces of scrap lumber and boxes if we were outdoors. If we were inside, we built them with pillows, blankets and sheets that sometimes would cover the entire living room and dining room areas.

We spent a lot of time playing "army" in our fort in the side yard at Shin Dang-Dong.

Our fort in backyard of Shin Dang-Dong

My older brothers usually let me play simply because there were only four of us available (my younger two brothers – Pat and Jamie – were too young: at the time, Pat was only two and Jamie was an infant). Naturally, given a choice, my brothers preferred playing against a "real" enemy than an invisible one, especially when chasing, shooting and pretend-dying were involved. While the shooting and dying might be fictional, occasionally, things did escalate into real fist fights, shoving matches, and the inevitable tears and crying. Mostly, though, we got along fairly well.

If nothing else, living in a large family teaches you negotiating skills (how to trade without losing your good stuff) and pecking order (who has the first and last say, and the seat by the window in the car). There was no choice.

Sometimes I didn't want to play with my brothers, preferring my dolls and my own play world to their war games. At other times, especially if they had a friend or two over to play, even if I wanted to join in, I was relegated to a role as "the nurse" or "the Indian squaw". These were, after all, fairly sexist times.

We were lucky to be overseas in a large family, though, particularly given our mobile lifestyle. I had several overseas friends who were 'only children', and I always felt a little sorry for them. Yes, they had more and better "stuff" than we did, but I know we had more fun. There were so many of us and we were close enough in age to enjoy many of the same activities. We were remarkably evenly spaced, as a matter of fact. My mother had a child every two years from 1946 to 1960, until our number had grown to the final count of seven.

Because there were so many of us, we always had playmates, and there was rarely a dull moment with seven creative minds at work! But, in Korea, we were still pretty young. We built forts, played "army", teased the dog, and did all the normal things that kids do – like going to school and waiting for our birthdays and making up elaborate Christmas lists. We may have lived in exotic places but we were still fairly typical kids.

That also meant we occasionally got injured. In fact, there was one summer in Taiwan when my mother was in the military hospital's emergency room with one of us nearly every other week – a broken arm, a sprained ankle, or on an off week, maybe just a few stitches. In Korea, we had a few unscheduled hospital visits, as well.

The only stitches I remember getting were from playing on a homemade swing at the Shin Dang-Dong house. We had hung the swing between two sturdy little trees in the front yard. Basically the swing was made of a sturdy rope strung between the two trees with a thick rectangle of wood as the seat. We could raise and lower the level of the swing by moving the rope up and down from one set of notches on the trees to another.

I played on the swing for hours and taught myself all sorts of simple acrobatic tricks on it. For instance, I would flip myself upside down and swing like a trapeze artist. The key to this trick was to always double-check that the swing was set at the highest notches. Once, when I neglected to check, I flipped upside down and scraped my face along the ground before finally letting go.

Why do scrapes on your face and head bleed so much more than any other part of your body?

I stumbled bleeding and crying into the house and the next thing I knew I was at the local Korean hospital being held down by several nurses while a doctor sewed up a deep cut on my lip. I was told it was important to put in stitches, or "I might never be able to wear lipstick when I grew up". That reasoning held little appeal to me at seven, but I quickly discovered that I had no say in the matter.

It was a frightening and painful ending to a fairly humiliating experience. I tried to figure out how to blame one of my brothers for changing the level of the rope swing, but in the end, I only had myself to blame for not checking. I had several weeks of scratches and scabs to keep the memory and shame of the event fresh.

First Christmas at Shin Dang-Dong

The holidays are hard when you are away from home. But, I suspect they aren't as hard on children as they are on parents. For us kids, Christmas was Christmas wherever we were, once we had been assured that Santa would be able to find us. My parents, though, had to do all the real work to make the Christmas celebration happen.

For one thing, they had to buy the gifts way in advance – in fact, months in advance! Usually our gifts were ordered from a huge four-inch thick Sears catalog and if our prayers were answered, they ordered most of our gifts from the Toys section at the back of the catalog, not from the clothes section in the front. It was either that or they made our gifts. My mother was a whiz with her Singer sewing machine. Occasionally, they found local items to give us as gifts – Korean kites, pointed Korean rubber slip-on shoes, spinning tops or bouncy balls.

Being a girl, I was given a pretty set of Oriental dolls, which apparently were for show and not to be played with. They were adorned in finely crafted silk Korean and Japanese costumes, frozen into elaborate dance poses, and then nailed to wooden pedestals.

Their bodies were all wire and stuffed bits, pathetic as play things to my seven-year-old eyes. Once you take off their glued-on clothing, there was no putting them back on again. Believe me.

Japanese doll

It wasn't just the gifts my parents had to organize, they also had to locate a Christmas-like fir tree and find the ornaments and decorations that may have only just arrived in our shipment of household goods from the States.

All our worldly possessions were shipped via ocean carrier. The crates had to be cleared through Korean Customs, trucked to Seoul from the port of Inchon, and then unpacked in our house in Seoul. It was like a small Christmas when everything arrived and we got to open all the boxes and crates. After so many months of waiting, it was exciting to see all our stuff again. There was even a kind of Christmas-like sense of "surprise" in discovering what did and didn't get lost or damaged in transit.

How was our Christmas at Shin Dang-Dong? For us kids, it was all about toys and food. For my mother, though, it was an opportunity to teach us about sharing the Christian Christmas Spirit with the Korean children who lived in the lean-to shacks in the shantytown outside our gate. I suspect she also wanted to keep us busy, because we were no doubt driving her crazy with Christmas questions, like when it would come, whether Santa would find us, and would we get what we really, really, really wanted?

What she did that first Christmas was to organize us around the kitchen table so that we could wrap up candy into individual packets made of napkins tied with red and green ribbon. By Christmas Eve, we had a huge pile of these little Christmas favors and it was finally time for the distribution phase.

We opened the gates of the compound and started handing them out to the children in the streets outside. Within minutes we had dozens, and then a surging crowd of children all with their hands in the air begging for these Christmas treats. By the time we were done, every child under the age of twelve in a two or three block radius knew how to say "Merry Christmas" (which sounded like "melly ka-li-sama").

The fact that it stands out in my mind fifty or more years later makes me think my mother might have been on to something. As chance would have it, she was able to combine her two favorite projects: giving back to her community while at the same time civilizing her own little army of kids.

Shin Dang-Dong and the Slicky boys

At Shin Dang-Dong, we were the only foreigners living in one of the poorest areas of the city. We lived in a compound surrounded by a wall topped with cement embedded with broken glass and curled barbed wire. In the front yard next to the gate, we also had a very mean watch dog named Sparky. It was clear from the beginning that Sparky was a watchdog and not a pet, because even we were afraid of him.

Sparky had a ferocious bark that rose to a whiny yelp as he went into his vicious paroxysms whenever a visitor, particularly a Korean visitor, came to our gate. He would repeatedly and wildly throw himself against the thick rope and collar that bound him to his area near the gate. And he was strong; so strong that occasionally, he snapped the rope.

Once he tore the long billowy skirt off a Korean woman, a friend of the landlady's who had come to visit her. He was restrained before he actually bit her, and as children, we thought it hilarious – like slapstick performed for our amusement. As an adult now, I'm just glad he never went after any of us! He was a real psycho dog.

The one time Sparky got loose and earned his keep, so to speak, was a night when burglars came over the wall. These burglars were locally known as "slicky boys". They broke into the house in the middle of the night while we were sleeping, and stole among other things, a tape recorder with the huge 5-inch reels containing my father's Korean language course tapes. For some reason, we thought the idea of Koreans stealing Korean language tapes was pretty funny and ironic, in a twisted sort of way.

We knew that there were two of them because, as luck (bad luck) would have it, my brother Mike actually saw them when he got up in the middle of the night to go to the bathroom downstairs on the first floor. He told us later that they were dressed all in black like Ninjas, and he saw them sneaking around like black shadows in the living room on the first floor. My mother found Mike afterwards, scared stiff and still pressed up against the wall near the bathroom, his eyes as round as saucers. By the next day, when he retold the story Mike had regained some of his swagger, but I don't think he ever went downstairs in the middle of the night by himself again. I know I never did.

My father, some of the servants, and of course, Sparky, the psycho dog, chased the two *slicky boys* in the yard around the house but never caught them. Knowing my dad, I suspect he was glad he didn't actually catch them. I mean, what would he have done with them? My dad wasn't a physical sort of guy; he was the intellectual brainy sort. Would he have yelled at them in inflection-perfect Korean? Told them to stop this silliness and go on home? Or felt compassion for them and helped them pack a few more things? With my dad, the one sure thing was that he was unlikely to resort to violence.

The *slicky boys* somehow got back over the wall, but not before Sparky bit one of them in the seat. The men were never caught. But, that wasn't the interesting part for us kids. We figured that between the glass and barbed wire on the wall and the dog bite, there must be blood. My younger brother, Jerry, and I walked around and around the house the next day looking for gruesome blood stains. I don't think we ever found any, which is just as well.

First School: Seoul Foreign School (1957-1958)

Since we arrived just after Labor Day, we were immediately enrolled in school and I entered the second grade at Seoul Foreign School. I think we only attended that school for half the year and then transferred to the Catholic school, Sacred Heart Academy. I have only a few memories of Seoul Foreign School, but even so, they are vivid ones.

Singing Protestant Songs

One memory of the classroom is a funny one involving my brother, Mike, who was in the second grade with me. (Note: In fact, Mike and I were in the same grade for most of our schooling. I started first grade at age five because of my December birthday, while he started school late because of his July birthday and we were only eighteen months apart; between that and his being held back a year, we ended up in the same grade most of our school years, and with our similar names – Michael and Maureen – people often assumed we were twins).

This memory must have been from around the time we found out we would be transferring to the Catholic school. Seoul Foreign was a Protestant missionary school. In keeping with its religious leanings, each morning we were expected to stand up, say a prayer and then sing a Protestant children's song, like "Jesus Loves Me". I loved that song and quickly learned all the words. That particular morning I sang heartily along until I got an elbow nudge in the ribs from my brother, Mike, who told me to stop singing that song because "It's a Protestant song and we are Catholics!" (Since I wasn't really sure if it would somehow affect my entrance into Heaven some day, I only sang it quietly to myself after that.)

Mike & Denny Find a Bomb

The other memory of the school also involved Mike, but was a much more serious event. Seoul Foreign School didn't have a lot of playground equipment. In fact, we had our recesses in a large packed-dirt area behind the school that was bordered by bushes and trees and these provided the boundary of the play yard. There may even have been a fence, although I don't recall it.

We spent a lot of our time playing tag and other made-up games, as kids do. Probably there were a few kick balls with which to play four-square and soccer and I remember being introduced to hopscotch and marbles in the dirt, as well.

One day, my older brothers, Denny and Mike, and their friends decided to investigate the area beyond the bushes. My brothers were natural ringleaders and were always testing the arbitrariness of adult rules and boundaries.

There was a ditch beyond the bushes and the ground there was uneven. It was back among the trees and bushes that Mike and Denny found a live hand grenade left over from the recent war (Korean War, 1950 – 1953). Naturally, they brought it back to the playground to show everyone, and luckily, it didn't explode. Instead, the U.S. military bomb squad was called, classes were dismissed and we were all sent home. We thought it was terribly exciting. There's nothing like an unscheduled holiday to brighten a kid's day!

Now, as an adult with children of my own, I know how fortunate we were. It's a fine line we walk between life and death, tragedy and luck. In the spot where Mike and Denny found the hand grenade, the military police found a whole cache of hand grenades and weaponry.

Catholic School - Sacred Heart Academy (1958 - 1959)

Sacred Heart Academy had originally been an all-girls Catholic boarding school. In 1958, it opened its doors to little boys and became a coeducational elementary school for the growing population of English-speaking children in Seoul.

Sacred Heart Academy, Seoul, Korea

One of my first memories about our switch to Sacred Heart was of taking a different school bus and hearing the kids from our old Seoul Foreign bus jeering at us out of the bus windows, "Sacred Heart! SCARED Heart!" Other than that jolting memory, I think the transition was fairly painless.

In fact, I liked Sacred Heart. I had gone to a Catholic school for first grade, so it wasn't entirely unfamiliar territory. Catholic schools, particularly those run by actual nuns are unique places. And by "real nuns" I mean ones where the nun wear the whole regalia of full-length Gothic habits, white coif and guimpe (don't be impressed, I had to look the terms up, too), and sporting huge rosary bead belts.

At Catholic school back then you went to Mass a lot, and religious education – learning the Baltimore Catechism – was reshuffled to the top of the academic priorities. And, there were uniforms. At Sacred Heart, we girls wore navy blue jumpers with white blouses and the boys wore navy pants with white shirts. No doubt we looked deceptively angelic.

We went to Sacred Heart for a year and a half – through my third grade school year. While there, I had my First Communion. My First Communion class was made up of six children: me, my brother, Mike, and four other little boys. Coming from a family of brothers, I felt right at home in a circle of male cohorts, and if nothing else, they set off my stunning white dress in the group photo. We couldn't have looked more innocent and saint-like.

We might have lasted longer at Sacred Heart but my brother, Mike, got expelled, and that pretty much sealed the deal for us, as a family. He got caught in a prank that went terribly wrong. It was the end of winter and we'd had quite a bit of snow. For recess we were sent out to the playground and we did all the winter things we could think of: building snow forts and snowmen, and having snowball fights when the playground nun wasn't looking.

On that particular day, Mike and his friends started building a huge snowman. They were a competitive lot and they were going to build the biggest snowman anyone had ever seen. The boys patted the first big snowball together and rolled it around until it grew and grew to a formidable size. Then they placed it at the very top of a very steep hill at one side of the playground. Someone (it could have been my brothers) came up with the idea of sending the snowball down into the play yard, as a sort of manufactured avalanche.

The nun in charge – Mother Riley – was standing with her back to the steep hill when the boys sent the huge snowball churning its way down. It was a very steep hill and this snow-boulder traveled much faster than anyone had predicted. Much to everyone's delight, it crashed right into Mother Riley. She ended up with a broken leg, but that might be an exaggeration that got added on to the story as it was embellished in the retelling over the years. At any rate, there was no exaggeration in the ire of the school towards my brother, Mike.

It was his own fault – instead of running away when the snowball started down the hill as all the other boys did, he alone stood at the top of the hill to watch it hit the nun. Even then, he still might have gotten away with it had he looked a little more horrified and a little less gleeful.

Second House: Itaewon (1958 - 1959)

After we had been in Seoul for a year, we moved to a new home in a recently completed development of houses on the side of a hill called Itaewon. This area was closer to the military base, but still outside of it.

Itaewon neighborhood

This house was a "modern" split-level. It only had three bedrooms so I shared a room with my two youngest brothers, Pat and Jamie; the other three boys were in the second bedroom; my parents had the third. There was a railing overlooking the foyer, and the living room and kitchen were on the main floor, with a family room at the bottom level. We had a small backyard that still had the sparse vacant look of a construction site. There were no trees, grass, or plants around the house until my mother started planting her own flowers and trees. It would be one of many yards, in many different countries, that she would landscape over the coming years.

Living in a quasi-American neighborhood was a whole new experience for us kids. Suddenly, we could ride our bicycles on paved streets, and play during the long afternoons and weekends with a pack of other American kids.

Malaria and other mosquito and insect-borne diseases were prevalent in Korea. It was the practice of the American military at the time to drop DDT "bombs" from airplanes over whole neighborhoods to kill the mosquitoes. As children in those early evenings we would hear the plane diving down to unload its bombs of smoky DDT and we loved it! We would run around in the chemical smoke and fog. Later on when we lived on the military base, instead of dropping the chemicals from planes they released it from the back of a jeep that drove up and down the streets of the neighborhoods on South Post. I cringe to think about us playing in all those chemicals now, but at the time it was exciting and great fun.

My memory of the DDT planes at Itaewon took a particularly horrific turn once, though, when I managed to get some of the chemicals into my eyes. It burned and my eyes teared up and became so sensitive that I couldn't open them.

My parents happened to be on a trip somewhere – Hong Kong, I think – and had left us with a baby sitter, a secretary friend from the Embassy, who stayed with us at the house while they were gone. She took me to the base hospital to get my eyes checked out and the doctor put some salve in them and covered them with eye patches, like the ones sleeping rich women wear in old movies. My key memory of the event, though, was of going out for ice cream afterwards and not being able to see it. I don't remember how long I had to keep the eye patches on, or how long I spent with the shades pulled down in my darkened bedroom, but luckily, there appears to have been no permanent damage. In fact, for years I took great pride in my sharp 20-20 eyesight.

Third House: Life on Yongsan Army Garrison, South Post (1959–1962)

Our house on South Post, Seoul, Korea

Another year passed and we went on our first home-leave (more about that later) and when we returned to Korea, we moved on base for the first (and the last) time. It was great to experience living in what we considered to be a "real" American community – not just with American neighborhoods, but an American Dependents' School, an American movie theater with its kiddie matinees every Saturday morning, a church, and the PX and commissary shopping – and it was all on base. The base was a miniature American city.

Indeed, there are advantages and disadvantages to living on base. The advantages are that we had lots of other American kids to play with and we spent a lot of our time in large groups of kids, playing, riding bikes, going to the movies, bowling, and taking swimming lessons at the Officer's Club. The disadvantage was that you were only nominally in Korea; if you closed your eyes, you could be on any base in any country in the world.

Our house on South Post was on a corner lot. Beyond our house the street went into a cul-de-sac with a huge circle that we used to ride our bicycles around. Our driveway and the parking spot for our station wagon was above the level of the house. To get to the front door of the house, one walked down a steep set of steps and then followed a sidewalk around to the front door.

The front door was oddly situated on the back side of the house, facing a large stone retaining wall. The inside of the house was all on a single level.

As you came through the front door, a large living room with a fireplace was to the left. To the right was a hallway with four bedrooms off it. Mine was the first one on the right. My brother, Jamie, and later Chris, shared my room. The next bedroom was Pat and Jerry's bedroom. Later, Jamie moved in with them when Chris was born. At the end of the hall was the kids' bathroom. On the other side of the bathroom was Mike and Denny's bedroom.

When Denny was in high school, my mother reshuffled the room assignments and created a separate bedroom on the back porch for Denny, complete with tatami flooring and sliding rice paper doors. That allowed her to cut down on some of the tension and fights that go on with growing boys.

At that point, she moved Jerry and Mike into one bedroom, Pat and Jamie into the other, and baby Chris in with me. Down another long hallway was my parents' master bedroom suite with its own bathroom off their large bedroom. I remember their room best at Christmas time when my mother would lock the bedroom door before Thanksgiving so she could accumulate and wrap all the presents, away from our prying eyes. With seven children, there were a lot of gifts. We would spend endless hours trying to figure out how to get a peek into the room to see what we were getting for Christmas.

Our Pets: Cats, Dogs, Chickens & a Duck

This was the first house where we had pets. We hadn't had a dog since our Labrador retriever, Sally, back in Maryland, if you don't count Sparky, the psycho watchdog in our first house. In the house on South Post, we started with a couple of cats. One was a large Siamese cat named Kimchi. He eventually ran away and went wild, and for the next year or so we would put food out and occasionally see him darting across the road and behind bushes, but he never came back to live in the house again. The other cat, a pregnant black cat, whose name I don't recall since we always called her "the black cat", was given to us by a departing family. The cat promptly had a litter of kittens and we suddenly had lots of pets until we managed to find homes for them.

One Easter we were given several baby chicks and a duck. The duck was mine and I named him "Duke". He would follow me around whenever I was outside, which was comical. Poor Duke had a tough time initially, though, because the baby chicks knew there was something different about him and pecked at him. It was the Hans Christian Andersen story, *The Ugly Duckling*, come to life, only in Duke's case, he did it one better by becoming the leader of a flock of chickens.

Watching the chickens following him around the yard was a sight to see. I never figured out whether he thought he was a chicken or they thought they were ducks.

We also had the first (of two) miniature dachshunds named Schnitzels. This first one was brown; the second one we later acquired in Taiwan was black with touches of brown. Schnitzels (both of them) became Pat's dog, as many of our dogs did over the years. For some reason, dogs always seemed to gravitate to him.

South Post: Living on a Military Base

We enjoyed living on base and my parents seemed to relax a bit and gave us free rein (well, pretty much) to go anywhere on base that we could walk or ride to on our bikes. So where did we end up going? Under the base fence to the Korean side, of course! Just behind our cul-de-sac of houses and across a large field was the tall wire fence that surrounded the base. Beyond it were the rice paddies where we would catch frogs in the spring, come home with leeches on our legs in the summer, and where we would ice skate in the cold winter months.

Ice-skating was, let's say, "interesting" on a rice paddy. For one thing, there were the frozen tufts of rice grass to maneuver around, but on the positive side, even if the ice was thin, the water beneath was never very deep. We might go home with freezing wet feet, but there was never a danger of drowning. The boys picked sides and played ice hockey with makeshift pucks and sticks, or we organized races or played crack-the-whip. Usually, it wouldn't take long for the Korean kids to show up.

The Korean kids didn't own ice skates; I don't think that ice skates were a part of their culture. But they did figure out how to have fun on ice, like other children. Instead of ice skates, they created skate-sleds;

Korean ice sled

small, square boards with two runners on the bottom. They would kneel down on the board and move across the ice maneuvering the sled with long ice picks. It was amazing how quick and agile their skate-sleds were!

The residential base housing was expanding as the U.S. Armed Forces were increased due to the Cold War, and as a result, more and more American families moved to Korea. There was on-going construction going on behind our cul-de-sac of houses and we happily played in the construction sites as often as we could.

A mobile basketball hoop was set up in the open field behind the houses, but as it turned out, it wasn't completely secured to the ground. One day we all climbed to the top, and on a dare, hung over the backboard to reach down to see if we could touch the net below. That's when the whole thing tipped over. The rest of us – perhaps four or five kids – all let go and went flying, but my younger brother, Pat, who was probably four or five at the time, hung on for dear life. He ended up splitting open his chin on the metal bar he was clutching. That was one of many family trips to the military base hospital for stitches, slings or arm casts.

Even so, the field was a great place for an adventure. We dug caves, built forts, and in the evenings as the fireflies and crickets came out we played long games of hide and seek, flashlight tag, and told scary stories about cats with ruby eyes sparkling in the dusk. Behind the houses on the opposite side of the street was a hill, where we played king of the mountain. You were "king" if you were the first to touch the base fence at the top of the hill, while everyone else was also scrambling for the honor.

In the late balmy summer evenings, frogs in the rice paddies croaked, fireflies flitted in the tall grass, parents drank highballs, and we played baseball or rode our bikes just like we would have, had we been back in some Stateside neighborhood. Our little American community was mimicking the life it might have led in the States. I think so anyway, except there was one huge difference in that our fathers were either U.S. military officers or diplomats with the State Department or American Embassy.

Occasionally, local political situations arose that made things unsafe for us. For instance, it seemed that every spring the Korean students rioted, or North Korea rattled its sabers, or some corruption was uncovered at the highest levels of the local government. At these times there was talk of evacuating American dependents and the allowable single suitcase per family was packed and placed near the front door, just in case. There were also natural disasters. Like the time the Han River overflowed its banks in a flash flood and half the base was under water.

I was in school at the time of the flood and word went out that we were all being sent home until the water receded. The school buses arrived, but for some reason two of my girlfriends and I got left behind at the elementary school. We decided to hike up to the high school which lay on higher ground and was not too far away, up the street. We thought hiking through the waist-deep water would be very exciting, that is, until we saw dead animals floating in the floodwater, and swirling storm drains threatened to suck us down. Suddenly, we realized we might be in actual danger. That's when the fun turned into something a little more serious and desperate.

We struggled on, leaning on each other and trying to keep up each other's spirits. It was scary and we were so relieved when we finally arrived at the high school some time later. Luckily for us, it was a chaotic scene of buses and parents and military police and no one noticed our soaked clothing and streaming hair as we got pulled into the hubbub. We never told anyone what we had done or how close we came to becoming a statistic. As frightening as it was, the thought of the punishment we might incur seemed even scarier.

Living on base was quite an adventure, even without natural disasters. There was so much in such a small area. There were swimming pools, a theater that showed kiddie matinees on Saturdays (tickets were fifteen-cents for kids and twenty-five cents for adults), the PX (the Post Exchange – sort of a big department store) and the commissary (grocery store), and a Toyland that was set up in a huge warehouse annex near the PX from Thanksgiving through Christmas. We had activities like Little League baseball for the boys, girls' softball leagues for me (my mother was my team's manager and we had two young soldiers as our coaches), the library and its summer reading competition (yes, even nerds could win at something!). It was a magical little village, in many ways. But, it was also very much a military base. At precisely 5 PM every afternoon (in fall or winter; 6 PM in the spring and summer), the cannon was fired on the Main Post and a bugle sounded. Every vehicle on base came to a stop; men in uniform would jump out and stand frozen at attention and saluting, as the American flag was lowered. It was out of respect for the flag, but for us it was also a reminder that we were living under the protection and rules of the U.S. military.

There were other ways we were reminded that we were living on base. For instance, we used the military currency called "MPC" that looked a lot like Monopoly® money. There were no coins in this currency because even the change was some pastel-shade of paper money. Periodically, and without much warning, they would do a changeover to a new MPC currency in order to slow down the black market. I'm not exactly sure how that worked. Apparently, only Americans could get their money exchanged, so any MPC that had made its way onto the black market was suddenly of no value. It was a small lesson in how ephemeral trust and value are: one minute a piece of paper is "worth" $1.00 and the next, it can be totally worthless. Is anything inherently valuable? Or does value always require our acquiescence?

My Mother's Activities in Korea

Thanks to the luxury and low cost of having servants, my mother became the "Madam" of the house, which made her a sort of house manager rather than a housekeeper. That left her with more free time than she would have ever had back in the States, particularly being a mother of seven children. Even so, she was always very busy.

I think my mother viewed her community activities as "her job", of equal importance to the work my father was doing for the government. She headed up the women's club to found orphanages and plan clothing and food drives for the poor, she joined the Grey Ladies, an auxiliary nursing organization, to help out at the military hospital, and to relax, she joined an off-off Broadway theater group and got small parts in *Auntie Mame*, *Guys and Dolls* and *The Crucible*.

She also traveled from one end of the country to the other several times over with the RAS – the Royal Asiatic Society – a tour group dedicated to seeing the "real" Korea and as much of it as possible. Sometimes she took a few of us kids along and they are some of my fondest memories of Korea and the serene beauty of the country. We visited Buddhist temples on quiet mountainsides, swam at empty white sand beaches on the East Coast of Korea, and hiked in pine-shaded mountains.

Buddhist Temple - Korea

We did a lot of walking and hiking in Korea. In fact, my tenth birthday was spent on an all-day hiking trip with my ten favorite friends, and was finished off with birthday cake back at the car at the end of the afternoon. It is a happy memory combining a number of favorite activities: being outdoors, doing something physical and refreshing, sharing the experience with my family, and being surrounded by good friends who were there to wish me well. What more could a person want from a 10th birthday?

Dad & Maureen - hiking on 10th birthday

OEC Picnic at King's Tomb

In addition to the scenic wonders of South Korea, there was also the long history of the country to discover — back all the way to the Three Kingdoms of the first century BC. Legends go back even further to the man-god Tan Gun who founded the Cho-sen or Joseon (meaning "Land of the Morning Calm") Kingdom in 2333 BC. We visited many museums and historic sites in our five and a half years and absorbed much of the country's long story. Its history is so much longer and deeper than our blink-of-an-eye American history and I think becoming aware of it gave us a better appreciation and respect for the country.

Sometimes as Americans we become so obnoxiously full of ourselves and our country's wealth and luck that we forget that even so-called "Third World" nations have something to offer us – a different kind of wealth and wisdom that we can learn from.

The American Embassy and OEC (the U.S. foreign aid organization) had picnics, dinners and events to celebrate the Fourth of July or other American holidays. They were a relaxing time to come together as an American community, but also gave even the reluctant families a chance to go off base and see a little of the country and experience some of the local culture. One of the OEC picnics was held at the Kings' Tombs, where traditional Korean dancers in their colorful costumes danced with fans and elaborate movements to the beat of drums and Korean twelve-string zithers. There were presentations of Oriental marital arts, singing of Korean folk songs, and much pageantry. In addition, there was also fried chicken, sack races, and American-style games and fun.

Blonde hair was a novelty in Korea in the late 1950's and because I was a small child, people didn't feel the least hesitation about reaching out and stroking my head. It's disconcerting enough to be stared at wherever you go, but to have people reach out and touch your hair was a bit hard to take, particularly for a shy kid like me.

The other thing I won't soon forget was the bathrooms, or lack thereof. I learned to squat over holes in the ground from a very early age. The squatting, particularly for a limber child, was no big deal; but the smell of the binjo ditches (open sewers) and out-houses on a warm day is not something you quickly forget, much less get used to. And then there was the honey-bucket man who carried the sewage in buckets strung on a pole balanced across his shoulders to the rice paddies to use as fertilizer. Now there's an aromatic job, if ever there was one, and an example of the most basic form of recycling.

My younger brothers – particularly the two that were born in Korea – Jamie, in 1957, and Chris, in 1960 – were raised by amahs, which were their nannies or nursemaids. The amahs would treat the infant American children just like Korean babies. They carried them on their backs swaddled tightly in a Korean blanket. They fed them a gruel of mushy rice when they began transitioning to solid foods, and they shared the Kimchi (fermented cabbage), soups, stews, and Bulgogi (marinated barbecued beef) from their own plates when the kids moved on to real food. They loved their charges and the children were well cared for, dare I say, completely pampered.

The problem was that the servants spoke only Korean to them, fed them rice, and basically treated them as little Korean children. So, when the family went back to the United States for home leave every two years, it was an interesting dilemma to find that the youngest children in the family craved oriental sticky rice, expected to be carried everywhere, and listened for familiar Korean endearments. In our family, when it became clear that they were starting to prefer the Korean way to the American, my mother put her foot down and decided she would have to cut back on the 24/7 usage of amahs for childcare. These kids needed to learn to become Americans, too.

Chapter 4 Intermission—Our Home Leaves

Home Leave of 1959

During our years in Korea, we took two home leaves – trips back to the U.S. – one was the summer of 1959 and the other the summer of 1962. It was required that a family return to the U.S. periodically – usually every two years, but sometimes it was extended to three, depending on the circumstances. Home leaves were vacations, of course, but they were also "working" vacations for my father.

He had to spend time in Washington, D.C., being debriefed at the State Department and working at the country desk, meeting and sharing information with his peers and superiors. For us, it was three months of fun. We visited relatives, renewed friendships, saw a good bit of the United States, and shopped. We also listened to music, memorized radio ad jingles, and watched a lot of TV. I guess you could say we were catching up on two years of changes in pop culture in an intense three-month stint.

I only have vague memories of our first home leave in 1959. I'm certain that we spent time visiting relatives in Omaha and Boston, and I know we spent time in Washington, DC, as we always did on home leaves. I also remember a road trip out West. The reason it sticks in my mind, though, isn't for the scenic beauty. I recall two things about that trip: one was riding a horse for the first time, and the other was of being attacked by bees.

The horseback riding was fun. We went on a trail ride in the mountains and for years afterwards, like many little girls, I wanted to own a horse. The bees were another matter entirely. We were staying in a log cabin in the mountains of California, or it could have been Colorado, I'm not exactly certain. My mother had sent us outside to play and I had my new Bozo the Clown puppet – a brightly colored rubber Bozo head on a red polka dot cloth body.

Jerry, Mike, Pat and I wandered around in the woods outside the cabin, and I spied a huge old hollowed out tree stump. "Let's put on a puppet show!" I said. "That stump can be the stage." I quickly jumped into the crater of the stump with my puppet. For a second or two, all was well. Then I felt something crawling on my wrist. I looked down and saw that it was a bee. I wiped it on my brother, Mike, and he immediately jumped back.

The next second, all hell broke loose. There were angry bees everywhere! We all went screaming in different directions. I ran for the cabin. My mother came to the door and quickly saw what had happened. She pulled me into the cabin and started smacking at the bees around me. I had bees in my clothes and in my hair and I was hysterical. My mother stripped off my clothes while my father swatted at the bees still flying around the cabin.

My mother finally stuck my head under running water in the sink to drown the ones caught in my hair. I had a lot of bee stings, but I don't remember being terribly swollen or even that I had THAT many welts. Still, I was deathly afraid of bees for years. In fact, whenever I saw one on a flower, I would walk way out of my way not to have to pass close by. I guess, looking back, I'm just glad that I wasn't allergic to bee stings.

The other memory I have of the 1959 home leave was that before returning to Korea, we spent some time in Honolulu and that we all fell in love with the islands. My parents decided to buy a house there, even though we would only be able to live in it on home leaves. Hawaii was becoming the 50th state, and we made it our home state. To this day, I still feel that Honolulu is my "hometown", and I know that many of my brothers feel the same way because two of them ended up living in Hawaii for many years.

Home Leave of 1962

We moved to Taipei after our home leave to the US in the summer of 1962. It was a great home leave – we traveled by ship, the USS President Cleveland of the American President Lines, from Yokohama, Japan to Honolulu, Hawaii. It was our first trip by sea, and it was fun, except for the whole seasickness thing.

Funny, how no one mentioned that possibility beforehand. I was excited to be going by sea because I really didn't like long air trips on propeller planes. It used to take 19 or 20 hours to get across the Pacific by plane, hopping from fuel stop to fuel stop – Seattle to Anchorage to Wake Island, to Guam, to Okinawa, to...well, you get the picture. It was a lot of up and down, all in unpressurized cabins. Planes didn't fly at the altitudes they fly now, and so instead they bounced around from air pocket to air pocket, or so it seemed to me. By the tenth hour of flight, the recirculated air in the cabin was beyond stale and everyone had used at least one airsick bag. It was nightmarish. So I thought, it's got to be better by ocean, right?

Wrong. And worse, once the sea gets churned up, you feel trapped in a way that is almost unbearable; way longer than a 19 or 20-hour plane ride. You know that you can't leave, you can only pray that the sea settles down – or that by some miracle your stomach does.

My mother and older brother, Denny, were just about the only ones on the entire ship who didn't get terribly seasick. My father tried to keep a good face on it – he had been in the Navy after all, even though the closest he came to a ship during WWII was a ride around Boston Harbor – but I think even he was feeling a little under the weather.

It wasn't just the seasickness. For me, the other strike against this particular ocean voyage was the children's activities. You see, I was eleven-and-a-half years old that summer – my birthday is in December – so I was ALMOST twelve. But, you had to BE twelve to move up to the teen-level activities so I was stuck hanging out with the "little kids" – me and about twenty other two to eleven year olds. It was humiliating to be almost a teenager (or so I thought), and end up being shunted into hanging out with the babies.

Children's costume party - USS President Cleveland

    I have since found that I love ships and cruising. Perhaps you have to grow into adult activities of eating and drinking to really appreciate traveling by ship?

    Our home leaves usually meant a trip across the U.S. visiting relatives and doing the usual touristy things in between lots of visiting. One thing we learned about my mother on these home leaves is that she can pull relatives out of thin air. Every time we came back to the States we met some long-lost relative of hers – a great uncle who was the first to plant rice in California, two grand old great-aunts — Lillian or was it Bessie and Maude? They were gracious and kind to us but, really, WHO were they? Well, you get the picture. Later, my mother would say, "you remember when we went to visit great Uncle Harry (or whoever), don't you?" Hmmmm? Well, maybe I do. I'm not sure.

    In my mother's hometown of Omaha, we would spend a few days visiting, picnicking, and (we hoped) staying in a motel with a pool. Occasionally, my mother's sisters would invite a few of us to stay with them, particularly if there was a cousin within 3 or 4 years in age and of the same gender; it was a chance to get to know the cousins, explore our roots, as it were. However, my mother's family learned not to invite too many of us at once – to weigh the house too heavily with Sullivans could result in chaos breaking out in totally unexpected ways. For one thing, we tended to side with each other, and to encourage each other's more creative (and occasionally destructive) ideas. Somehow we found trouble, or it found us, and we managed to attract a lot of it.

Once in Medford, Massachusetts (my father's hometown), we nearly burned down my grandparents' house playing with these really cool strike-on-anything matches. Naturally, we had to go around and strike them on everything to test them.

Another time in Omaha (my mother's hometown) we convinced one of my younger brothers to slide down the laundry chute in my Aunt Inez's house. Luckily, she had a laundry basket to catch the clothes (and brother Pat...or was it Jamie?) in the cellar. We hadn't checked first, so that clothes basket turned out to be fortuitous.

The Sullivan relatives, Danbury, CT 1962

We especially loved my Grandma Corkin's house in Omaha. The first house she lived in was across the street from a huge public park and only a block from a movie theater, convenient to everything that was important, in our minds.

In her second house, she had a piano in the cellar and we played it with abandon (which explains why it was in the cellar perhaps?). She had lots of interesting old things to look at, too, and although we weren't allowed to touch her china teacups from around the world nor play with her demitasse spoon collection, she was good to us and didn't seem to mind the noise and confusion of our visits. We tried to thank her in our own way. Jerry and I had discovered that watermelons come from seeds that summer, so we planted a bunch of them along my Grandma's front walk. We waited and were a little disappointed when she never thanked us for them in her letters. Imagine, walking out your front door and picking a watermelon! We thought we had given her the most amazing gift.

We were infatuated with everything in America. In many ways, we couldn't have been more foreign. For instance, we thought it was a great trick to be able to actually drink from the faucet, since we always had to have water boiled and filtered overseas. We thought round-the-clock TV was utopian and we would watch anything and everything, without discrimination. We treated elevators and escalators as amusement rides, and would line up to use them again and again, much to my parents' chagrin.

By the end of the summer, we would have all the current commercials and songs on the radio memorized so that they would last us for the two years until the next home leave. We also loved drive-in theaters – doesn't everyone? Maybe you don't have to live overseas to love the novelty of watching a movie in the privacy of your car in the dark, eating popcorn, and listening to a double feature through a small squawk box attached to the driver's window.

During the intermission, we would race to the grassy playground below the screen and play on the merry-go-round or the slides and swings. My father would come and round us up during the concessions advertising before the second feature to herd us to the bathroom and then wrap us in a blanket in the backseat, knowing that we would all be asleep and would probably have to be carried in to the motel beds.

Home leaves were magical times when we were thrown together as a family – Mom, Dad, and seven kids in a station wagon – with no servants, no amahs, no one to make our beds or pick up our clothes, as my mother often reminded us (in a sometimes less than loving tone, I might add). But we saw a lot of our country, too. My parents took our learning about our own country pretty seriously. We drove across the U.S. several times in those years, visiting the Grand Canyon, the Rocky Mountains, Yellowstone and Yosemite, the beaches of California, as well as Maryland and Delaware, and of course, long expanses of the Midwest because we always had to stop to see my mother's family in Omaha, Nebraska, and then to quaint historic New England to visit my father's folks.

My mother would try to dress us up, teach us our manners, and generally tame her little army, and we sometimes basked in the compliments of the adults around us. At other times, we were just brats. Like any group of kids, particularly siblings who have been crammed into one too many motel rooms with the choice of sharing a double bed with a brother or sleeping alone on an uncomfortable fold-out cot, sometimes things would get ugly. It was inevitable.

Once, we were eating in a restaurant — a Denny's or HoJo's, I think — a coffee shop type place. With nine of us, we nearly always had to sit at two tables. It was usually the four oldest at one table, and the three youngest at a table with my parents. That was the split on this particular hot and sticky day. We had been in the car for hours and had finally stopped for the night. We had wanted to jump into the motel pool first thing, but my mother decided it was late and we should have dinner first. We went, but we were already in a mutinous mood.

The older kids ordered and the waitress brought us each a straw for our drinks. That was a mistake. First, Mike, then Denny shot the thin paper cover of the straw through the air until one hit Jamie, sitting at my mother's table, in the back of the head. He laughed. We laughed. My mother frowned. It went downhill from there. By the end of our meal, my mother had disowned us. In a fury, she came over to our table and announced, "You are a bunch of spoiled pigs. Get up and leave this restaurant right NOW!"

We knew she was angry — the rising red in her face and throbbing veins in her neck were plain enough — but somehow, we weren't quite done. We left the restaurant, of course, but having no place to go, we sidled back along the glass front and eventually stood right in front of my parents' table, leaned in and pushed our faces against the plate glass window, a line of little pig noses smearing the once clean window. If looks had velocity, the look my mother gave us would have registered an atomic blast. My father, much to her chagrin, hid a smile. Bad move. When we saw his reaction to our shenanigans, we got worse.

Mike put on a poor boy expression, dropped to his knees on the cement, and said in a pleading voice mimicking every beggar — real or scam artist — we had ever encountered, "Puleeeze, I have no mother, no father. Puleeze, give me money. I am so hun-gary!"

The rest of us doubled over with hilarity, each trying to egg on the other.

That wasn't the first, nor would it be the last time that we embarrassed my mother and pushed her to the limit. There was a time – way back when – when she really cared what other people thought, but we eventually embarrassed that right out of her.

That's not to say we couldn't still embarrass her in front of her family, of course. On the home leave in 1967 through Europe, a teenage Mike volunteered to be in charge of the movie camera. When the eight-millimeter films of the trip were developed and delivered to my aunt's house in Omaha while we were there, my mother made the mistake of volunteering to show the films to the entire family without first censoring them.

We had just spent a month traveling through Europe, touring the grandeur of the Roman ruins, getting a papal blessing from the pope at St. Peter's, taking a cruise up the Rhine with its amazing castles at every bend in the river, visiting the Tower of London and Buckingham Palace — but on Mike's films, there was very little of the historic or the sacred. Instead, Mike had taken movies of lots of pretty young Italian, German and British girls, all long legs and nubile in their mini skirts and tight blouses. There were a few family shots showing the backs of my younger brothers in the woods in Germany as they relieved themselves after a picnic stop. And there were lots of shots of us clowning around. It was more like the Marx Brothers in Europe than a serious travelogue. We found the films hilarious; and my mother learned the value of censorship.

Saying Farewell to the Relatives

My mother always had a hard time saying goodbye to her relatives after she had been home in Omaha. There was one memorable occasion when we were late getting to the airport. In a family of nine people, with seven of them under the age of twelve, add 23 pieces of luggage and numerous hand-carries, and it was apparent that we could have used a full-time logistics manager. But, we had Dad and somehow, we (he) managed.

Memories of an Overseas Childhood 45

On this particular day, we were driven to the airport in three separate cars by various relatives recruited for the duty. My father and youngest brothers, Chris and Jamie, arrived first with a portion of the luggage. My Aunt Inez drove Denny, Mike, and me, weighed down with another sizeable load of luggage. And my Uncle Bill was to drive my mother, brother Pat and Jerry in the final vehicle with the last of the luggage, which were mostly hand-carries.

The Omaha airport was a madhouse when we arrived in the second car. Luckily, my father was already in line with the tickets and the growing mound of luggage. My aunt's car arrived with us in plenty of time. So far; so good. We added the luggage from our car to the mountain in front of the check-in counter. People stared; the agents cringed and glanced at their watches, because, of course, it was getting late.

"The flight has already started boarding, Mr. Sullivan. If we hurry, perhaps...." the agent said in a fluster.

My father looked around with growing anxiety – he was always anxious when we traveled, and who could blame him? Now though, he wondered what to do if my mother didn't arrive at the airport in time? Should he leave with some of us? Should he tell the ticket agents to hold off putting the luggage aboard? What to do?

To make matters worse, my brothers were already fooling around. Airports were familiar playgrounds, after all. And this was long before security lines – at least, in America.

"Watch the hand-carries," my father would periodically holler at my brothers. But the only one who actually was listening was Chris, the youngest, perhaps three years old at the time, who perched himself in the middle of the busy check-in area on top of the toy bag – a red American Tourister bag that was as big as he was. We called it "the toy bag" because it was filled with games, plastic soldiers, cowboys-and-Indians, the occasional cap gun, a few decks of cards, and lots of stuff we had collected to play with. It was without a doubt the heaviest bag we traveled with.

The airlines allowed us 66 pounds of luggage per person; supposedly this was to include our hand-carry baggage, as well.

However, we knew that they only weighed the checked luggage. To make certain, my father always sent us far away with the hand-carries so there wouldn't be an opportunity of a by-the-book counter agent asking that the entire hand-carry luggage be added to the total weight. My father taught us early "out-of-sight is out-of-mind". I suppose we never considered that our overweight luggage might compromise the flying efficiency of the plane. Perhaps it did. Now that I think about it, we did seem to fly pretty low in the atmosphere in those days.

With the luggage finally checked in, my father herded us to the gate, looking over his shoulder for my mother, who still hadn't arrived. At the gate, the agent took the tickets, counted heads and asked where the other three were. My father said they were on their way. The ticket agent glanced around, waiting, and then finally suggested that he and those of us who were already there, get on board. She would hold my mother's tickets aside.

My mother's relatives – uncles, aunts, and cousins – lined up for the last good-bye hugs and kisses. My father led the way down the impromptu receiving line, shaking hands, hugging, kissing and saying good-bye to them, with Denny, Mike, Jamie, Chris, and me following in his wake. Then, having stalled as long as we could, we headed out towards the plane waiting on the tarmac. As we reached the plane's stairway, we turned to wave goodbye one last time and caught sight of my mother, Jerry and Pat who had finally arrived.

My mother, all smiles and out of breath, saw the relatives still lined up and she pushed my brothers down the line in front of her as she began her own goodbye hugging and kissing. Unfortunately, someone unrelated to us had stepped in at the end of the line and the momentum of the good-byes caused my mother to grab the man, give him a hug and a big kiss before stepping back and realizing she had never seen him before in her life. She shrugged, smiled, and waved, then hurried towards the waiting plane. Another home leave was over and we returned to our real life.

Chapter 5   Taipei, Taiwan (1962 – 1964)

The Sullivan Kids, circa 1962
Ages of the Sullivan Children upon arrival in 1962 in Taipei, Taiwan:

> *Dennis (Denny), age 15, sophomore*
>
> *Michael (Mike), age 13, 6th grade*
>
> *Maureen (Reen or Reeny), age 11, 7th grade*
>
> *Robert (Jerry), age 9, 5th grade*
>
> *Patrick (Pat), age 7, 2nd grade*
>
> *James (Jamie), age 5, kindergarten*
>
> *Christopher (Ku or Chris), age 3*

Grass Mountain – Yangminshan

In 1962, we moved to Taipei, Taiwan, on the island of Formosa. Once again, we lived in an American enclave, although not on a military base this time. Again, we had an approximation of living in an American neighborhood.

The place we lived was called (by the Americans, at least) Grass Mountain (Yangminshan, in Chinese) and it was one of the few times overseas where we did not live in a walled compound with a gate. Not only were we living in an un-gated American neighborhood, but we had the Grass Mountain Community Center with its American-style snack bar, bowling alley and movie theater within walking distance of our house, which for a family with seven children made it seem pretty close to heaven.

The Community Center was a place where we, as kids, spent a lot of our time after school and on weekends. There was a Taiwanese man named Smiley who worked behind the counter at the snack bar and who was a local legend for his perfect French fries – crunchy on the outside, soft on the inside – which we then smothered in ketchup.

The bowling alley was the daytime draw; the movie theater was the main attraction at night and on weekends. We all bowled on Saturday mornings in the kids bowling league. Even my parents became avid bowlers during those two years in Taipei. Both my father and my mother served on the Community Center board as vice president, one succeeding the other in that capacity. They have always been involved and generous about volunteering their time and energies to their community, wherever we lived. I don't know if it was entirely altruistic or if perhaps they felt an obligation to the community because with nine of us, we certainly used up a lot more of the services, resources, and activities.

The Neighborhood

Our neighborhood was a special American residential area on Grass Mountain. In fact, each group of Americans seemed to be separated into its own neighborhood. There was an area for us – USAID (the U.S. Agency for International Development) and U.S. Embassy families, another for Naval Intelligence, another for Army dependents (they lived in an area called Tien Mou, down in the valley below), and there were a sprinkling of Americans living throughout the city of Taipei itself. These were generally the missionaries and Americans affiliated with other groups that would today be known as "NGO's" (Non-governmental organizations), although that term hadn't come into vogue yet.

We loved living in Yangminshan. Even though we were living in an essentially American neighborhood, it was a different experience from the one we had while living on the military base or in Itaewon in Korea. In Korea, while living on base, we lived apart from the Koreans. That's one of the odd things about military bases – they are pretty much the same wherever in the world you were. Life on base – the facilities, schools, base housing, and myriad of activities – is essentially the same whatever base you're on and wherever in the world it's located.

In Taipei, although we were definitely living in an exclusively American community, we also lived surrounded by tangerine orchards, terraced rice paddies, and Taiwanese farmers. We had lots of contact with the locals and we were particularly happy about that. What's the point of living overseas if you aren't exposed to the local culture?

The Plum Club

Just up the way from our housing area, there was a little group of shops – cobbled together shacks really – marking the bus stop along the main road up the mountain. It wasn't far from our house so we used to walk up and buy fresh plums, dried salted fruit, and firecrackers.

The local fruit was amazing, in taste, size and variety! It's hard to describe if you haven't eaten fruit picked ripe from a tree. The tangerines were so ripe that the thick skins simply dropped away from the fruit when you began to peel it. The plums were not at all like the plums you find in a stateside grocery store, not even in the organic stores of today! The Taiwanese plums were huge with a deep purple hue, firm but not hard, sweet tasting, and dripping juicy.

I was 12 years old that first summer and my friends and I liked these plums so much that we organized a Plum Club in their honor. Literally the only activity of this club was to take our allowance, hike over to the Chinese store, buy a bag of plums each, and spend the afternoon eating them. I don't remember how long our club stayed viable – probably not long, given its limited appeal – but there were at least a few afternoons sitting contentedly on the front steps of my friend, Linda Milberger's house, eating juicy plums, talking and laughing, and feeling very privileged and full of ourselves, and of course, full of plums.

Exploring Grass Mountain

There was plenty to do around our neighborhood. Living on the side of a mountain gave us ample opportunity to hike the surrounding hills, swim in the streams (disease-ridden though they might be), and there were plenty of places to explore.

For instance, there were caves not far down the path at the back of our house along the edge of the tangerine orchard fence. We called those "the small caves" although it might have been more apt to call them "the bat caves" because as it turned out, they were filled with bats. We were really curious about these caves. We wondered if these caves might somehow be connected to the larger ones on the other side of the mountain.

One day, we decided to find out so we packed up some spelunking supplies (flashlights, a Cub Scout knife, a really cool fold-up camp spade, and plenty of snacks) and we headed down the path to the opening of the small caves. The opening was just a hole in the side of a small mound, but it opened up into a small cavity when you crawled inside. It was a short adventure, however, because as soon as we were inside and turned on our flashlights, the bats flew out, squealing and screeching above our heads. We flew out right after them with a bit of squealing and screeching of our own. We never did trace the origins of the tunnels in the back of the little caves. Perhaps they were connected to other caves, perhaps not; fear of bats prevented us from finding out.

The other caves, the ones we referred to as "the big caves", were located on the other side of the mountain. A long path led from the main road, through the cemetery and past the large houses of the Naval Intelligence group, and then down a small winding path. The path, partially hidden in thick undergrowth, eventually led to a waterfall with a natural slide.

One Saturday I counted nineteen American kids swimming there, ranging in age from eight to sixteen. Kids would jump into the shallow stream at the top of the falls and would be carried down a slippery green slide and over a small waterfall, maybe five or six feet high, into a tropical swimming hole. All around were jungle vines, trees and bushes. I don't know who was the first brave soul to try it out but it seemed that each group of American kids would rediscover the place and we always thought we must be the first to ever swim there.

We did our best to keep the location of the waterfalls secret from our parents. It was such a good place to hang out with our friends that we didn't want to ruin it, and they couldn't forbid us to go to a place they didn't know about. Or at least that was our reasoning.

The older teens would smoke and drink stolen bottles of beer or some rotgut Chinese liquor. But the rest of us simply wore out the seats of our swimming suits on that slimy rock water slide. Later we learned that the stream was fed by the run-off from the surrounding rice paddies and orchards and when a medical pathologist later tested the water it was brim full of hepatitis and God knows what other diseases.

Probably it was a lucky thing that we were a bunch of overseas brats who were inoculated every six months with nearly a dozen different shots. We regularly had shots against tetanus, typhoid, diphtheria, TB, polio, cholera, yellow fever, smallpox, typhus, plague, as well as gamma globulin for hepatitis, although, I didn't personally have to get that one because I had hepatitis when I was 4 years old (in Maryland, before I even went overseas!). At any rate, no one got sick from swimming there, at least, not that I recall.

The "big caves" were beyond the water slide, on the side of the mountain in an area of cliffs. There were three caves that we knew of, although there may have been many others. They were huge; not only were the openings large enough to walk through standing up, but once inside, there were tunnels that led into cathedral-ceiling rooms and others that you had to crawl through to get from one room to another. One tunnel continued on until, if you stood in the right place you could turn your face upward and see daylight coming through a hole above you.

We had heard a rumor that these big caves had been used during the war (WWII) for the Taiwanese to hide from the Japanese, or maybe it was the Japanese hiding from the Americans – that part was never really clear to me. The thought of finding something left behind from twenty years before – buried family treasures immediately sprang to mind – led us to spend a number of long afternoons exploring these caves. However, all we ever found were the remains of old fire pits and scraps of fabric that might have been from clothing or perhaps from threadbare blankets. There was no pirates' cache, at any rate!

Formosa, "Snake Island"

The downside of living on Grass Mountain – well, of living anywhere on the island of Formosa, for that matter – was the presence of snakes. They were everywhere. I had even heard people laughingly refer to Formosa as "Snake Island". Disgusted (and startled) by the number of snakes that found their way inside our house, particularly after heavy rains, my mother asked the servants to block up the drainage holes on the screen porch with small stones to keep the snakes from slithering in. These weren't innocuous garden snakes either; these were poisonous snakes – Hundred-Pace vipers, coral snakes, Russell vipers, bamboo snakes, and the fearsome Formosan cobras.

One day we were on the school bus on our way to school when we made a regular stop outside the gate of the house of an American family who lived about halfway down the mountain. The bus driver honked, but no one came out. We joked that they must have overslept. The driver honked again. Still nothing. Then someone noticed a movement at the living room window. It was then that we saw that the whole family was standing at the window excitedly gesturing towards something in their front yard. We looked where they were pointing and saw a huge snake – a Formosan cobra – coiled up and sunning himself next to the driveway. We heard later that the family waited most of the day for it to slither away. Imagine an excused absence from school because you were trapped in your house by a large snake!

photo of Formosan cobra

I was never really phobic about snakes. Sure, I didn't like snakes and I was certainly afraid of them – most were poisonous, after all – but that fear never stopped me from going outside or from exploring the mountain. In fact, I remember once thinking it would be great fun for my brother, Jerry, and me to carry a dead snake on a stick back home to my mother to scare her. We envisioned her screaming and climbing on a chair or something equally dramatic. Much to our chagrin, she took it in her stride and just told us not to bring it into the house.

Our House on Grass Mountain

Up on Grass Mountain, we lived at the edge of the American housing area. My mother had a lot of fun landscaping our huge back yard during our two years living in the house. She created a Japanese rock garden with a koi-pond in the patio just outside the screen porch in the back, off the living room. We thought the fishpond was a great idea, like having a tiny swimming pool, although we soon discovered the only time we were allowed to play in it was to clean it. My mother planted flowers, a border of rose bushes and several trees in the yard, and our house became quite a showplace. In fact, my parents used the fishpond patio area as an extension of the living room and had many indoor/outdoor parties. Entertaining was a part of my father's job and my mother was very good at helping him in that area of his work.

Front of house on Grass Mountain - Taipei

The house itself was all on one level and had a garage, servants' quarters and kitchen on one end and our living quarters on the other. In between was the dining room/living room with its huge fireplace and a long screen porch along the back. The house had four bedrooms. My parents' master bedroom suite was at the back of the house and the three bedrooms for the kids were off a hallway in the front of the house. There was a smaller screen porch along the backside of the house, too, and my parents' bedroom and my brother's bedroom both opened on to the porch.

Stealing Tangerines

Taiwanese tangerine orchards bounded the length of our backyard. This close proximity to one of our favorite fruits only caused a problem once when Jerry and Mike got caught stealing tangerines from the orchard. The farmers had padlocks on the gates to the orchards, but the fencing around the field was flimsy, at best.

Maureen in backyard of house –Grass Mountain, Taipei

We soon discovered that we could easily wriggle under the fence, pick the ripening fruit and hightail it back into our yard. This particular time, though, the farmer saw them and followed Jerry right back to our house. There was a noisy confrontation with the angry farmer, with our servants translating and my parents anxiously hoping to sidestep

Maureen in backyard of house (tangerine orchard fence behind)

an international incident. My father stepped in to smooth things over with the farmer, supplicating in fluent Mandarin, mixed with a bit of local Taiwanese vernacular, about how the farmer's delicious ripe tangerines were too tempting, even for these terrible American boys.

In the end, my father agreed to generously compensate the farmer for the stolen produce and we were told, in no uncertain terms, that we should turn our attentions elsewhere. My father wasn't a disciplinarian – that was my mother's job – so it was unusual for him to get upset with us or to set rigid boundaries on our behavior. When he did get angry, though, it usually meant that we had stepped across some undefined but sensitive international protocol. Because he so rarely got really angry with us, we took him seriously when he did. We stayed away from the tangerine orchard; well, at least, we stayed away from that particular orchard.

The Difference between Firecrackers and Bombs

We turned our attentions elsewhere and luckily there were a lot of things that we found interesting. One area of great interest to us (need I say, "fascination"?) was firecrackers. The Chinese invented firecrackers, and in Taiwan, they were exploded at every celebration, large and small.

It wasn't long before we discovered that the little Chinese store on the mountain road sold every variety of them. Some were like small pencils that you struck against the side of a matchbox and quickly tossed before the explosion, others were sparklers that glowed and jetted small bursts of sparks but didn't explode, and still others were crackerballs that were the size of small marbles and that you threw on the ground to make them pop and explode.

Once when I was striking one of the pencil-type firecrackers on the side of a matchbox, the entire matchbox burst into flames in my hand. My fingers and the palm of my hand were burned – not so badly that I had to be rushed to the hospital, but badly enough that the pain was excruciating for the rest of the day. I had to keep something cold constantly pressed on the burned area and I vividly remember buying and carrying around cold cans of Coca-Cola to ease the pain. Naturally, I hid the resulting blisters from my parents – it would be bad enough to have to explain about playing with firecrackers, but getting burned was humiliating – the ultimate "I told you so", not to mention, "It serves you right!"

Of all the firecrackers, though, it was the skyrockets that got us into real trouble. One day, Jerry had a really terrific idea. "Let's build the biggest firecracker anyone's ever seen!" How the word "bomb" never occurred to us, I can't explain.

Jerry convinced a group of neighborhood kids to pool their money together and we went up to the little Chinese store and bought a bunch of skyrockets. We brought the rockets home and gathered in our backyard to cut them open and collect all the gunpowder inside. We took a fat section of bamboo and sealed one end of it, then poured all the gunpowder into the other end. Next we soaked a rag with lighter fluid and stuffed it into the bamboo container with a piece sticking out to serve as the fuse. We debated about who should get to light it. I'm pretty sure it was Jerry who won, but it may have been Mike. The rest of us hid behind some bushes and rocks, close enough so we could see the explosion. It was our money, after all, and we didn't want to miss anything.

Jerry lit the fuse, then hit the ground and covered his head, most likely imitating something he had seen in a war movie. The gigantic "BOOM" shook windows in houses several blocks away. The crater – yes, there was a small crater in our backyard – was a foot and a half in diameter. I think Jerry had ringing in his ears for the rest of the day.

Of course, everyone in the neighborhood who was at home that afternoon came running down to see what had happened in the Sullivans' backyard. We were so dumbfounded by the size of the explosion that we never thought to run away. There wasn't much we could say in our own defense, except that we never thought it would be that big, or that LOUD. Later we found shards of bamboo stuck in the trees nearby. Thank God that Jerry dropped to the ground – if he had been running away after he lit the fuse, he probably would have been badly hurt, if not killed. It was pretty amazing, though.

Neighborhood Activities

It was great fun living in a neighborhood full of children. There was always plenty to do and plenty of people to do it with and we were always trying to find ways to make money to spend at the snack bar, bowling alley or movie theater.

One of our moneymaking schemes was organizing neighborhood carnivals. We put on shows for the younger kids (we charged a dime to get in to the roped-off area of someone's backyard) and created all sorts of carnival acts for the amusement of our audience, or at least, for our own amusement, since we were as much actors as participants.

Once my brother, Jerry, and I concocted a drink made out of dozens of root beer and cherry-flavored Fizzies® (for people who have never heard of them, Fizzies® were a sort of flavored Alka-Seltzer® that you dropped into a glass of water to create a carbonated drink). We gave tiny paper cups full of this concoction to kids (a nickel a pop) and then took them into a darkened box for their "space ride". I guess you could say this was an early attempt at homemade hallucinogenic trips. Little did we know! The stuff was pretty gross and no one took more than a tiny sip, which they promptly spit out. But, it was all in good fun, right? And what a shame we couldn't get kids to go on the trip twice.

Halloween and the Taiwanese Children

The Taiwanese children that lived around the American enclave on Grass Mountain were sometimes mystified by us and by our activities. No doubt, our culture was as strange to them as theirs sometimes was to us.

For instance, we never could get the hang of their traveling Chinese Opera shows with all the screeching vocals and wild masks. For their part, they never really understood our Halloween tradition. But that didn't stop them. The Taiwanese kids caught on to walking up to the front doors and putting their hands out. They didn't even need to say "Trick or Treat" to get the candy. The problem was that they didn't realize it was only one night a year!

For our part, we thought Chinese funerals were pretty strange, too – they wore white, for one thing, they burned paper money, for another, and they hired professional mourners – people who didn't even know the deceased – to grieve. If I remember correctly, only the Chinese Christians were actually buried in the ground while the Buddhists preferred cremation with the ashes reverently placed in religious urns. I can see the point of being cremated, but I don't understand burning money so the dead person will have something to spend in the afterlife. As for the idea of professional mourners, I'm ambivalent – who really knows anyone anyway? And, besides, it's nice to be missed, even by people you never knew.

As children, we had the normal fascination with death. Having a cemetery so close by the neighborhood gave our fascination a little more immediacy. We did all the usual things – scaring each other with horror stories about walking alone near the cemetery and reporting strange lights and eerie goings-on and that sort of thing.

But all the made-up stuff got swept aside the night the cemetery caught on fire. I don't know if it was started by lightning or something else, but I remember sneaking over to the cemetery the next day with some friends and seeing charred wooden coffins that had been broken open, I assume in an effort to put out the smoldering embers. It was very odd, in a black humor sort of way, to realize that some dead people were apparently meant to be cremated, planned or not.

Earthquakes

Our house was a ranch style – all on a single level and made of cement and stone. I suspect that was a good design for the earthquakes and typhoons that we soon discovered were prevalent on the island.

Formosa has literally thousands of earthquakes each year, although most are so slight that they are hardly felt. The big joke in our family was that the earthquakes only happened when my father was down-island on a business trip and that he was somehow tipping the island. I don't know how he managed it but he never seemed to be home when we had one. The rest of us weren't so lucky.

During one such earthquake, my mother was at a Ladies' Club meeting on the top floor of one of the new skyscraper hotels downtown. She said the whole building swayed and the furniture slid from one side of the room to the other. She hung on for dear life, but said she was amazed that many of the panicked women, who should have known better, actually tried to escape by getting onto the elevators! Luckily, no one was injured.

During my first earthquake I was so frightened by the rolling sensation that I hid under my bed. I thought it was the right thing to do should the ceiling cave in. The second time I climbed into the closet – another brilliantly wrong move. After being scolded and instructed by my mother to leave a shaking building, I learned to race outside at the first jiggling movement.

Still, we noticed that our servants were pretty casual about leaving the house since apparently, no earthquake in their memories had ever been bad enough to cause them much disturbance and they were quite blasé about them. Because we never came to feel that kind of over confidence ourselves, my mother had to order them to go outside during earthquakes, to serve as role models for us children, if not for their own safety.

The Great Alaskan Earthquake of 1964

At Easter of our second year (March 27, 1964), we were vacationing at the very southern tip of Taiwan, in a place called Olanpi. It was a wonderful place with beautiful long white beaches and we stayed in a Western style lodge with cabins on the hill above the beach.

Sullivan and Clapp families - Easter at Olanpi

    We heard via shortwave radio that there had been a bad earthquake in Alaska and that there were tidal wave warnings, a potential tsunami, throughout the Pacific as a result. The lodge building was on a bluff pretty high above sea level, but we all went out to "see" the expected wave anyway. In my imagination, there would be this single huge wave traveling at the horizon towards us. In fact, it turns out that I saw it so vividly in my mind that to this day that huge wave occasionally shows up in my dreams. But, in the end, there was no wave. They said the sea level may have risen perhaps three feet as a result of the earthquake but that was all. Being kids, we were disappointed. Ah well.

Typhoon & Floods

For all the beauty of the island, it had its share of disaster and bad luck. There were the many, many typhoons that blew through the island during the summer and autumn months. During really bad typhoons the whole city flooded, but since we lived on a mountain, the rainwater quickly drained away.

Even so, we had some great neighborhood Typhoon Parties, and once we were out of school for three weeks after the very destructive Typhoon Gloria in 1963, a particularly bad storm. After the typhoon was over, all of us were commandeered to go down to the school to help with the cleanup. It was really awful. The cleanup work required wiping each book individually and laying it in the sun to dry out. All those brand-new textbooks and library books – some 8,000 of them – ended up swollen from the drenching and smelling so badly from rot and mold as they were drying that when school started up again, students retched from the lingering stench when they opened the book covers.

The American school was located in the Shih Lin area down in the valley. Because of the threat of flooding, it was built with huge protective dikes with watergates to keep the floodwater out of the school grounds. Unfortunately, the story goes that some maintenance person opened the gates "to let the water out" not realizing that he would be letting in even more floodwater, and so the school was flooded.

The City of Taipei

While we spent a lot of time on our mountain playing in our neighborhood with other kids, many of our other activities were spread all over the city, so we saw quite a bit of Taipei.

Jerry and I took piano lessons and our teacher was downtown in the middle of Taipei. Denny went to the American high school, which was located downtown. Our Catholic church was also downtown, as was the Officer's Club where Denny was the lifeguard and where we would go every Sunday after Mass for the Sunday brunch. The PX (a sort of military department store) and Commissary (the military grocery store) were downtown in the same area.

The swimming pool where we took lessons in the summertime, and the Teen Club (which I was unfortunately too young to enter because one had to be in high school to be considered a "teen") were located in Tien Mou, where the military housing was and where most of the military kids lived.

Denny at 16

Taiwan was a pretty cool place for teenagers, or so I've heard. The older teens had the Teen Club that was quite the swinging place – although that's hearsay, since I never personally saw the inside of it. I was too young. My oldest brother, Denny, was in high school in Taiwan, though, so in our family he was the first to test the waters of adulthood, so to speak, and the rest of us watched in awe as privileges and honors seemed to be heaped upon him.

He worked as a lifeguard in the summer at the Officer's Club, had plenty of of his own money, and seemed to have quite the independent life. He went to dances at the Teen Club on weekends, went to parties, dated girls, and later had a steady girlfriend. He even managed to talk my parents into buying him his first motorcycle and with "wheels" he had a freedom that the rest of us could only dream about.

Denny on his first motorcycle - Taipei

He even went on a weekend camping trip with his buddies, Steve and Clark. Plus, he was the oldest, the first-born son, and my parents adored him, and innocents that they were, they trusted him. Of course, because of some of his antics, they never truly trusted any of the rest of us when our turns came along. I'm not saying that we deserved any more trust than he did, but it must have been fun to go out and experience the world with a set of trusting parents supporting you and cleaning up your messes. The rest of us received more on the lines of grudging toleration. I guess you could say that Denny ruined it for the rest of us. My parents weren't anywhere near as naïve when the rest of us headed into our teen years.

Denny wasn't a complete tyrant. Occasionally, he shared his good fortune with us, his younger siblings. Like the times he was supposed to be baby-sitting us, but instead he invited his girlfriend, Sandee, over and told us to go to the movies so they could have the house to themselves. We were happy to oblige.

On one particular occasion, though, we went to the movie theater down the block and during the film something broke: the film or the projector, I don't remember which. Anyhow, when the lights came on we looked around the theater only to discover to our horror that our parents were sitting just six or seven rows in front of us. We slid down in our seats and waited for the lights to go out. It was the longest ten minutes of my life. Once the lights were safely off, we hightailed it out of there and got home before the movie was over, just to make absolutely sure that we would get into the house before my parents got home!

My Mother's Parties

After six years overseas, my mother had developed a pretty notable reputation for her parties. She was one of those people who knew how to plan, organize, cater, and throw a party. Sure, it was part of her job to entertain, but it was a talent that she apparently had some facility for. In fact, I have been told that some of her parties were considered legendary.

For instance, once she organized a moveable feast – a progressive dinner – where she hired pedicabs (rickshaws pulled by a guy on a bicycle) to carry the dinner guests from house to house: a stop at the first house for drinks and appetizers, at the next for drinks and soup, then the next for drinks and the main course, the next for Irish coffee and dessert, then someplace else for after-dinner drinks and snacks. (You get the picture.) By the end of the evening, the Taiwanese drivers were nervously laughing in the back seats as the tipsy American men were furiously pedaling their pedicabs in chariot races down the street. (Yeah, these were our parents!)

My mother entertained a lot because of my father's job and position. There were the quiet cocktail parties for visiting dignitaries, the formal multi-course feasts for Taiwanese bigwigs, and at other times it was an old-fashioned American block party. It didn't matter; she excelled at them all.

One of the benefits of all this entertaining was that she accumulated an incredible repertoire of exotic and gourmet dishes, that she eventually compiled into a cookbook that is treated like a cherished family Bible with favorite recipes dog-eared and bookmarked (copies available upon request).

The downside of these parties was probably all the alcohol consumed. One of our classic family stories is about our cook, Johnny (his Chinese name was Hwan), collecting what remained in all the drink glasses after a party and then drinking the concoction himself. To make matters worse, he then got on Denny's motorcycle, good and drunk, and with a Tarzan yell he crashed it in the street outside our house.

His wife, Yuki, had to do all the cooking for the next couple of days while he recovered from what must have been the mother of all hangovers. Johnny was an outstanding cook and my mother taught him her recipes while in exchange, she received her first Chinese cooking lessons and recipes from him. She forgave him the motorcycle accident (although I'm not sure that Denny ever did).

Our Pets in Taiwan

Speaking of Johnny (Hwan), our cook. He was not only a fabulous cook, but a budding entrepreneur, as well. He owned a chicken farm "back home" in his fishing village and the one job supplemented the other. He was determined to build his wealth and leave a great inheritance for his family.

Johnny gave us some baby chicks as a gift. Of course, he didn't immediately see the problem with a few hens pecking around the back door and how they might (or might not) get along with our two pet dogs.

Guang-Go, toy poodle

Guang-Go was a haughty white toy poodle that totally ignored the chickens, but Schnitzel was another story. He was a miniature dachshund, black with brown markings, and by nature and temperament, he was a hunter. There was nothing he enjoyed more than a romp around the yard chasing the chickens. He would have left them alone if they didn't always take off running and set off his "chase" instinct. Several times he managed to catch one of them and it was not pretty. When he did, I had assumed that we would be having chicken for dinner but Johnny, ever the resourceful chicken farmer, just picked up the squawking hen and sewed her wing back on. He didn't believe in eating a potentially good egg provider. The wing healed and she was as good as new, as far as we could tell.

We had a pet kitten for a short while; another Siamese. I don't remember its name but I do remember that he seemed a bit insane, perhaps inbred or something. For instance, he would go from completely calm to suddenly leaping up and dashing around madly, running helter-skelter, climbing the curtains, and that sort of thing. During one of these weird episodes, he ran up a six-foot rattan screen and the whole thing fell over on top of him, killing him instantly. There was nothing Johnny could do to bring him back, and so we found a shoebox and had a very fine burial in the backyard for him. He was the last cat we had as a pet; after that, we always had dogs, guinea pigs, geese and monkeys, but no cats.

Preteens in Taipei

We, the younger Sullivans, had a good time in Taiwan, too. For those two years, it seemed we were just under the radar with my parents, who were busy and otherwise occupied. During February of 1963, my mother left for a couple of months to return to the U.S. in order to have a hysterectomy. She stayed with her sister, my Aunt Fern, and Uncle Philip, in California. During her stay, my father was left in charge of the seven of us back in Taiwan, so he had his hands full. Still, I don't think it was much of a hardship for him since he had the help of a cook, a baby amah, a wash amah, and a gardener. Plus, we were in school all day while he was at work.

In general, my father was a calm and fairly relaxed man at home, as long as things were going along smoothly. To make certain he stayed calm and relaxed, we felt it was our job to assure him that everything was indeed going smoothly. I don't know if he actually trusted us to act responsibly, but he made us think he did. It was quite a gift that he was able to instill in each of us a sense that above all else we didn't want to let him down.

One of the positive things that came out of my mother's absence for those two or three months was that my father began to talk to us kids. Sure all parents talk to their kids, but I mean that for the first time, he had real discussions with us about world events, history, science, language or whatever we were studying in school.

He teased us and baited us and asked open-ended questions and it was as much a revelation for us to discover how funny and smart he was as it was for him to discover that sometimes we could hold our own in a discussion, too. Perhaps, it was an inevitable change in the family dynamics, but in some ways, my mother's departure threw us in his way so that he finally noticed that we were getting old enough to have interesting conversations with.

It was the beginning of what we later called, "talks around the Round Table", although we hadn't yet acquired our big custom-built round dining table with its lazy Susan and elbow room for nine. But it was the beginning of our spending time together as a family just talking, and when we did, it usually happened around the dining room table after dinner.

World Events

People of my age and older remember where they were when certain world events happened – it was Pearl Harbor for my parents' generation, but for my generation it was Friday, November 22, 1963, the day President John F. Kennedy was shot in Dallas, Texas.

In Taipei, we weren't in school or at work when it happened due to the time difference. For us, in fact, it was Saturday, November 23rd at 2:30 a.m., and because of that difference, I'm pretty sure that I was asleep in my bed, totally unaware that the world had changed.

In 1963, living overseas as we did, there wasn't any instant TV access to news footage or moment-by-moment coverage. So in many ways, I guess you could say that I "missed" it. Yes, it still affected us, and we read the *Stars & Stripes* (military newspaper) account of it, and later more detailed accounts in the *Time* magazine and *Newsweek*, but it was months before I saw the news clips that everyone else remembers and I think because of that, it never had the immediacy that it had for our fellow Americans back in the States.

Becoming a Teenager

Of more interest to me at the time was three weeks later on December 7, 1963 when I turned 13 – a teenager at last!

Becoming a teenager changes a person. In America we don't have Coming of Age ceremonies to move a child into adulthood, as they do in so many cultures around the world. In fact, we tend to prolong childhood into a person's 20's due to the extended financial dependency during the college years.

But even if we don't celebrate it as a "Coming of Age" experience, a girl begins menstruating as she enters her teens and that certainly is a deal-changer. As your body changes, you begin putting away the Barbie and Ken dolls and begin looking at real boys a little differently. Of course, when you are raised with six brothers, it takes a bit longer to overlook the downside of "real boys" – the gross humor, constant wrestling, and crude language – but even I got past all that eventually.

In school, the social groups started congealing. The more mature girls started going steady with the more socially forward boys and the talk centered more on fashion, music, boys, and, of course, gossip.

My brother, Mike, eighteen months older than me, discovered this new teen world and decided that it was one in which he could rule. Although he might not be getting the top grades in school, he had always been a sharp dresser, super-conscious of how he looked, and it wasn't long before he began to make a career of being "cool".

Sure, he managed to get into a good bit of trouble along the way – for fighting, for drinking on weekends, for disrupting the classroom – but he also managed to figure out how to sweet-talk the principal or superintendent of schools and there was always a teacher who admired his spunk and liked him and became his advocate. They saw something in him – perhaps it was his intelligence, a kernel of goodness, or maybe just his sense of fairness that belied his actions.

Because we were so close in age, and he was the leader of the so-called "cool" group at school, I was drawn into his orbit for the first time. He checked out his friends and picked out the nicest one for me to go steady with. Frank West was a good-looking and very sweet boy and he became my first boyfriend. We went to the school dances together, held hands and kissed at make-out sessions held in a clearing near the cemetery.

Weird now to think about, but boy, did we think we were mature. Our "gang" ruled our social world, small though our world might be. It was my first, and last, experience of being a part of a "cool" group at school. While I'm glad I had the experience, I'm aware now as an adult and as a parent, that I was very lucky that my experience was so short-lived. At 13, I probably could have been talked into just about anything. I was too young and too inexperienced to understand how peer pressure had me under its sway. I'm relieved that I didn't get talked into anything dangerous or life altering – "lucky" is how I describe it now – but at the time, I admit I never wanted that time to end. It's left me with a deep sympathy for little girls who succumb to the "coolness" siren.

By the end of 8th grade, my close girlfriends and I had high school all figured out. It was the spring of 1964 and we were anxiously looking ahead to starting high school at TAS (Taipei American School) that fall. TAS was a sort of "teen heaven" in our eyes. The school had sports teams filled with cute boys, cheerleaders who got to date them, and parties and dances every weekend at the Teen Club, and if all that wasn't enough, TAS even had high school fraternities and sororities.

We decided that we would try out for cheerleading. We had been on our eighth grade cheerleading squad for the junior high's intramural basketball games, and we thought we had an "in" because the sister of one of my friends was a cheerleader. She told us that our getting on the squad would be a breeze. Plus, as I said, we were already "cool".

In my little world, it didn't seem that life could get any better. Then over that summer, the bottom fell out of my world. The U.S. and Taiwan governments decided to end the USAID program in the country and as a result, my father was going to be transferred.

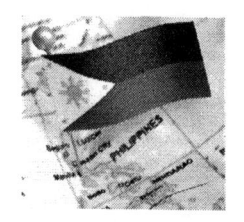

Chapter 6   Manila, Philippine Islands (1964 – 1966)

The Sullivan Kids, circa 1964

Ages of the Sullivan Children upon arrival in 1964 in Manila, the Philippines:

Dennis (Denny), age 17 (at KMI)

Michael (Mike), age 15

Maureen (Reen or Reeny), age 13

Robert (Jerry), age 11

Patrick (Pat), age 9

James (Jamie), age 7

Christopher (Ku or Chris), age 4

Our Mid-Tour Move to the Philippines

My mother had the round dining table built in the Philippines. I don't know all the details; I just know that she custom-ordered it, and it quickly became an important part of our home life. The table was large and circular and had a huge lazy Susan in the center upon which the serving dishes were placed. For the first time all nine of us could sit around the table and have enough elbow room. Almost immediately there were fewer territorial disputes during dinner (as in, "He's touching me", "Mike just kicked me", "Mom, tell him to stop breathing on my food. If he doesn't, I'm not going to eat it," and so on).

OK, maybe it wasn't just the table. A lot of things changed between Taiwan and the Philippines. Our ending up in the Philippines was just the beginning because it wasn't the usual State Department transfer.

Originally, we were scheduled to go on home leave the summer of 1964. My mother had even put down a deposit on berths on the USS President Roosevelt to take us from Hong Kong, via Japan, to Hawaii. But in the end, none of that ever took place. Instead, my father went on TDY (temporary duty) to Jakarta, Indonesia and naturally we assumed that Indonesia would be our next post.

I'm sure Jakarta is a lovely place and, indeed, I would love to go there, but it presented a problem for my family because it didn't have an American high school. At the time, Denny was going into his senior year of high school and I was going to be a freshman. My parents would have to scramble to find alternatives for us.

As it turned out, Denny took his future into his own hands. His girlfriend, Sandee, had just graduated from high school in Taipei that year and her father, a Colonel in the military, was being reassigned back to the States to Ohio. Denny, in love for the first time, wanted to go back to the States with Sandee. So he found a military school to attend that wouldn't be too far from where Sandee would be going to school. The school he chose was KMI (Kentucky Military Institute) in Lyndon, Kentucky, near Louisville. My parents, perhaps a bit perplexed by his sudden interest in the military, agreed to the arrangement because they figured a military school would keep him out of trouble. So with that, his schooling was no longer an issue.

Denny - KMI cadet

The attention then turned to me. But unlike Denny, I wasn't anxious to go anywhere. In fact, I wanted very much to stay with my friends in Taipei.

Up until then, I had assumed that we would be in Taiwan for another two years. On that assumption, my friends and I had figured it all out, as teenagers do. The plan was that we would go to TAS (Taipei American School), we would become cheerleaders and by extension, we would end up in the coolest group in high school. This new change of plans ruined everything.

Can there be anything worse for a 13 year old (nearly 14) than to lose her circle of friends, her high school plans, and her whole teen world the summer before beginning high school? It was a waking nightmare, and I felt alone in my agony.

My mother, ever the practical one, proceeded ahead to find me a high school. One option was to go to boarding school in Switzerland, but my parents decided that with Denny going away to school, it would be too expensive to send me that far away, too. So they looked for something closer by, and voila, it turned out there were all-girls boarding schools in the Philippines. Great. My mother contacted a few of the schools and the next thing I knew she and I were on a trip to Manila, via Hong Kong, so we could check out the schools, take the entrance exams, and find me a school.

The Beatles in Hong Kong

I was a reluctant participant in this boarding school idea. However, before we got to Manila to look at schools, we had a couple of days of shopping in Hong Kong. And, it was there that I touched the Beatles. Literally. Yes, them!

I was 13 years old and had been crazy about the Beatles from the first time I had heard a pirated copy of I Want To Hold Your Hand. That summer of 1964, they were on their World Tour and had a concert scheduled in Hong Kong. By the time we decided to go to Hong Kong, tickets to the concert were long since sold out, but as fate would have it, it turned out that we were staying at the same hotel as the group – The President Hotel in Kowloon.

The Beatles, circa 1964

No, we hadn't planned it. In fact, we didn't find out they would be there until we checked in and noticed that the hotel staff was buzzing about the expected arrival later that day of The Beatles. I promptly found out the time and positioned myself in the lobby, along with hundreds of other girls, to see these heartthrobs close-up.

The screaming began as soon as the wailing of the police escort sirens could be heard. As the limo drew up outside the lobby's glass doors, the crowd, me included, surged forward. Then the limo door opened and three of the four Beatles ran the gauntlet from the car to the waiting elevator. Ringo wasn't with the group in Hong Kong because he had been left behind in London with a sore throat. Instead, there was a substitute drummer, Jimmy Nicol, traveling with them, so I saw all except one of the Beatles.

As I was pushed and elbowed in the frenzied crowd, I closed my eyes and stuck out my hand and was rewarded with a touch of the sleeves of the Beatles' jackets as they ran past. Ah! I'll never wash this hand again. (OK, I wasn't THAT far gone, but it was definitely pretty cool.)

With the Beatles gone, the lobby slowly cleared and the excitement died down. I was too keyed up to go back to the hotel room so instead I went out and walked and did some shopping in the little shops around the area. I was in a daze.

I returned to the hotel later, entering the hotel on the ground level where there was a shopping arcade below the lobby. I got on the elevator and pressed the button for my floor, which was one of the upper floors, and I leaned back against the elevator wall as it started to climb. Suddenly the elevator stopped and the doors slid open to a scene of mayhem and the next thing I knew The Beatles charged into my elevator, together with a couple of their security men. My eyes must have been the size of saucers as I hugged my shopping bags to my chest and stared open-mouthed.

The doors closed and one of them, John perhaps, noticed me and asked, "Who's the bird?" meaning me.

They all turned to look at me and I would have dissolved into the wall if I could.

One of the security men cursed and pushed a button on the elevator panel. "How'd you get in here?" he demanded.

The others smiled and joked, "Actually, I think she was in here first," one of them chuckled.

The elevator stopped at the next floor and the security guard took my arm and guided me off the elevator, not unkindly, but not gently either. They all hollered "goodbye" and waved as the doors closed. The moment – MY moment (sigh) – was over. I stood in front of the closed elevator doors for a long time wondering what had just happened.

Eventually, I made it back to our room. My mother was in the room with a family friend who lived in Hong Kong. Ironically, he asked me if I knew that the Beatles were in the hotel?

I nodded.

"Would you like to go to their after-concert party? They have booked the entire floor, just below yours, and I've been invited to it."

I stared at him in disbelief, but before I could answer, my mother quashed the idea, "She's only 13 years old. She's too young for that sort of thing." And that was the end of it. She was right, of course, but oh, to be a few years older! (OK, a few years older and not traveling with my mother). But, still, I was happy with my brush with The Beatles. In fact, it's one of my cherished memories that, to this day, never fails to make me smile.

Choosing a Catholic Girls School

After my brush with celebrity, it was hard to get back to concentrating on the task at hand, which at that point meant touring boarding schools and taking entrance placement exams. We visited a few schools and I sat for the exams and walked the campuses and viewed the dorms; but the truth is, I was still in a coma of denial.

Maureen & Mom arriving in Manila, 1964

I prayed so hard that my father wouldn't be transferred to Jakarta that I shouldn't really have been surprised when my prayers were answered. Indeed, we weren't going to Jakarta – instead my father got orders for a transfer to Manila! How weird is that?

The Move to Manila

Back in Taipei, we packed up our stuff, went to going-away parties, said our goodbyes. We arrived in Manila the last week of August 1964. Because it all happened so quickly, and our household goods wouldn't be arriving for another month or two, we lived in the Manila Hotel until my mother found us a house.

The Manila Hotel, Manila, P.I.

The Manila Hotel was a grand old luxury hotel located right on Manila Bay. Normally, living in a hotel would be a good thing because we loved hotels (and still do). But this time, it wasn't quite as much fun because even though it was still only August, our summer vacation was prematurely terminated.

It turns out that the school year at the American School in Manila began the first week of August, and that meant that we had already missed a month of classes! Take a moment and let that sink in: I was thirteen years old...a month late for my freshman year...at a new high school...where I knew no one. It was devastating. If I hadn't already been a shy person by nature, this set of circumstances would certainly have caused me to become one.

Our House at 26 Cambridge Circle, Forbes Park Estates, Makati, a Suburb of Manila

Still, life in the Philippines wasn't a complete disaster. For one thing, my mother found us a fabulous house to live in. In fact, it was, by far, the nicest house we lived in overseas, bar none!

It was in a very expensive gated community called Forbes Park, where quite literally, millionaires lived. The house was ultra modern and set in its own compound. It had a large metal double gate, as well as a pedestrian gate with a sidewalk that led to the front door. There was a two-car garage with direct entry into the kitchen. The grand front door opened into a living room with soaring ceilings giving it an open and airy feeling, even in the breathless humidity of tropical Manila.

Jerry in front of Forbes Park house in Manila

The dining room, in a separate alcove off the living room, was to the left of the front door and that is where the famous round table was placed. The kitchen beyond was large, although I never spent much time in it, and there were servants' quarters – two small bedrooms and a bathroom – located behind the kitchen. The huge living room opened on to a high-ceilinged screen porch, which then opened out to a patio area with an expanse of grassy yard beyond.

In the center of the backyard was a Nipa hut playhouse (a miniature of the traditional Filipino huts, made out of wood and matted grass and built on stilts about three feet off the ground). The Nipa hut was a Christmas gift for my younger brothers that first Christmas (1964) and had been set up in the middle of the back yard for my brothers to play in.

To the right of the front entryway of the house were the bedrooms and a family room. The bedroom end of the house could be closed off from the living room with a tall floor-to-ceiling flexible room divider that could be drawn shut like a huge curtain. My parents closed it, in fact, when they had parties.

We had a pool table in the family room with a television surrounded by comfortable rattan furniture. This was the first overseas post where we had English-language TV programming pretty much around the clock, or so it seemed. The shows were older than what were being shown in the U.S., but who cared? They were new to us.

The house had five bedrooms and two of them were off the family room: one was Mike's room and Jerry and Pat shared the other one with a shared bathroom between the two bedrooms.

Up two steps from the family room was a long hallway that led to the other bedrooms. My bedroom was the first one on the right; then there was a shared bathroom between my room and the next bedroom, which Jamie and Chris shared. The only lock between the bedrooms was on the opposite door of the bathroom, so if I wanted to keep my brothers out of my room – and I normally did – I had to lock them out of the bathroom, as well.

All the bedrooms had built-in drawers and shelves along the outside wall beneath the windows, along with the room's air conditioner. On the inside wall was a huge double closet next to a built-in dresser with a large mirror above it. The only furniture required was the beds themselves, a desk and chair, and perhaps a bookshelf.

At the end of the long hallway was the master bedroom suite. My parents' bedroom was large, so large in fact that in addition to the normal bedroom furniture, it contained my mother's full-sized desk as well as a chaise longue where my father would stretch out after work in air-conditioned comfort, have a cocktail – a dry Martini with a splash of Vermouth, usually – and read Time magazine before dinner.

The living room had ceiling fans but no air conditioning, so on really hot days we would gravitate to the air-conditioned bedrooms of the house.

My parents had a king-sized bed and my mother had splurged on a set of satin sheets. The reason that sticks in my mind is that when my parents weren't around, my younger brothers made a game of sprinting down the long hallway, leaping on to the bed and sliding across the slippery satin only to crash on to the floor on the other side. They thought it was hilarious fun.

The master bedroom had its own bathroom but what was memorable about it was that the toilet, sink and bidet were a dark shade of olive green. It was odd since the rest of the house was painted in soft shades of off-white and all the other bathrooms had fixtures in the usual pastel blues, greens and yellows.

The bidet was a novelty to us and was the first one my brothers had ever seen. My mother never explained what it was used for and my brothers ended up deciding it was probably a water fountain for the dogs. My mother never disputed their interpretation and she ended up putting a potted plant in it for decoration.

Mike and the LaSalle School for Boys

I attended the American School along with my four younger brothers – Jerry, Pat, Jamie and Chris. My brother, Mike, didn't get accepted into the school because, we suspect, his records from previous schools marked him as a "trouble-maker" and as a private school, the American School in Manila didn't have to accept him. They were correct that his track record was pretty ragged. He was held back in first grade and flunked the third grade, so for a couple of years he was a year behind me in school. He was also one of those tough kids, just as comfortable using his fists as his mouth – neither of which endeared him to the school authorities.

Mike had always had a rough time with school and schoolwork. It could have been that he just wasn't suited to a mobile lifestyle where you transfer from school to school. Some kids seem to need more consistency and stability than others.

Over my 12 years of schooling, I attended five elementary schools and three high schools. Probably today Mike would have been tested for ADHD, dyslexia, reading or other learning problems, because he certainly had difficulties, but back then, they just figured he was a bad egg and treated him accordingly. Naturally, he reacted accordingly – getting into fights, receiving low grades, and all the rest.

Since Mike couldn't attend the American School, he was sent to an all-boys Catholic school – LaSalle School for Boys – where he actually did remarkably well on their entrance exam and ended up skipping the eighth grade and going straight into the ninth grade at the school.

When we arrived in Bangkok two years later, he and I were again in the same grade for our junior and senior years and graduated together in June of 1968.

The American School in Manila

As I mentioned, we were a month late for school that year. By the time we arrived, all the sports teams had been picked, cheerleading squad try-outs were over, and I had a lot of make-up work to do to catch up in my courses.

One mistake I deeply regret was in deciding to take Spanish that year. It wasn't long before I discovered that many of the kids in my class had been speaking Spanish practically since birth. In fact, their taking a Spanish class was comparable to my taking an English class – it was more about grammar than about learning the vocabulary and pronunciation of a new language. Eventually, my mother found a tutor for me, but by then, I was so hopelessly lost that I dreaded going to my first period Spanish class every single day. It pretty much ruined language courses for me, which is ironic given our lifestyle, and belies the fact that at the time I could already get by in several languages; just not in Spanish.

The other aspect of life in Manila that was totally new for us was to be attending a school where the majority of the students weren't transients like us. Indeed, most were expatriate residents of the Philippines who were American citizens, but they didn't move every two years like we did.

At school, we were outsiders in a way we never had been before; we were "the new kids" in a social world where the cliques had been established in early elementary school. I remember feeling almost shunned. OK, it wasn't that dramatic, but then again, when you're 13, it felt that dramatic. The boys at school – some of them, at least – were curious about me and I went on my first real "date" in Manila.

The girls weren't as welcoming; teenage girls can be cruel. They closed ranks and I felt ostracized. It was subtle and also harsh. I spent a lot of lonely lunch hours in the library and went home to listen to records alone in my room, daydreaming about the way I wished my life could be, the way I thought it would have been had we stayed in Taiwan.

I had never stopped to consider that the schooling I'd had up to then had been among "my own kind of people" — people who moved every two or three years, whose parents worked for the U.S. government or the U.S. military. Here I was in Manila, among the sons and daughters of expatriates who had married and merged into the local Filipino society, and I found it to be something of a closed society.

It took me a year – yes, a YEAR – to make a single good friend. I have never felt so alone and confused as I was during those two years in the Philippines. Being 13 and 14 years old, I was convinced that the problem was me, as teenagers do, and I concluded that I was some kind of misfit. It took me years to regain my self-confidence and to realize it wasn't me.

Still, I was off to a rocky start in high school in Manila. In fact, it was a huge relief when we moved to Bangkok two years later and were back among kids like us – military and diplomat's children. It felt like coming home.

The thing about moving every two years is that you become open to making friends quickly – you have to because you aren't going to be there long enough to let nature take its course. There is more flexibility in social relationships and groups that you don't find in more stable school settings back in the States. You would think that the friendships would be all surface without depth, but that wasn't the case. In much the same way that boot camp or sharing an emotionally-charged experience with others can foster deep connections that have no relation to the amount of time spent together, so being a part of an overseas mobile community can establish deep and abiding friendships. There is a bond made, almost like being a part of some medieval secret society, where without even the need for a secret handshake you recognize one another, you "get" each other at a nonverbal level. Isn't that what we all really want after all – to have someone "get" us?

Being a Teenager in Manila

Life wasn't all bad in Manila, of course. One of the cool things about living in the Philippines is that big stars and rock groups actually stopped and performed in Manila. That was a first for us. Up to then we had lived in Third World countries that generally were ignored by the famous celebrities of the day.

Even minor celebrities like Rod Serling (of the Twilight Zone TV series) came to Manila. In fact, Rod Serling gave a talk at our school and afterwards, I got a chance to meet him. He was an articulate and interesting speaker and told us, in his distinctive narrator's voice, tales of his first visit to Manila, parachuting in with MacArthur's "I-Shall-Return" invasion forces as they re-took the Philippines from the Japanese during WWII. It was a great story and resonated with me since he mentioned landing near Manila Bay and fighting his way into the Manila Hotel, a hotel I knew pretty well after spending a month living in it.

Many rock groups also made stops in Manila, including the Dave Clark Five, The Animals, The Rolling Stones, and others. My parents felt I was too young to go to the concerts, but I had a best friend at the time who made it a point to stake out the backstage areas so we could, at least, SEE the groups as they ran between their limos and the arena doors. That, it turned out, was even better! I wish now that I had been the avid autograph hound that she was; those scribbled names on dog-eared photos and folded album liners probably would be worth a fortune now. I wonder if she kept any of them?

Life in the Philippines

Perhaps it was the times – 1964 to 1966 – when the Vietnam War was ramping up just to the southwest of the Philippine Islands. Or maybe it was simply the Philippines itself, but at any rate, living in the Philippines was the first time overseas that I ever felt less than safe. Today, not feeling safe overseas is apparently a common experience for American diplomats and their families in far flung posts around the world. But in the mid-1960's it was a new experience for us.

Up to then, we had felt safe and fairly secure wherever we lived. Korea and Taiwan had welcomed us – perhaps envying us our comparative wealth – but even so, the local people were always friendly and gracious. Yes, there were student riots and some unrest when we were living in South Korea, but it wasn't directed at Americans in particular, and we never felt personally threatened.

In the Philippines, though, Americans weren't welcome or, at times, even liked. It felt more like we were merely tolerated. Because of the Vietnam War there was an incredible build-up of American troops and that resulted in added pressure on all Southeast Asian countries, including the Philippines. In addition, our history with the Philippines had not been particularly rosy. During World War II, for instance, MacArthur swore he would never leave the Philippines to the Japanese, but then he left. And although the resulting death count was extremely high for our American troops left behind, it was even higher for the local Filipino troops and worse, for the Filipino non-combatants, civilian women and children.

It wasn't a pleasant experience for us to live in a place where we felt a constant undercurrent of resentment. But even as I write that, I must admit that it wasn't like that everywhere we went in the Philippines. When we traveled outside of Manila, for instance, up to Baguio, over to Bataan, or on various other trips, we weren't scorned, threatened or made to feel unwelcome. Mostly, in fact, we had a pleasant experience with the Filipinos and enjoyed our travels to the beaches and visiting historical sites. The Philippines is a beautiful, tropical paradise and has much to recommend it to tourists and long-term visitors alike. But even so, in Manila during those times, there was a palpable anti-American sentiment.

Gabe, Our Driver

We employed a driver, Gabriel, for the first (and last) time while living overseas. Gabe's job was not only to drive us to and from school and our activities, but also to protect us and to keep us safe from street thugs, anti-American zealots, and anyone else who might wish us harm. I don't know if his duties were actually made that explicit, of course, but we were all aware of the dangers and learned to be cautious. Whether it was explicitly in his job description or not, Gabriel did take our safety seriously.

Manila was the first place I had ever seen everyday citizens carrying firearms and it made me uneasy and occasionally frightened. How pervasive were guns? I once went over to the house of a high school friend and a group of us spent the afternoon spraying the back yard with a machine gun his father had let him play with! Whew! Sure, it was no doubt illegal, and we certainly didn't broadcast that we had been playing with live weapons, but I'm amazed now that such a thing could even occur! I was 14! I also received the gift of a switchblade "for protection" from my brother, Mike. Where he got it, I have no idea. It was a noble gesture, I suppose, but, really,...a SWITCHBLADE? Still, it was a sincere gift and I still have it tucked away in my dresser drawer.

Mostly though, we ignored the undercurrent of menace in the city, if we noticed it at all, and we just carried on. Our house was broken into once, which is not an uncommon occurrence anywhere overseas. It's like the old saw: Why do people rob banks? Because that's where the money is. But being robbed in Manila was different from the time we were robbed in Seoul, for instance. For one thing, the Filipino police actually caught the robbers and even recovered our stuff. The disturbing part was that the robbers were never penalized nor did the police ever return any of the stolen articles. It left us with a sour taste. The underlying sense of pervasive corruption and seediness was disheartening.

The Philippines, after all, had been a protectorate of the U.S., a U.S. territory, and very nearly a state. When they became an independent nation, they wrote a constitution that is almost a word-for-word copy of our U.S. Constitution; and their government structure is a mirror of ours. That's why it was so disturbing to see the rule of law so twisted and misinterpreted.

On a positive note, though, I was impressed by the Filipino press and the freedom the reporters appeared to enjoy in reporting, commenting on, and yes, even openly criticizing their government. I thought at the time that their press enjoyed much more diversity of opinion than our own American press enjoyed back home. I don't know the current state of the press in the Philippines, so it may no longer be true, but I admired their courage and honesty at that time. It couldn't have been easy, given the state of their government and its political intrigues.

Christmas in a Christian Country

My social unhappiness lent a pall over my memories of the Philippines. It took me years to realize that upon reflection I actually had some truly happy times while living there. Many parts of the country were incredibly beautiful and fascinating, and most of the local people were friendly. It was also an interesting experience living in a country that was so westernized. But it was especially interesting to live for the first time in a Christian country that celebrated all the holy days – Easter and Christmas, in particular. We had lived in Buddhist countries where these holidays weren't even acknowledged. Back then if you lived in a non-Christian country, you could easily miss Christmas entirely.

I was 14 that first Christmas in Manila and was finally adult enough to stay up and go to midnight Mass. That year, my parents had been invited to a huge Christmas celebration with some Filipino friends and Mike and I were invited to go along. It was a chance to experience a different Christmas tradition and to see how very differently and fervently they celebrated Christ's birth.

It began with a sumptuous party at their huge home. This was a wealthy Filipino family – it was clear from the size and luxurious furnishings of the house and the number of servants, not to mention the glitter of their gold jewelry and the rustle of the silk of their Christmas finery. There was a grand sit-down dinner, crowded with their large family, relatives and close friends and other guests, perhaps a hundred people in all. I wasn't used to being up late and was tired after the dinner which didn't end until around 11 p.m., but that was only the beginning.

Next came the high Mass at the Cathedral. The church glittered with flowers, candles, and pageantry. The singing and music were deafening but beautiful, and the church was packed with people – shoulder-to-shoulder, standing room only. It was a solemn and long, but joyous service.

Afterwards, it was the family tradition of our hosts to open presents after attending midnight Mass, so we returned to their house for the post-Mass party. We didn't get home until four in the morning. I was envious that they got to open presents earlier than we did, and I was particularly envious that day because I knew that they would now be able to sleep in and we couldn't. My younger brothers were up an hour or so after we went to bed, already begging to open the Christmas presents we had only just put under the tree. It was days before my sleep and waking schedule got back to normal.

Easter in the Philippines

As joyous and elaborate as the Christmas celebration was in the Philippines, and for as much as we enjoyed the newness of sharing our Christian holidays in a Catholic country, Easter time was something else again. Easter is an important church holiday, but we learned that the Filipinos take Ash Wednesday and the Lenten period very seriously and to an extreme that we weren't prepared for.

It was nothing to hear of severe fasting, the wearing of hair shirts, people covering themselves in ashes, and others ritually whipping themselves to expiate their sins. It all culminated on Good Friday when penitents would even parade through the streets carrying huge replica crosses in imitation of Jesus' suffering, and occasionally a few even volunteered to be nailed to crosses.

After the reverence for life found in Buddhism, it was a bit disconcerting to wonder at how this kind of self-loathing could have ever been connected with the Christian love that is the foundation of Christianity. It's still a mystery to me. I understand the desire for forgiveness for their sins, but what type of God did they believe in who would demand such payment?

Beaches in the Philippines

We found the beaches in the Philippines to be equal if not superior to those we had enjoyed in Hawaii, and that is high praise since we were enamored with Hawaiian beaches, and still are. The big advantage the Philippines has over Hawaii is its greater size and number of islands. There are simply MORE tropical beaches to choose from than in Hawaii.

Filipino party rafts

We went to the beach at least one or two weekends a month during our two-year stay. We had a few favorites – one let us rent rafts that we anchored offshore in the calm waters of a coral reef. The "raft" was a floating grass-roofed party platform – it had a built-in picnic table and benches where we could eat and sit in the shade out of the glare of tropical sunlight.

On shore, we rented open-air Nipa huts (traditional Filipino grass huts) that were similarly outfitted. We kids would spend our beach days swimming, snorkeling or just paddling around on air mattresses and tubes while the adults played rounds of bridge, gin rummy or poker at the shaded picnic table, either onshore or anchored offshore.

On shore Nipa beach hut

Visit to Corregidor

We visited the many historic sites around Manila. Corregidor was a personal favorite, as it required a trip on the hydrofoil shuttle to reach the island in Manila Bay. The island itself was fascinating. We were there in 1964, just two decades after the momentous events of the Second World War. While it seemed to us that a long time had passed since the war even then, I'm amazed at how immediate the history seemed as we walked around the bombed out hospital and barracks. The guns were silent, but the history still lived on.

The local guides at these historic sites were still young enough to remember the actual events. We spoke to people who had lived through the bombardment and siege and had personally known the soldiers and nurses. Some had later been imprisoned at Santo Tomas in Manila and other

Corregidor gun emplacement

military and civilian POW camps after the fall of Corregidor. It is a stunning reminder of a very difficult chapter in America's past, not just for us but also for the Filipinos who fought and died alongside our troops.

We also visited the site of the Camp O'Donnell prisoner-of-war camp and the depressingly huge cemetery at Capas National Shrine where many victims of the Bataan Death March and prison camps were buried. It is a stark reminder of the cost of war and of man's inhumanity to man. About 2,200 Americans and 27,000 Filipinos died at Camp O'Donnell. It is a staggering waste to contemplate.

Pagsanjan Falls

My older brother, Denny, came home from Kentucky for a month at Christmas on his school break. It must have been very weird for him. He had been away at a military school, away from the family, not really "on his own", but no longer living with the family anymore either; like purgatory, I guess. Anyway, he came home, and my mother intended to show him a good time.

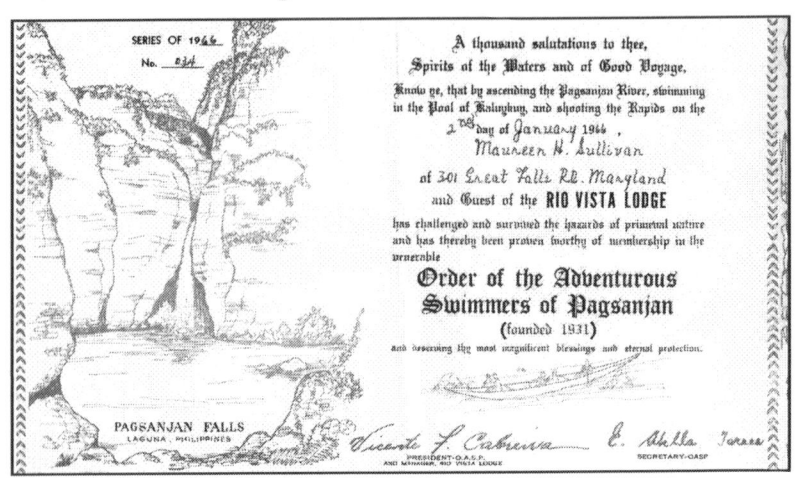

Pagsanjan Falls certificate

We went on trips – to the beach, of course, but also to some special places. One was a trip to Pansanjan Falls. This was a particularly fun trip. It was a couple of hours outside of Manila and required a canoe trip up a river to see the falls. On the way back we ran the rapids in the canoes.

We traveled from Manila in two cars. In the first car was my parents, the Filipino friends who had brought us to the falls and my youngest brothers. My brother Denny drove the second car with the rest of us. Being in a car without an adult meant we were supposed to "be on our best behavior", but what my mother didn't know wouldn't hurt her, right?

Stopping at open market along the road

She thought the little walkie-talkie transistors between the two cars would be enough to keep us in line. At one point, we stopped for a break and as a treat the Filipino friends bought all of us coconut milk (still in the gourd). We were polite and said, "thank you", but once we got back on the road, we heaved them out the window like liquid hand grenades. Yuck.

I love coconut...the white sugary concoction they sell in the bakery section of the grocery store, but who knew it began as this chalky, thin liquid surrounded by bland, white meat? Unfortunately, my mother saw the coconuts fly through the air and immediately we got a staticky reprimand, her icy voice barely covering her fury.

None of us knew how to respond until Denny picked up the walkie-talkie and in a clipped military voice, said, "We read you, over!"

Going to the PX and Commissary

Once a month we would do our shopping at the PX (Post Exchange) and Commissary. We had been shopping in PX's and Commissaries for the past seven years overseas. But the difference in the Philippines was that we weren't living on a military base; in fact, we weren't even living CLOSE to a military base. We had limited options: we could drive a few hours south to Subic Bay, the Naval base that had a decent size PX and commissary, or we could take the hydrofoil across the bay to Sangley Point, a much smaller base that only took an hour or two to get to, but didn't have much of a grocery selection; or we could drive a few hours north to Clark Air Force Base, probably one of the largest military bases in the Pacific.

Usually, we headed north. It was a full day's trip and we couldn't ALL go because when you shop for a family of eight for a month's worth of groceries you will definitely fill a station wagon. Of course, not everyone wanted to come along each month – it could be a pretty boring trip – but, even so, we each managed to go on the trip with my parents several times over the two years. Personally, I liked sitting in the backseat in the warm sunshine with the wind in my hair. I would daydream as I watched the greenish blur of tropical jungles and sugar cane fields whip by.

Jeepney in Manila

There was traffic – the occasional water buffalo, bicycles, diesel trucks, not to mention the decidedly Filipino Jeepneys. Jeepneys were gaudily painted and betasseled ten to twelve person buses. They were basically open-sided trucks but had a roof to protect the riders from the hot sun as well as the occasional monsoonal shower. They carried it all;

people, chickens and cargo of all sizes and shapes strapped to the roof racks and making the vehicle look top heavy and ready to topple over on the next sharp curve.

Clark Air Force Base was a huge noisy military base. There were planes constantly taking off and landing and the din was deafening. Many of the planes were medical flights. Clark had a huge efficient hospital and it was the first stop for the military wounded being flown out of Vietnam. Clark was also the first stopover for the soldiers on their way back to the States or on R&R leave to Japan or Hawaii, so there was a lot of activity, traffic and people on base.

We would spend most of our time at the Commissary, shopping for groceries and we certainly stocked up. There was usually a train of shopping carts – four or five, minimum – being hauled out to the car and then my parents had to shift the goods around in the back to make it all fit for the long drive home. We brought along coolers for the refrigerated foods and filled the car to the rafters. That's why only one or two children could come along on the trip because even the backseat would get filled and there would only be a small hollowed out spot to sit for the ride home.

When we got back to Manila, it would be another long unloading process, but at least we had servants to help out. Well, yes, they helped out all right, and it turned out, helped themselves to the food on occasion, too. We had one cook, Virginia, whose husband would mysteriously show up on the Saturday nights we had been to Clark. It turns out – and it took us several months to realize what was happening – that he would quietly pack up a fair amount of our Commissary groceries to sell on the black market the next day. Needless to say, when she discovered the theft, my mother fired Virginia.

Pets in the Philippines

Over our years overseas we had a menagerie of pets – in addition to the normal cats and dogs, we had some exotic pets like monkeys in Thailand and a huge tortoise in Ethiopia, and some of our pets belonged more in a barnyard than in a backyard, like the rabbits (Korea), horses (Ethiopia), a duck (Korea), geese (Thailand) and chickens (Korea and Taiwan).

In the Philippines our pets consisted of the two dogs that we had acquired in Taiwan – a dachshund named Schnitzel and a white toy poodle named Guang-Go – and we added a guinea pig or two to the mix in Manila. I don't remember how we acquired the guinea pig or which of us he belonged to, but he was a memorable pet.

We kept him in a cage in the garage and he would regularly sneak out of the cage to eat the dog food left in the dogs' dishes then he would run around the yard and would hide in the landscaping drainage pipes. Somehow my brothers had taught the guinea pig to imitate their whistle, so that when one of us whistled a certain set of notes, he would whistle them back at us and would sometimes even come to us. At the time I didn't find this particularly odd. I thought all guinea pigs did it. It turns out, he was just another weird Sullivan pet.

Home Leave of 1965

Because we hadn't had our normal home leave after leaving Taiwan in 1964, we went back to the States the summer of 1965 instead. One of the highlights of the vacation was going to the World's Fair in New York City.

We also stopped in Kentucky to visit Denny at school. We were there for their end-of-year parades and celebrations and I even got to attend one of his end-of-year dances, complete with formal floor length dress and long white gloves.

By mid-summer, we had concluded visits with the relatives and my father had finished being debriefed at the State Department in Washington. It was time to relax. So we headed out to Hawaii to finally live in our house in Honolulu for a few weeks.

My parents had bought the house after our 1959 home leave because they had fallen in love with the Hawaiian Islands with its gorgeous weather, tropical beaches, and mix of Asian and American cultures. After their years of living in the Orient they felt it would be a comfortable and fitting place to retire to eventually.

The house was built on one of the ridges overlooking Honolulu. It was just off Wilhelmina Rise in Kaimuki and had a spectacular view looking down into the crater of Diamond Head on the left and to the right the entire Waikiki skyline spread out before us with the airport and Pearl Harbor way off in the distance.

Denny's school year in Kentucky didn't begin until late September, however, our classes in Manila started the first week of August. We left with my father for Manila while my mother and Denny stayed on in Hawaii for another month.

Denny painting garage in Hawaii

They made us jealous with their photos and stories about painting the house in the cool mornings and then spending every afternoon at the beach; Denny surfing and my mother leisurely reading novels on her beach mat. Rough life, that. We, on the other hand, were back toiling away in the heat of Manila getting into the school year routine. It didn't seem fair.

Jamie's Birthday and the Round Table

Jamie's 8th birthday on September 19th in 1965 took place before my mother had returned from Hawaii, so my father and I were in charge of organizing the birthday festivities. Jamie invited some friends and my dad and I planned the birthday party, complete with party games, prizes, and food, including a hot dog and beans lunch, before Jamie could blow out the eight candles on his birthday cake and open his presents.

Things went well with the games outside in our large backyard and I rounded up the kids to go into the dining room for the planned lunch. As always seems to be the case, there's one kid who just turns out to be annoying. Naturally, we had one at the party. He had been whining about wanting to be first for every game, complaining that someone was cheating when he didn't win, and just being an all-round pain in the neck.

At lunch, I wasn't surprised when he ran ahead inside to be first at the table. If there had been a head of the table, no doubt he would have tried to sit at it, but just his luck we had the round table. The food – beans and franks – were already placed on the lazy Susan in the center of the table. The kids – keyed up as only 7 and 8 year olds can be – scrambled for the seats around the large round table. In the confusion of everyone getting settled, the obnoxious kid reached out and started spinning the lazy Susan, tentatively at first, and then with an evil grin, he spun it faster and faster.

No one defies the laws of gravity for long. After a turn or two, the centrifugal force caused the huge bowl of baked beans to fly off the lazy Susan and with a perfect sense of rightness, it landed squarely in the obnoxious kid's lap.

I looked up in surprise and saw that my father was standing across the table from me. I swear I saw a glint of amusement in his eyes and perhaps the slightest twitch at the corner of his lips, but that was all.

We cleaned the kid up and Dad even managed to keep a straight face when he turned the damp and stained boy over to his bewildered mother an hour later. After the last of the kids left and Jamie had carted his haul of birthday presents into his bedroom, my father and I finally relaxed in some comfortable chairs on the porch.

I glanced over at him. "Well, that went well, don't you think?" I asked.

He nodded thoughtfully, and then added, "Except for bean boy." His lips twitched and then I saw a huge grin spreading across his face. We laughed until my stomach hurt and tears were streaming down my cheeks. It was priceless.

Next Post: Bangkok, Thailand

In the spring of 1966 my father went on TDY (temporary duty) to Bangkok and by the end of May he received orders that he was being transferred to Bangkok. Once again we were on the move and there was the usual chaos of boxes and crates in the living room in the Manila house with burly Filipino movers going in and out as my mother tried to keep track of what was packed in which box.

On the trip from Manila to Bangkok, we stopped in Hong Kong and spent a week shopping and tramping around Kowloon and the island of Hong Kong.

Family in Hong Kong, 1966

 over the years my mother had acquired her own Hong Kong tailor, Petone's, who kept her measurements and preferences on file. On a visit, we would stop in to see Peter and his brother, Tony, the first day or two of a visit, armed with ripped out magazine pictures of dress ideas. There we would pick out the fabric, and leave, stopping back in for a fitting during the next day or two. By the end of our stay we would leave with a wardrobe at a fraction the cost we might have spent in the States, and with clothes that fit us to a "t".

Besides visiting the tailor, we also spent a great deal of time in the English-language bookstores, of which there were many. It was one of my favorite activities – one I could share with both of my parents, who were also avid readers. The musty smell of old books always brings to mind the long afternoons spent wandering up and down the aisles of floor-to-ceiling shelves of books in some ancient bookshop tucked away on a side street in Kowloon.

That trip, we flew from Hong Kong to Bangkok at night. I looked out the window and saw the fires and streaks of tracers far below us in Vietnam. It was the first time the Vietnam War was something real and immediate. It became more so over the next two years in Thailand.

Many of the kids that I went to school with had been evacuated from Saigon and while their mothers and families lived in the safety of Bangkok, their fathers were still living and working in Saigon.

Initially, they had received optimistic reassurances that Saigon was well behind the lines and out of harm's way. That was more or less true until 1968. During the Tet Offensive in January of 1968 the North Vietnamese attacked the US Embassy in Saigon and were fought off by the Marine Guards.

When your father works for the American Embassy – ANY American Embassy – just hearing that the grounds of an Embassy had been penetrated brought war and calamity way too close to home to be comfortable.

Chapter 7 Bangkok, Thailand (1966 – 1967)

The Sullivan Kids, circa 1966

Ages of the Sullivan children upon arrival in 1966 in Bangkok, Thailand:

Dennis (Denny), age 19 (in the Marines, California)

Michael (Mike), age 17 (high school junior)

Maureen (Reen or Reeny), age 15 (high school junior)

Robert (Jerry), age 13

Patrick (Pat), age 11

James (Jamie), age 8

Christopher (Ku or Chris), age 6

Welcome to Bangkok, Part 1 – May, 1966 to May, 1967

We arrived in Bangkok at the end of May, 1966, and from our first sight of the city – a late night drive from the airport to the hotel – the lights of the city glowed and twinkled around us and we already began to sense that Bangkok was going to be an exotic and fun place to live. As it turned out, we were right. Thailand was (and still is) a beautiful country filled with warm, friendly people; our school – the International School of Bangkok (ISB) – was a great school where we made many good friends, and over our two years in Thailand, we had wonderful times and collected lots of lasting memories.

The Erawan Hotel

For our first week in Bangkok, while my mother was house-hunting, we lived in three rooms at the Erawan Hotel. The Erawan was a really fabulous old hotel (Note: it opened in 1956 and was eventually demolished in 1987 to make way for the Grand Hyatt that sits on the site today).

The Spirit House in front of the Erawan Hotel

The Erawan was noted for its famous spirit house, the Erawan Shrine. In fact, it was such a big attraction that even after the Erawan was demolished, the shrine was kept on the grounds of the Grand Hyatt. The Erawan Shrine spirit house was built to protect the hotel and to correct the bad omens that were believed to have been caused by the laying of the foundation on the wrong date.

This was a country that had teetered between the Buddhist and Hindu cultures, taking on a bit of each and mixing them into a unique cultural concoction. The people have a deep spiritual sense of luck, fate, spirit worlds, astrology, and an alignment of the chi of the universe.

Apparently, the original construction of the hotel had been besieged by a number of mishaps and an astrologer was finally brought in to suggest a solution to the bad luck; the shrine was his remedy. The Hindu Brahma statue housed in the spirit house was designed and built, and with much religious and secular fanfare, put into place at the corner of the hotel site, where no shadow of the building would touch it (which would have caused even more bad luck). With the Shrine in place, the hotel gained providential good luck, as did many of its visitors over the years.

Hotels weren't the only places protected by spirit houses; in fact, nearly all the homes in Bangkok had them. That is, all except the house my mother found for us.

The House in Bangkabua

Obviously, spirit houses were integral to the mix of Buddhist and Hindu heritages in Thailand. A savvy traveler learns to respect the local culture and customs, or be prepared to suffer the consequences. My mother had a tough time house hunting. With eight of us, it wasn't easy to find houses large enough, especially when it came to the necessary number of bedrooms and bathrooms. We were, therefore, astounded when she was able to find us a large, really amazing house after only a week of looking. Keep in mind that many families spent weeks, if not months, living in hotels while they searched for the right house. My mother had done the job in just over a week!

The house my mother found seemed perfect. It was 100 years old and located in the Bangkabua section of the city, an older area off the beaten track. The house was described as "a Christian house," which didn't seem like a bad thing to us. It was built by an early convert, who perhaps in an effort to turn away from his former "heathen" ways, did not commission the building (and therefore, the blessed protection) of a spirit house. That was a spiritual no-no in this Buddhist country, and may explain why the house was empty and available when my mother went looking.

In the eyes of the local Thais, our not having a spirit house to protect the house (and us) meant that it was jinxed and we were warned any number of times that we would have nothing but bad luck. Perhaps. I suppose the truth of it depends on the longevity of the curse and how much you believe in that sort of thing. Let's face it; everyone's life is filled with a mix of good luck and bad luck. We can lay credit or blame for each turn of fate to the rabbits' foot in our pocket or the spirit house in the corner of our yard, or to our fervent prayer to God or our patron saint, or even to astrology. In the end, life is simply a mix of good luck and bad luck.

Arriving at house in Bangkabua, Bangkok, 1966

Still, the lack of faith surrounding the house was pretty evident. The Thais around us were always expecting the worst. For instance, once in middle of the night there was a huge fire in the crowded slums just down the road from the house. Our servants wasted no time in packing up their belongings and fleeing, so sure were they that the fire would spread to our spiritually unprotected house. The fire didn't reach our house, but I'm sure we all had moments that night where we wondered, What If...? I know I did.

Even though the place didn't have a proper spirit house, it was still an imposing structure. It was a large wooden Victorian style house. The front had an open porch that ran the length of the house. There was a tall (over seven feet) double-door front entrance and huge shuttered windows in every room, upstairs and downstairs. Since it was the tropics, there were no glass panes in the windows, only screens and wooden shutters that we pulled closed when it rained and to keep the bugs out at night.

Upon entering the front door, the stairway to the upstairs was to the left (the telephone was at the foot of the stairs next to a convenient bench to sit or lie on). Directly ahead on the opposite side of the foyer was a short hallway leading to a small breakfast room, where we ate most family meals, and beyond that, was a long narrow galley kitchen.

To the right of the foyer were double doors that opened into the living room and a small formal dining room that my parents used for entertaining but that the family only used for Thanksgiving, Christmas and Easter dinners. Off the living room there were tall double doors that opened outside to a large patio area and beyond that, the huge yard surrounded by landscaped tropical greenery, trees, and flowering bushes and shrubs. There were servants' quarters located out behind the house in a separate outbuilding.

Upstairs in the house were four huge bedrooms. To the right of the stairs was my bedroom. It had tall seven-foot high double doors, with bolt locks and upper and lower pin bolts that dropped into the floor or were pushed up into the doorjamb to close and lock the door in place.

Dad in Bangkabua house, Bangkok, 1966

All the bedrooms had high ceilings with huge languid fans; the ceilings and the fans were designed to stave off the worst of the tropical heat and humidity, moving the air, if not actually cooling it. All the rooms had multiple doors – one leading to the center hallway and the others connecting to the bedrooms on either side. I suppose, in theory, the entire upstairs could have been opened into a huge ventilated space, but we rarely opened all the doors at the same time.

The bedrooms each had a window air conditioner, but these were only used on the hottest of nights, because using all of them at once overloaded the very sensitive and ancient electrical circuits. Even without the overload we lost the electricity regularly. My parents' bedroom had the only air conditioner that was on most of the time but it was no match for Bangkok's stifling heat and humidity.

There were two large bathrooms upstairs. The better (cleaner) one was the one I shared with my parents. It was "better" and "cleaner" not through any inconsistency or lapse in the servants' daily housekeeping routine. It's simply that the other bathroom was the boys' bathroom and it was always a disaster scene of damp towels strewn on the floor and grit on the bottom of the bath stall, except for the fifteen-minute period just after the maids cleaned it and just before one of my brothers used it.

Front entrance to Bangkabua house, Bangkok, 1966

We didn't have bathtubs nor even Western style showers in these bathrooms; instead we had a bath stall – a four feet high tiled wall with an opening on one side, and a phone shower head on a short hose. The height of the stall was short enough to see over, but high enough to provide some privacy. It also had the added benefit of not needing a shower curtain, which would just have gotten moldy and gross in the double-whammy of hot water and humidity in Bangkok's tropical climate.

Originally, I had the room next to the bathroom; but later, when Judy Harper moved in with us, she and I were moved to the larger bedroom on the other side of my parents' bedroom.

My younger brothers – Chris and Jamie – shared my original bedroom and Jerry and Pat shared the other bedroom across the hall from them. From Jerry and Pat's bedroom there was access to a small attic room that Mike claimed as his bedroom. To get to it, he had to climb a short ladder with perhaps six rungs that led to a staircase that took him to his room in a turret of the house. Personally, I found it creepy up there, but it didn't seem to bother Mike. During the day, the rest of us were envious of his little kingdom and privacy, but at night I must admit that I, at least, was glad not to have to sleep up there.

Backyard of Bangkabua house, 1966

Between the two bathrooms at the end of the hallway was an upstairs screen porch where the TV was located – since it was "outside," the rabbit-ear antennae got slightly better reception. We didn't have a lot of English-language TV shows in Bangkok – particularly by comparison to Manila – but we occasionally enjoyed the few we did have.

Surrounding the house was a huge lawn and a tall – perhaps seven or eight foot high – metal fence with a double-door gate that the gardener would open when the car horn was honked.

The Thai Neighborhood

Our house was located off a small dirt track in a poor neighborhood. Beyond our house were another one or two houses before the beginning of a huge slum. Many of the kids from the slum gravitated to our gate out of curiosity and boredom. They were curious about us, naturally, but we also became their source of entertainment at times, as well; and they, ours.

One game the street kids would play was to imitate every word or noise my brothers would utter. Many an hour was spent with my brothers yelling something on one side of the gate and having a group of kids on the other side repeat it back at them. Some times it would be phrases, sometimes lyrics from silly songs, like "Monkey see, Monkey do," only when the Thai kids repeated it, it sounded more like "Monk-kay, SEEEE! Monk-kay DOOOO!"

Some times things escalated from silliness to missiles flying back and forth. First, some innocuous pebble might be tossed over to catch someone's attention, then next, a stone or mud clod or two, and then spoons!

The Spoon Incident

Let me explain about the spoons. In one of the houses on the other side of our wall, we had a neighbor who was dying of TB (tuberculosis). The poor guy hacked and coughed up his lungs from his back porch on the other side of our wall nearly every morning. Over the months, as the back-and-forth increased between my brothers and the gate kids, once in a while, things would get out of hand.

There was the time my brothers filled up water balloons and heaved them over the wall scattering the kids with shrieks of surprised laughter. Unfortunately, that was the same week that the sick man died. In answer to the water balloons, the Thai kids retaliated by throwing "death spoons" over our gate. What are death spoons?

Apparently, in an effort to prevent the transmission of his highly contagious illness, the man's family didn't just wash the implements the sick man used, they would throw them away. These were cheap metal spoons and chipped bowls, primarily. Because the gate kids were upset with my brothers over the water balloon incident, they began to throw the spoons over our gate. Ugh.

With five boys in the family, we had a number of minor incidents that caused friction between our neighbors and us. I don't blame the neighbors for complaining; heck, most of the time I agreed with them about how annoying my brothers could be.

Sometimes it was baseballs that were hit or thrown over the back wall and into a neighbor's house. Sometimes, it was fruit stolen from a neighbor's tree. Though, that time it wasn't my brothers' fault, it turned out that our monkey was the culprit.

My father learned to always carry a few Thai Baht (currency) in his pocket when the neighbors asked to speak to him. It was rarely good news, and normally a few dollars soothed their hurt feelings.

Overall, though, I think the neighbors appreciated having us living in the house. As long as wealthy Westerners were paying the bills, things improved for everyone in the neighborhood – the telephone line lost some of its static, the electricity worked most of the time, and the water flowed through the water pipes and appeared, if not cold and pure, at least not as brown when the faucet was turned on. I think it was reasoned that putting up with my brothers and their antics was the price everyone paid for these working utilities.

Pets in Bangkok: The Monkey

Whenever we talk about living overseas and the strange pets we have had, invariably we bring up the monkey, or monkeys, because actually we owned two of them while we lived in Bangkok although the one we usually talk about – our favorite – was the first one.

The monkey in the tree, Bangkok 1966

The monkeys were both gibbons, a highly intelligent small ape that is also an endangered species. Our monkey was without a doubt the best pet we ever had.

Initially, my mother was dead-set against getting a monkey. Jerry and I were the first to spy a monkey for sale in the open-air Sunday markets in Bangkok. Heck, it turned out you could get a baby monkey cheap and we quickly pooled our money and bought a tiny little monkey that turned out to be way too young.

We brought it home, figuring that we could hide it from my mother, but when it didn't seem to thrive – wouldn't eat at all, in fact – we had to show her and she immediately realized that the monkey wasn't well. I suspect now that she was concerned it was carrying something lethal that we might catch (and – God Forbid! – that it might be something we had not been inoculated against). We rushed the baby monkey to the vet and he gave it a glucose shot, explaining to us that the baby had been taken from its mother before it had been weaned, and that it didn't have enough teeth nor the metabolism to live on anything but its mother's milk. Sadly, it died that night. It was awful. We had him in a little cage and he was motionless, looking like a tiny old man curled up and fast asleep. We gave him a great burial, but even that didn't take the ache away.

A week later my mother came home with a small gibbon monkey. Now that I think about it, it's really shocking that she did such a 180-degree turnaround about getting a monkey, but perhaps she talked to other Americans and discovered that monkeys were pretty common pets in Bangkok.

Dad and the monkey, Bangkok, 1966

Of course, she made sure the monkey she bought was old enough to survive. His name was Boom-bai, but he only really understood the word "mah" which meant "come" in Thai and we never called him by a name.

When Mom came home with the monkey, she had him in a cage in the back of the station wagon. She showed us the monkey and explained that he must get acclimated first. At some point, she took him out of the cage and held him. It was the sweetest thing to see him with his arms wrapped around her, like a baby clinging to its mother.

Then suddenly something startled him (probably all of us crowding around wanting to take a turn holding him). At any rate, he screeched and took off running, long arms raised in the air for balance, and "ooh-ooh-oohing" as he swung himself into the huge tree near the gate of the compound. Gibbons are fast and gifted gymnasts. They can travel nearly 35 mph swinging from branch to branch through a forest, and have been said to be able to make leaps of up to 25 feet. If he wanted to get away from us, there wasn't much chance of our catching him.

My mother persevered. She stood patiently under the tree, calmly repeating "Mah... Mah!"

I remember that we thought that was hilarious and teased her about it for years. She was so serious and had just learned this great word command in Thai and was using it to great effect, showing off even. Then the most astounding thing happened. The monkey scurried down the tree and swung himself back into her arms. Needless to say, from then on my mother became his greatest proponent and defender.

This particular monkey was a character, to say the least. He was smart, as gibbons, and all apes are. He had no tail; his fur was thick, wiry and black with a white circle around his face and hands. His face was black and looked like the wrinkly little face of a very old man. His eyes were lively, dark and observant.

Mom and the monkey, Bangkok, 1966

The cutest things about him, though, were his hands. I suspect that the hands are always the most fascinating part of a monkey. They are so much like ours; they manipulate things just as we do, and it is the hands and the things the monkey does with them that demonstrates how very bright he is, way smarter than we gave him credit, at times. We taught him a lot of things; and I know he taught us a thing or two, in return.

My father used to get up very early in the morning. We all did because in Bangkok everything was done before the heat of the day, in the tradition of the tropics. Our school bus would show up at 6:30 a.m. and we started classes at 7:30 a.m. Of course, it also meant that school was done by 12:30 p.m. and that was nice as it gave me the whole afternoon to hang around with my friends.

My father was the first to get up each morning and when the monkey heard him moving around he would "hoo-hoo" and knock against at the shuttered windows until my father opened the bathroom shutter. The monkey would then slip between the bars and would sit on the edge of the sink as my father shaved, observing his every move.

Eventually my father taught the monkey to turn the water on and off and he would imitate my father, as monkeys do (yes they really do that). We were never able to teach him to drink from a cup – he always drank by dipping his hand into the liquid and sucking it out of the very fur around his wrist. He liked to have his feet tickled. Sometimes he would lie down and raise his feet up in the air, patiently waiting for someone to caress his hands or feet.

If he were perched on the couch behind your head, you would sometimes find him grooming you as he searched for lice in your hair. No, he never found any that I know of, but it was hilarious and actually quite a soothing sensation. After all, we were his family, his troop, and it was part of his social nature to groom us. Although, seeing him occasionally pick at something and put it in his mouth was disconcerting, to say the least. Did he do that automatically or did he actually find something edible in our hair?

Between the back door and the servants' quarters was the tree where the monkey lived most of the time. There was a rope strung between two trees so he could swing himself back and forth, but we didn't usually keep him tied up except when my mother had parties or if we were leaving the house for a while.

He didn't like being tied up with the rope and would sometimes make a huge scene if he thought he could garner some attention. Once he was hooting and hollering and when we came out he was pulling at the rope as if it were choking him. It was his way of expressing his annoyance with being restricted. Anything for a little sympathy. When we didn't fall for his shenanigans, he would get upset with us and would occasionally try to pee on unsuspecting people walking under his tree. As is the way with boys, my brothers rooted for the monkey and his aim. Crude humor, but sometimes surprisingly funny.

We had no choice but to keep him tied up during my mother's parties though, because, as it turns out, monkeys have a real affinity for alcohol and due to their small size it doesn't take much to get them drunk, nor long to create an alcoholic.

My parents used to give lots of parties; entertaining was part of my father's job and besides that, the parties were fun and my mother was good at putting them on. The parties in balmy Bangkok, particularly in a house without air conditioning, were generally held out of doors. We had a huge patio and yard and my mother would set chairs all around the yard for her guests to sit in as the hour grew late.

The monkey, normally chained up when my mother had parties, would sometimes get loose, and when he did he would sneak up to the highball glasses left carelessly on the ground beside a chair, and he would dip his hand into the drink and then suck the alcoholic cocktail from his wet fur. If we didn't catch him in time, he was soon rip-roaring drunk. We never meant for it to happen, but he was pretty entertaining when he got drunk.

For instance, he would reach out to swing up on a tree branch and miss it entirely and would then look surprised by the whole incident, shaking his head and looking around to see what might have pushed him off course. And, just like his human counterparts, the next day he was made to pay for overindulging because he also suffered hangovers. Poor little guy.

Jamie & Ku with Schnitzel, the dachshund, Bangkok, 1966

In addition to the monkey, we still had our two dogs – Schnitzel, the dachshund, and Guang-Go, my white toy poodle. The monkey loved playing with the dogs. But there was no question as to which had the upper hand. Initially, we were concerned that the dogs would hurt him, but we shouldn't have been concerned. The monkey was so much more intelligent than the dogs and he had the advantage of being able to climb and swing into trees and bushes. The dogs found him endlessly fascinating; and he, in turn, loved teasing them.

We also had two huge geese that kept the snakes out of the yard. The dogs didn't bother the geese much, particularly after being chased and bitten by them. Heck, we didn't go near them either. You only need to be bitten by a goose once. You won't soon forget that pinching sting, nor the nasty bruise it left that took weeks to fade. Before we owned them, I would never have guessed that geese could be so surly.

Tropical Pests

Speaking of pets and pests, in addition to snakes, which the geese kept at bay, there were huge frogs in the swampy foliage at the front of the house. We never saw them during the day, but at night we could pick out their lumbering masses with flashlights as they crawled across the yard, and boy, could we hear them! They sounded like sheep "baa-ing". It was an unearthly sound after a heavy rain on a dark and humid night.

We also had ants – army ants, to be specific. It was the tropics, after all, and I suppose we should have anticipated them. We learned early on that whatever you do, don't break their lines, because if you did, they would swarm and sting. They weren't quite as bad as the ants we later found in Africa – these weren't as big, nor did they adhere as tenaciously – but the sting was certainly as painful. To this day I get a creepy-crawly sensation whenever I see a bunch of ants together.

Once (I warn you this is gross) I was hungry and went into the kitchen in search of something to snack on. I spied a loaf of bread in a plastic bag and quickly reached in, grabbed a slice and without looking at it, took a bite. My tongue felt like a hundred needles had pricked it. I spit the piece of bread into the sink and was appalled at the seething swarm of ants on it. I spit and spit and cringed at the thought of all those ants. My skin still crawls at the thought! For days afterwards, I would flinch at the sight of an ant, not to mention an army of them.

Family Lingo

One of the novelties of a mobile lifestyle is that we created a family lingo that was a mixture of a number of favorite phrases in multiple languages. Even our nicknames sometimes resulted from some foreign incident. My youngest brother Chris got the nickname "Ku" because the baby amah in Taiwan couldn't pronounce the "r" sound in his name so she called him "Ku-shee" (her version of "Chrissy"). We shortened it to "Ku" and that was his nickname for an embarrassing number of years. We still occasionally refer to him that way.

Families tend to create their own inside jokes – usually funny only to members in on the origins of the joke. Well, we took it one step further and sometimes created whole performances.

For instance, there was a chant that Mike, in particular, brought into the family lore: The "Di-Mak, Mak" chant. Basically, he would chant in a low singsong voice, "Di-Mak!" and my younger brothers would respond in unison: "Mak! Mak!" Then he would chant again a little louder, "Di-Mak!" and they would chant back at him "Mak, Mak!" and so on and on. I believe the number of chanting interactions depended on how annoying they wanted to be. What does it mean? Basically, it's Thai for "Very Good!" or "Life is Good". With the refrain, "Good! Good!" I suppose that would be the translation anyway.

As I say, it was an irritating chant, and perhaps I'll regret having recorded it here for posterity. I'll mention the creation of a couple of other "oldies but goodies" in the Ethiopia section, where things occasionally got out of hand.

Summer School at ISB

We arrived in Bangkok in May of 1967. The previous school year in Manila ran from the beginning of August to May and we left for Bangkok shortly after the end of the school year. It would be nearly four months before the start of the next school year in Bangkok so my mother thought it would be a great idea if we all went to summer school that summer. I think it had more to do with wanting to get us out of the house, keep us busy and thereby out of trouble, but she said it would be a good way for us to meet other kids and in that regard, she was right.

That summer, I signed up for a typing class that was probably the most useful course I ever took. The return on that investment of time has been incalculable, particularly now that I spend about ten hours a day on a computer keyboard.

Learning to type back then meant that I could write more quickly and people could actually read what I wrote. I had been an avid writer since the seventh grade in Taiwan when Mrs. Finkelstein, my seventh grade teacher, complimented me on a short story I had written. That compliment was the fulfillment of a dream that took shape the year before when I was in the sixth grade in Korea.

My sixth grade teacher had given our class a creative writing assignment. Creative assignments are pretty common in classrooms today, but back then they were a rarity. My teacher asked us to write a short story about Christopher Columbus' trip to the New World. I wrote a very straightforward, and certainly very boring story that I no longer can remember the details of. I got a "C" on the assignment, which I do remember, so I'm pretty sure my story wasn't very good. I know that I included no dialogue, and I'm sure it didn't have even the most basic beginning-middle-and-end of a story arc.

The teacher read the story that got the "A+" to the class and I was totally blown away. It was written from the perspective of a mouse on the ship (and this was 25 years BEFORE the animated "An American Tail" movie, too!). It was funny, touching, and clever; and for me, in many ways, it was a paradigm shift. I thought that if I could write something half as good as that story, I would be in heaven.

In the seventh grade, I finally was complimented for my writing and I have considered myself a writer ever since. Let this be a lesson in taking the time to compliment and encourage children in whatever they pursue. A small compliment or word of encouragement can make a huge difference and pay dividends you couldn't begin to imagine.

Learning to type took care of the practical side of pursuing my dream. Once I learned to type, I honestly felt I had it made. Could a Pulitzer or at least an Alternate Selection for Book-of-the-Month be far behind?

ISB, International School of Bangkok

We attended the International School of Bangkok during our two years in Thailand – my junior and senior years of high school – although because we had an extended home leave in 1967, I also attended Kalani High School in Honolulu for the first semester of my senior year until we returned to Bangkok in December of that year and finished out the school year. Mike and I graduated in June of 1968.

ISB was an international school with children representing nations from around the world. Their parents worked in the embassies, international aid organizations, and of course, the U.S. military and diplomatic corps. However, during those years in the late 1960's because of the build-up in Vietnam, the majority of the students at the school were from the United States, which meant that perhaps 90% of the student population was American.

ISB outdoor lounge

ISB had high caliber teachers, most with masters degrees or higher, and an American curriculum. The sports and after-school activities were similar to what you would find at any stateside high school – and there were the requisite dances, fashion shows, and a variety of clubs and sports. Our class sizes were small compared to big city high schools, but still large enough – there were 175 graduating seniors in my class, and that was about average, I think.

Bangkok, "Teen Heaven"

I loved Bangkok – I believe we all did. Looking back, I think part of the attraction was that Bangkok was a sort of teen heaven. Taipei had that reputation, too, but I wasn't in high school when we lived there, so I can't judge whether it was true or not, although I know that Denny certainly loved Taiwan and had a lot of fond memories of his high school years there.

During our Bangkok years, Mike (17), Jerry (13) and I (15) were all teenagers. As teenagers, we had a lot of freedom in Bangkok, particularly by comparison to Manila where our driver, Gabriel, kept an eye on us. In Bangkok, there were few adult eyes looking over our shoulders.

The minibus picked us up for school between 6:00 and 6:30 a.m. (school started at 7:30 a.m.) and we didn't usually see my parents until dinner time. This was primarily because although my mother had always been a busy woman, in Bangkok she took a full-time job working as the publishing coordinator for several international conferences. She loved the job and she gave it her usual 110%, which meant she was very busy and happily focused on it; so for us, it meant, blessedly, a lot less scrutiny of our activities.

Chavalit Hotel, the after-school hang-out

My mother will tell you that one of her child rearing philosophies is that teens need a certain amount of freedom to test their wings. When you are raising teenagers overseas, in fact, it's critical that they learn to become self-reliant before you put them on a plane and send them all by themselves thousands of miles away to college. It's probably better that they make any missteps close to home, where parents are around to encourage, discipline, and occasionally, to just pick up the pieces. Naturally, our intent in Bangkok wasn't to learn self-reliance so much as to just have a good time; the city was our oyster and by some miracle we had pretty much been left to our own devices to enjoy it. How cool is that?

But leaving philosophy aside, we were high on the heady freedom of it all. Since we were living in the tropics, our school day started early and ended early – in fact, the second year when I was a senior I was done with my classes by noon. We would have lunch (Singha beer and khao pad, the amazing Thai fried rice) at some corner noodle shop (mostly run by Chinese merchants rather than Thais).

The rest of the afternoon we spent with our friends, hanging out together at the Chavalit coffee shop located at the end of the soi (road) the school was on. Like most teenagers, we moved together in packs and we never tired of being together; talking, planning parties for the weekends, listening to music, or just doing nothing, but always doing it together. Sometimes we would take samlors (a sort of motorized three-wheeled pedicab) or klong boats (water taxis that ran on the remaining open canals of the city) and we might go see a movie, or to the teen club, or shopping in the open-air markets. Oh yeah, and occasionally, we did our homework.

The Teen Club

The teen club was on the other side of town (closer to the embassy) near Lupini Park and we actually spent a fair amount of time there and made a point of always starting out at the teen club every weekend night – Fridays and Saturdays – primarily because it was the only place we admitted to our parents that we were going. It was an "approved" spot for us. And to give it its due, it was a fun place with music (juke box and our own live bands), dances, ping-pong tables and a snack bar. There were adult chaperones that ran the teen club and organized the activities. They liked kids and because they weren't our parents, they became our confidants and de facto counselors.

The fact that the teen club was an "approved" place from our parents' perspective was also its fatal flaw. It had all those parental rules, like no drinking or drugs, and you had to be 16 to smoke in the smoker's patio out back. So we would spend an hour or so at the teen club, dancing and meeting up with our friends, then we would leave and go have some real fun, hitting the bars and nightclubs on Patpong Road or wherever we heard "the action" was.

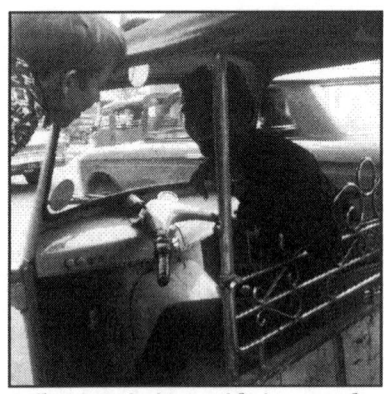

Mike negotiating a ride in a samlor pedicab, 1966

We went clubbing at a lot of the same places the GI's went, although most of us stayed away from them, and they from us. It was a "no-no" for any of the American high school girls to date GI's although it certainly happened; but the girls who did ended up with very shady reputations.

It's odd that we didn't have more contact with the GI's actually. After all, we were only a few years younger than most of them – many were 18, 19 and 20 years old; and we were 16 and 17. But the experience divide between them and us was a chasm; we may as well have been from totally different generations. As high schoolers, we were still caught up in the self-centered, innocent, narcissistic life of American teenagers; they, on the other hand, had seen war and death and it had aged them and seared their souls. About all we shared was our preference for rock music, American cigarettes and occasionally marijuana and hashish. Need I say that recreational drugs were ubiquitous in Bangkok and throughout Southeast Asia in the late 1960's?

To be honest, I don't recall my parents in many of my memories of Bangkok – I think that's probably true of teenagers everywhere. Teenagers are notoriously self-centered, and we were certainly that. I think now that my parents really had it tough with so many teenagers in the house at once. In Bangkok, I was 15, 16, and 17; Mike was 16, 17, and 18; Jerry was 13, 14, and 15 – three teenagers in the house at the same time; four, when Denny came home for visits. I don't know how my parents managed! And worse, they would have multiple teenagers living at home for at least the next 6 years. Perhaps that's the real reason my mother went back to work? She may have needed a dose of adult company and a respite from us.

Settling in to Thailand

Our first summer in Bangkok, the summer of 1966, was great fun and we met a lot of other kids and became acclimated to our new life in Thailand. My father was thrilled with his new position as Enterprise Officer at the USAID (U.S. Agency for International Development) mission. He liked the people he worked with and was comfortable being back in an Asian culture. You could tell that he truly reveled in it. While the Philippines may be fascinating, it really isn't "Asian" – their language, their culture, and certainly the Spanish, Catholic, and Polynesian influences far outweigh their geographic closeness to the Asian continent. My father's language skills and years of experience, background, and education were in Chinese, Japanese, and Korean – certainly those were also his preferred spheres, as well. He was never so happy with a post as he was in Bangkok and he seemed to relax and relish it.

klong boats on the Chao Phraya, Bangkok, 1966

Holidays at Pattaya Beach

We spent our first Labor Day weekend at Pattaya, a beach resort about two and a half hours south of Bangkok on the Gulf of Thailand. It was located about an hour north of Sattahip, the US Naval base and nearby U-Tapao airport that was built during the Vietnam War for the influx of soldiers being flown to and from the war zone. Pattaya came into its own during the late 1960's when the soldiers used it as their preferred R&R destination. It was a gorgeous beach resort with clear warm blue waters, sandy beaches, coral reefs, and very little surf. There were motorboats to rent for waterskiing, fishing boats that would take you out to the islands just offshore and, at night, the place was like a beach party movie only more exotic!

Pattaya Beach picnic, Thailand 1966

It was in Pattaya that many of our lasting friendships took root, and it made sense that it would happen there because all the Americans, or so it seemed, spent the holidays (Labor Day, Thanksgiving, Christmas, Easter vacation, Memorial Day, July 4th) in Pattaya. The first time we went, we stayed at the Pattaya Nipa Lodge (later called the Nova Lodge), located right on the beach. A lot of our friends rented bungalows and over the long weekend we had a relaxed time waterskiing and lying on the beach during the day, hanging out at the GI's snack bar that had a jukebox with fairly recent rock music from the States in the afternoons. And at night, we had beach parties, hung out at the local noodle shops (I guess these might be called open-air beer hangouts at night) or if we were feeling really rowdy we would head to Barbo's or the Marine Bar, which were where the GI's and their Thai prostitutes drank and did drugs. Wild AND off-limits, what could be more attractive to a group of teens?

We would drink beer, we would dance and listen to music on the beach, and we would play endless drinking games. Some of the kids were already looking to size up future dating potential, but mostly, at least over the Labor Day weekend at the beginning of the school year, the boyfriend-girlfriend relationships were still at the getting-to-know each other stages, so we tended to party as a group rather than pair off.

There were fist fights, whose seriousness could be gauged by how much beer or hard liquor had been consumed by the participants. When things got out of hand, there were MP's (Military Police) and the need for a lot of fast-talking. The MP's didn't necessarily want to get us into trouble, but sometimes we just pissed them off. (And, of course, we were underage, so they had that on their side). Occasionally, we managed to calm them down and they left us alone after we promised we would (1) be more quiet, (2) stop drinking, (3) would go home before midnight, or whatever promises seemed appropriate at the time.

Mike at Pattaya Beach, 1966

Judy Harper

That first year in Bangkok was my junior year of high school. Judy Harper – a freshman that year – moved in with us for the school year. Judy had long straight blonde hair (all the rage in the late 1960s), and she was pretty, petite, and a lot of fun. Her father worked for USAID in Vientiane, Laos, where there was no American high school. The high schoolers that lived in Vientiane were either sent to boarding schools in Switzerland or Singapore,

Judy Harper, Bangkok, 1966

or they did a home school correspondence program. Unfortunately, the teens who did the correspondence program for high school were notorious (heck, we heard about their escapades down in Bangkok!). The stories generally involved drinking, drugs, and even an occasional pregnancy.

Judy's parents thought it best for her to live in Bangkok and attend a "real" high school, so my parents volunteered to let her to stay with us for the school year. Maybe my folks hoped she would be like the sister I never had, or at least, be a ready-made friend. I think they were concerned about me and how reclusive I had become in Manila. They needn't have worried. The problem was the environment in Manila, and for me, life changed dramatically for the better when we moved to Bangkok. But it was fun having Judy living with us, and I was glad to have her around during that year.

Judy Harper, Bangkabua house, Bangkok, 1966

Easter, 1967 – Air America to Vientiane, Laos

I went home with Judy to Vientiane over the Easter vacation in 1967. My father arranged for us to get a ride on the cargo plane that flew daily between Bangkok and Vientiane. It was operated by Air America, the CIA airlines (although we certainly weren't aware of the connection at the time). It was a very different flight experience than the usual air trip you would expect.

First of all, it was a cargo plane with the only seats being the benches along the inner sides of the aircraft. Second, Judy and I were the only passengers on the flight. There was presumably a pilot and copilot in the cockpit, although we never saw them; and there were two guys working in the back with us. We took off and within fifteen or twenty minutes, one of the guys swung open the cargo bay doors at the back of the plane. It was stuffy in the plane and there was a rotten odor coming from what turned out to be the science project for the young son of the ambassador – some dead sea dweller – Squid? Clams? I'm not sure what it was, but it smelled like rotten seaweed. The bay doors were also opened so that the two guys could heave huge crates out along the way. We watched the crates sail down under their white parachutes into the canopy of green below as we flew over northern Thailand and southern Laos along the Mekong River, whose meandering brown water snaked through the jungle below.

What was in the wooden crates? Who knows? It could have been medical supplies, or food, or perhaps even guns. There was no telling because there were no markings at all on the outside of the crates. The guys wore a kind of harness while they were working, pushing the crates into place and getting ready to send them out of the plane. For safety's sake, they hooked themselves to the parachute line along each side of the ceiling of the plane. Once they were done, they invited Judy and I to stand at the opening to look out. We thought that was very cool.

We were flying low and it was mesmerizing to watch the jungle canopy disappear under us. Occasionally, we would pass over tiny villages, just a couple of huts on stilts in a small open space in the midst of the undulating greenery. Sometimes – particularly along the river – the people would look up and wave at us and we would wave back and smile down at them. It was a wonderful flight.

Vientiane, the capital of Laos, was once part of French Indo-China when the French had colonized that part of Asia. The city was so different from Bangkok. Thailand, called Siam originally, had been the only nation in the region to retain its independence during the colonial period. The primary reason it was left alone was that it conveniently served as a buffer between the French colonies of Vietnam, Cambodia and Laos, and the vast British Empire that stretched from Burma, through the Indian subcontinent and over to the edge of Afghanistan.

It was to everyone's benefit to let the Thais remain independent and the wily King of Siam managed to play his cards right to maintain his sovereignty.

Judy and I took pedicabs around the town and to me Vientiane seemed to be right out of a B-movie from the 1930's. There were the seedy French hotels and rundown restaurants slowly rotting in the tropical heat. There were the French colonials who had stayed on after independence and who carried on as if they were still living in a foreign outpost of Paris. And, there was a royal family that had a sordid reputation for gambling, drugs and corruption. It was all fascinating and completely new to me. I enjoyed the trip to Vientiane immensely.

We returned to Bangkok and finished the school year and by the end of the year, my parents decided not to extend an invitation for Judy to live with us the following year. I think they found it hard to discipline her. And personally, my loyalties were often divided. On the one hand, she and I had become good friends, but on the other, she was having conflicts with my parents over her dating and she got caught lying to them. I could see both points of view – indeed, I think I agreed with both points of view – but it left all of us at odds with each other. On top of that, my brother Mike was getting more and more involved in drinking and drugs and my parents really needed to be able to focus on him.

Seeing Thailand – Trips Outside Bangkok

"Bridge over the River Kwai"
(Mae Kong River)

We took a lot of family trips around the country while living in Thailand, as we always did in the countries where we lived. One of my favorites was the afternoon spent at the Bridge over the River Kwai. We had seen the movie, so visiting the famous bridge was high on our list. It is located two hours by car to the west of Bangkok near the border with

Memories of an Overseas Childhood **125**

Visiting temples outside of Bangkok, 1966

Burma (now called Myanmar). Actually, the name of the town nearest the bridge is Kanchanaburi and it's located where the Khwae Noi and Khwae Yai rivers converge into the Mae Klong River. This is where in 1942 the Japanese built the famous Bridge on the River Kwai with the labor of British prisoners of war (POWs). Nearby, we also visited the Kanchanaburi War Cemetery, where many of the POW's who died in the effort were buried, and the Chong Kai allies' cemetery, which was created by the Thai Government to honor all WWII Allied soldiers who died in the fighting in Southeast Asia. It's a somber sight with its sea of white crosses, as are all military cemeteries.

Not too far away is a magnificent Buddhist temple called Wat Tham Phu Way that features a series of grotto shrines in a large limestone cave system. Each grotto features a statue of The Buddha at a different stage of his life. I don't know what sorts of restrictions may be in place now on the temple grounds, but when we were there we were allowed to climb all over the buildings, and did so. I enjoyed the temple as much, if not more than seeing the bridge.

Jamie & Ku at temple at Kanchanaburi War Cemetery, 1966

Chapter 8 Intermission – Home Leave - June to Dec., 1967

The Long Home Leave

The homeleave of the summer of 1967 was one of our oddest home leaves. It was twice as long as any other we'd had, my father wasn't with us for most of it, and nearly everything that was originally planned ended up being changed because of uncontrollable circumstances.

It all started with my father being invited to go to a special six-week program at Harvard University. My mother thought the idea of spending six weeks with seven children in a hotel in Cambridge, Massachusetts sounded like one of Dante's circles of hell. What to do?

In the end, she decided that a leisurely ocean cruise from Singapore to Europe was just the thing to kill some time until my father's program was finished.

The plan was to take a train from Bangkok to Singapore, stopping at Penang and Kuala Lumpur, on the way; then we would board a ship and sail to Europe, with stops at ports in India and East Africa, up through the Gulf of Aden, then across the Red Sea, through the Suez Canal and from there, to Europe via the Mediterranean. After a short trip through Europe we would then fly to meet up with my father in Cambridge just about the time his course was ending.

Mike, Pat & Jerry fishing in Penang, 1967

Great plan, but that's not at all what actually happened. It started out as planned. My father flew alone back to Boston for his course and my mother, brothers and I boarded the train to Singapore, with wonderful stops in Penang, an island off the coast of Malaysia, and Kuala Lumpur, the capital of Malaysia.

The train trip was an adventure – traveling down the long Malay peninsula, and stopping at the British resorts on the island of Penang, where we lolled on the beach, the boys fished, and we soon discovered our normal diet heavy on rice had left us craving lots of starchy carbohydrates. At breakfast, the waiter set down a silver platter with nearly a full loaf of buttered toast. We dove on it like starving waifs, embarrassing my mother, as the waiter, completely nonplussed, replenished the platter several times. Now when I think of Penang, I always remember the great toast.

Snake Temple, Kuala Lumpur, 1967

In Kuala Lumpur, we toured the city and visited a Snake Temple where the monks draped poisonous snakes, drugged by the temple's heavy incense, around our necks. My mother volunteered to take pictures. There would be no snakes around the neck for her!

It was an auspicious start to our trip, but when we arrived in Singapore, everything began unraveling. We learned that the Suez Canal had just been closed due to the war between Israel and Egypt. With the Suez Canal closed, a sea voyage would take several weeks longer since we would have to sail around the Cape of Good Hope. My mother cancelled the ship reservations and then spent the next couple of days in Singapore making up a whole new itinerary for us. Instead of a leisurely cruise across the Indian Ocean, we flew from Singapore to Rome, where we commenced a road trip through Europe.

We spent several days in Rome, where we toured St. Peter's and Vatican City, walked through the ruins of the Forum and the vast Coliseum, climbed the Spanish Steps, threw coins in fountains and did every other touristy thing we could think of. We ate lots of Italian food – everyone's favorite – and missed Dad, who could have actually read and translated the Latin inscriptions on the monuments and would have really appreciated the blessings of Pope Paul VI.

After Rome, we flew to Lausanne, Switzerland, where we rented a yellow Mercedes. One of the memorable stops in Switzerland was Geneva where we happened to be on July 4th. My mother found out that the American Consulate was inviting all Americans who happened to be in the city to stop by to celebrate Independence Day. What I remember most about the picnic on the Consulate grounds that day, besides the spectacular sunny weather, was being touched by the playing of the Star Spangled Banner. There's something about being outside the U.S. and hearing our national anthem that seems to reach me on a subliminal level, constricting my throat and bringing tears to my eyes. Pride and patriotism seem to be just a little closer to the surface when I'm traveling, I guess.

We drove to Frankfurt, Germany next – stopping over night in Strasbourg, France (by accident). It was totally unexpected and not on our itinerary. Somehow we found ourselves on a bridge with a border guard checking passports, and the next thing we knew, we were in France.

In Germany, after a lovely boat trip down the Rhine, we flew from Frankfurt to London. What was memorable about that flight was that my suitcase got lost. That was the unhappy news, but it turned out to also be good news when the airlines gave me compensation money to go shopping. If this had to happen, it was nice that we were in London with all the wonderful department stores and great fashion! And the bigger plus was that eventually they found my suitcase and I got it back about a week later after we arrived in Boston.

As my mother had originally feared, we did end up spending a few weeks staying in the Commander Hotel in Cambridge, just off Harvard Square, while my father finished up his course. But somehow it didn't seem so bad after the wonderful trip through Europe.

My dad was in his glory in Boston. Suddenly, his Bostonian accent came back and he talked about "pahking the cahr in the yahd." We, of course, teased him endlessly, but he was thoroughly enjoying himself and loved showing us the world he grew up in. He had been raised in nearby Medford, so he wanted us to know that this was definitely his turf. He took us to Boston Red Sox games, his pride and glory. This was back when only the fanatics stayed true to the team, although to give them credit, that summer of 1967 season they came pretty close to winning it all and my father followed every inning of every game right into the post season pennant race. Being in New England, in addition to his beloved Red Sox, he talked up the clam chowder and baked beans, and we spent several afternoons strolling the Public Gardens and Boston Commons.

This was 1967 and Harvard Square in Cambridge was a crazy, psychedelic mix of hippies and international summer school students. My parents couldn't explain what in the world was happening on campuses and in the streets. But we teenagers knew. This was the Summer of Love, baby!

After he finished up his course and we said goodbye to his relatives, my father bought a station wagon and we drove it from New York City to L.A., then shipped it to Honolulu, and eventually to Bangkok. All I can say is, it was no way to treat a brand new car. Who breaks in a car by driving it across the country filled with 2 adults, 7 children, and 23 suitcases and hand-carries? My dad, that's who!

He was the guy who talked his way out of traffic tickets using his Foreign Service ID card and an appeal to the officer's patriotism. He was also the guy who spent weeks wondering what "XING" meant and why it was written on the streets near intersections (which might actually explain the traffic ticket stops).

One of the highlights (or lowlights, depending on your perspective) of the summer came at a huge get-together in Omaha with my mother's relatives. My mother has four sisters, and the five of them and their husbands, have twenty children between them, so it was quite a reunion. We had a huge picnic at a local park and lots of time to start getting to know our cousins.

This was the home leave mentioned earlier where my mother decided it would be a good time to show her European home movies from our recent expedition across that continent. She had forgotten that Mike had been in charge of the Super 8 movie camera and that he had focused his lens on two things: women's low-cut blouses and their high-cut miniskirts.

There was nary a scenic vista on any of the films unless it was in the background behind some blonde or raven-haired beauty. It proved embarrassing in front of an audience of relatives, although I must admit that we Sullivans found it absolutely hilarious.

There were, in addition to the study of the European female anatomy, a number of shots of my younger brothers caught in the act of "being themselves". One memorable sequence was of Jamie and Ku coming out of the woods where they had apparently gone to relieve themselves. Catching sight of the camera instead of looking chastised, they immediately started making faces and acting like doped up monkeys. It was comic, sure; but not exactly for public consumption, and certainly not for Mom's relatives to see. Live and learn. Or better yet, live, learn, and then quickly move on! Which we did...on to Hawaii.

Cousins, Grandma Corkin, Hope, Omaha 1967

Chapter 9 Hawaii (Aug. – Dec., 1967)

The Sullivan Kids, circa August, 1967

Ages of the Sullivan Children upon arrival in August, 1967 in Honolulu, Hawaii:

Dennis (Denny), age 20 (in the Marines, California)

Michael (Mike), age 18, high school senior

Maureen (Reen, Reeny), age 16, high school senior

Robert (Jerry), age 14, high school freshman

Patrick (Pat), age 12, 6th grade

James (Jamie), age 10, 4th grade

Christopher (Ku or Chris), age 7, 2nd grade

Home in Hawaii

We arrived in Honolulu in time to get registered for the fall semester of school. Mike and I, both seniors, attended Kalani High School; Jerry, a freshman, went to Kaimuki Middle School; and Pat, Jamie and Chris (6th, 4th, 2nd grades) went to a Catholic school not far away.

Kalani High School

While I was excited about the prospect of going to school in the States, the reality turned out not quite what I thought it would be. Having endured a fair amount of loneliness in the Philippines as an outsider to the school's status quo, I was a little more prepared for exclusion this time around. It didn't come as such a big surprise and letdown when I was ignored by the reigning cliques and clubs at the school.

This time, I was a senior and not the intimidated freshman I had been in Manila. Over the previous three years I had developed a thicker skin, a strong inner life, a good sense of humor, and a studied nonchalance about isolation. In fact, I almost enjoyed the mystery of no one knowing who I was or what my back story might be. Of course, that may be just the wishful imagination of an outsider speaking.

I made a few friends to eat lunch with and to talk with about papers and tests, but I don't remember the adjustment to the new school as being as soul-wrenching as it had been for me in Manila. Plus, I had the knowledge that this would be short term and that we would, indeed, be returning to our friends and beloved ISB and lives back in Bangkok at Christmas time. So instead of feeling miserable and an abject outcast, I relished being in Hawaii, going to the beach, shopping, listening to music and writing and receiving letters from my friends overseas. It wasn't all that bad.

Jerry at Kaimuki Middle School

Jerry managed a bit better than Mike and I in regards to "fitting in" to the local teen scene. He had a number of things going for him. First and foremost, he looked the part. He had the type of skin that develops a deep dark tan in the sun, so after a month or so he was as dark as any of his Hawaiian friends.

He also was a natural mimic and picked up the local pidgin slang with ease, so not only did he look Hawaiian, but he also sounded authentic. Even so, I think the main reason for his easy acceptance was that he took up surfing and became quite proficient at it. He and his friends surfed every single day after school and on weekends. And, in the end, that's really the key to "making it" as a teenager in Hawaii, at least, it was in 1967.

The "Little Kids" go to the Catholic School

One interesting family story that came out of our sojourn in Honolulu and going to school in the U.S. was that Jamie's IQ was tested for the first time.

Up until then, Jamie had been a daydreamy, middling student, and so no one ever expected anything but middling scores from him.

At the Catholic school he attended in Hawaii they tested him and when the results came back, they called my mother to have him brought back in for more testing. It turned out he scored as high as anyone ever had at the school and naturally, they wondered if it was a fluke.

We wondered that ourselves. He certainly didn't seem especially bright to us – but then, what sibling ever does? And we already knew he wasn't very athletic or coordinated. He was just Jamie, the fifth of six sons in a competitive household that tended towards loud, noisy wrestling matches, and lots of one-upmanship and showing off.

Jamie wasn't a natural fighter, wasn't loud, and tried to stay out of the way when the older boys were looking for a scapegoat. So we were all a bit surprised to discover he was also hiding a fairly high IQ. An interesting side note to this story is that when I mentioned it to him recently, he said he remembered the testing and retesting, but said he never knew what it was all about. He thought they had retested him because he had done something wrong. No one ever thought to tell him about his high IQ scores. I guess my parents didn't want to give him a big head about it.

In truth, I'm not sure if it made all that much difference to the rest of us either, but I like to think it evened some cosmic scores in Jamie's favor somehow.

Our House at 3741 Lurline Drive, Wilhelmina Rise, Kaimuki

Our house in Honolulu was built on the steep hillside of Maunalani Heights that overlooked Diamond Head and Waikiki. The road up Wilhelmina Rise went straight up from Waialae Avenue in Kaimuki to Maunalani Circle at the peak. It was interwoven with a series of switchbacks, with Lurline Drive being one of them. It was a wealthy area, with the houses growing more and more luxurious as you climbed higher and the views got better and better.

We had owned the house for seven or eight years by this time, even though we had never lived in it. My parents had looked for a house when we were in Hawaii on home leave in 1959 and finally settled on this one – a four-bedroom place with a spectacular view. While we were overseas, a local real estate company managed the details of cleaning the place and finding tenants, and keeping it in reasonable repair.

As with many hillside homes, the garage was above the house with steep stairs descending down to the front door. The kitchen door and the front door were nearly right next to each other, with the kitchen to the left, the front door straight ahead. There was also a third door, far off to the right, leading in to one of the bedrooms.

The front door opened directly into the living room. Directly opposite the door was a huge plate glass window that framed a breathtaking view of Diamond Head and all of Waikiki spread out below, with the blue Pacific Ocean beyond, as far as the eye could see. We could watch the ships coming and going in and out of Pearl Harbor, as well as the planes taking off and landing at the International Airport.

Lurline Drive, stairs from the garage down to the house

To further enjoy the tremendous view, there was a large deck, or "lanai" as they call it in Hawaii. The doorway to the deck was off the small dining room area to the left of the living room. There was a mango tree growing up through the deck and a hole had been cut around it so that we enjoyed both shade and fruit; in fact, you could literally sit on the deck and pull fruit from the tree and eat it.

In the house, a single long hallway to the right of the front door led to the three bedrooms. My bedroom was the first one on the left, next was my parents' bedroom, then the bedroom for the little kids (Pat, Jamie, and Chris). Mike and Jerry had a bedroom downstairs, and that was where Denny slept, too, when he was visiting.

In the far right corner of the living room, near the window was the stairway down to the lower level. The washer and dryer were downstairs as well as a bedroom and a large family room with a pool table that occupied the boys and their friends quite a bit.

There were also storage areas behind the walls downstairs, and that is where we stored some of our things when we left to return overseas. Sadly, in the interim years while we were gone, renters nearly always ransacked the storage area and we learned to expect that we would have to replace nearly everything on our return. This included masks and fins, Denny's surfboard, a few boogie boards, extra sheets and towels and dishes, pots and pans and other kitchen implements. Nothing of much value, I suppose, except to us.

There was no yard to speak of around the house, partly due to the steepness of the landscape, but also due to the value of the residential land in Hawaii. With its view and location, this was prime real estate, and the houses were built side by side, crowded on to the limited number of viable building lots.

Overall, we spent most of our time in the upstairs living room where the TV was, or out on the deck.

Pat playing pool at Lurline Drive house, 1967

The Red Sox World Series 1967

My father had to return to his job in Bangkok in November of that year. The rest of us would follow a month later, during our Christmas vacation. Before he left Hawaii, though, he got an unexpected early Christmas present when the Boston Red Sox made it to the World Series that year.

You have to understand about my father and his obsession with the Boston Red Sox baseball team. Well, it's true of any Boston Red Sox fan. In 1967, the Red Sox hadn't won a World Series since the whole Babe Ruth curse thing 49 years before. My father was born and raised in Massachusetts. He would go to the home games at Fenway Park as a young boy but in all those years he never saw his beloved team win the World Series. My father wasn't an athletic kid; he was one of those nerdy kids who knew all the statistics – the number of home runs, the batting averages, and so forth. And he loved his team with all the devotion of a Boston fan.

How much did he love them? Well, I remember him holed up in the bathroom in our house in Taipei in the summer and early fall with a suitcase-sized transoceanic radio to listen to staticky Red Sox games in the middle of the night. And these weren't even play-off games; it didn't matter as long as his team was playing, and even better if they were winning. As I said, he was a Fan (with a capital F).

So the Red Sox finally made it to the World Series in 1967 to play against the National League champs, the St. Louis Cardinals. My father was determined not to miss a game, not even a single play, so he took a radio into the bathroom, into the grocery store, anywhere and everywhere to hear every moment of the series. Keep in mind, this was old-school carry-a-radio-around, and was well before headphones and earbuds.

It wasn't long before my mother wanted him out of the house whenever the games were on. Hawaii is six hours earlier than the Boston games and five hours earlier than the St. Louis games. So, normally, the games started just after two in the afternoon in Boston, which was just after eight in the morning for us. This was just about the time, in fact, that my father had to drive us to school.

That first week of October (note: the first game of the Series was played on Wednesday, October 4) we listened to The Game on the way to school every day, and if it wasn't on yet, we listened to some reporter talk about the last game, or dissect the chances of winning or losing the next game. It was baseball, baseball, baseball.

The Red Sox lost the first game, 2 to 1, on their home turf. My father was beside himself. Could they pull it out? Then they won the next day, 5 to 0, again at Fenway. My father was ecstatic. Next, the Series moved to the St. Louis Busch Stadium and the Sox lost a little of their momentum due to the no-game travel day. That was unlucky for them because the Cardinals beat them, 5 to 2, at Saturday's game, and an embarrassing loss on Sunday, 6 to 0. It looked like the Series was over. One more game, to be played in St. Louis, to boot, and the Series would be history. My father was feeling pretty low.

That fifth game was played on Monday, October 9th, and again we were tuned in to the car radio on our way to school. Mike, Jerry, Pat, Jamie, Ku and I were all piled into our white station wagon, the game was on and my dad had turned the radio up a notch. Not only were we not allowed to talk, he wouldn't allow us to even breathe loudly. He drove the car as we wound down the snaking Sierra Drive, with my father riding the brakes as we cornered each hairpin turn, but he was barely paying attention to the road.

We came out onto Waialae Avenue, the major road through Kaimuki and turned left. The traffic was heavy and it was stop and go before we could turn right to head over to the Kaimuki Middle School to drop off Jerry. We were in the middle of an intersection when smoke started billowing from the engine.

"DAD!" We yelled in unison.

He seemed to be looking at the smoke, but it was obvious his mind was at the St. Louis Busch Stadium.

"Da-ad!"

Finally, he noticed the smoke and pulled the car over to the side of the street, but he didn't switch the engine off. Not in the middle of the game! He still didn't want to miss even a moment of this important game.

"Are we on fire?" Ku asked from the backseat.

"No," Dad answered without looking at him. "The car just needs to rest for a minute."

Jerry rolled his eyes. "My school's just down the street. I'm walking." And he got out and headed down the block, not even glancing back at his embarrassing family sitting in the station wagon with the wisps of smoke seeping out from the edges of the hood.

"Dad, we have to get to school," I finally pleaded. I hated being late to school and having to walk self-consciously into a classroom where all eyes would be turned to me.

He glanced at us, as if surprised we were still there in the car with him. "Uh, it should be OK now," he said.

He turned the wheel and pulled the car into the traffic still listening intently to the game and we continued on our way, tiny wisps of smoke occasionally escaping from the hood.

When he came to pick me up that afternoon, I knew the Red Sox had won the game because the grin on his face stretched from ear to ear.

"So?" I said as I got into the car.

"They won 8 to 4!" he crowed. "And the Series moves back to Boston!" All was right with the world again.

In Boston on Wednesday, they won that game, too, and it certainly looked like The Bambino's curse was about to be laid to rest. But then came Black Thursday, or so it was for my father. When he came to pick me up at school that afternoon, he sighed with disappointment but also seemed strangely resigned. It's a funny thing about Boston Red Sox fans in 1967, after 49 years of disappointment it seemed they really never expected to win. They wanted it, they dreamt about it, they prayed for it, but they didn't really expect it.

My dad grimaced a bit and then shrugged. "I should probably get the engine checked."

Sunday Breakfast or Dinner at Makapu'u

One of my favorite memories of Hawaii, whether when we were living there or just visiting, was our periodic visits to Makapu'u beach on the eastern shore of Oahu. We would go on Sundays, either early in the morning to get ahead of the weekend beachgoers or late in the afternoon to be at the beach when the last of the tourists and local bodysurfers were going home. My mother would prepare all the food, bring a small grill, towels and drinks and we would pile into the station wagon and head for Makapu'u, about 20 minutes from our house.

It was a favorite spot, a sheltered sandy beach below the highway, with the Makapu'u lighthouse on the point above the beach at one end, and the Beach Park with its bathhouse, picnic tables and parking lot, at the other.

Rabbit Island off Makapu'u Beach, Oahu, Hawaii

Sea Life Park is just beyond the beach and has an aquarium and entertaining shows of Hawaiian marine life. Rabbit Island – a funny looking island bird sanctuary sits in the ocean just across from the beach. It provides a sort of resting place for the eye as one stared out at the blue Pacific waves, and the tips of the whitecaps glittering in the sunshine. The little island is covered with rocks and birds and little else.

If we arrived at the beach early enough in the morning, we would have the place to ourselves for an hour or two before the bodysurfers and boogie-boarders arrived in ones and twos, dropped their towels, shook off their flip-flops and dove into the surf. In the late afternoon, while we waited for the coals in the grill to burn red, we would watch the sun-satiated families shake off the sand from their blankets and gather their toys, fins, and water wings together and trudge slowly up the hill to the showers and their cars.

In a little while, my mother would have the food frying – scrambled eggs and bacon in the morning; hamburgers or Bulgogi (Korean BBQ) with potato salad in the evenings. We would sit at the picnic table and eat, enjoying the privacy of the empty beach. Does it get any better than this?

The New Paperboy

One of the many things that you can do in the States, that you can't do overseas, is to work at a part-time job. Oh, sure, you can baby-sit or maybe figure out some make-work chore to get extra money out of your parents, but you can't really work a real part-time job. They just don't exist for American kids overseas. When we settled into our house in Hawaii, my brother Pat immediately decided he wanted to make some money with a paper route and soon one opened up for the *Honolulu Advertiser* in our neighborhood.

One of the reasons the paper route had opened up, he soon discovered, was because the former paperboy hadn't been a very good paperboy and as his services deteriorated he had trouble collecting money from his delivery customers.

Thus when Pat went out to do his first round of door-to-door collections, he found the customers refusing to pay for a variety of reasons: that the paper hadn't been delivered properly, or at all, or even saying that they had already paid. All the reported problems happened before he took over the route and he kept having to explain, "But I'm the NEW paperboy!" When he got home later that evening, he told us his story at dinner, and from then on, we had a new refrain whenever someone didn't understand you or misread a situation, we just said, "But I'm the NEW paperboy!"

Pets in Hawaii

We bought a German shepherd in Honolulu and named him Rebel. I'm not sure what my mother was thinking – buying a pet dog when we were only going to be living there for a few months. Personally, I suspect that she felt guilty for having given away all our pets in Bangkok before we left. We thought we would be getting them back when we returned, but apparently, she knew better. Anyway, she agreed to letting us have a new puppy, and like most of the dogs we'd owned in the past, he quickly became Pat's dog for all intents and purposes.

Rebel was a rambunctious puppy and got into everything, chewed on anything left out, edible or not, and was a troublemaker from the word "go". He got loose a few times and managed to cause a ruckus at the neighbor's house, too, getting into their garbage and being an all-around nuisance.

The neighbor thing was a little uncomfortable since we didn't know them that well. Soon my mother started taking Rebel to dog discipline classes, but he was still a puppy so I'm not sure how much good it did.

Still, in December we packed him up and sent him to Bangkok and he eventually grew into a pretty decent family pet.

The Genius Kid Down the Block

It wasn't long before my younger brothers had formed friendships with the neighborhood kids on our hillside overlooking Diamond Head and Waikiki. One of these kids quickly latched on to our family. I'll call him Keith, which might actually have been his name, but I no longer remember.

Anyway, Keith would show up early each morning and would pretty much stay all day, hanging around until dinner, and even later, if we let him. On school days, he would show up promptly after school. On weekends, he was sometimes there waiting outside the front door before we got out of bed.

At first, he was just another face around the house. My mother had always run an open-door policy with our friends – everyone was welcome in our house and friends were invariably invited to stay for dinner if they were around at that hour and if it was OK with their own parents. After a while, though, we noticed that Keith was always there.

Little by little, the story came out. Keith's parents were divorced and his mother worked pretty much all the time – from early morning until late into the night – a waitress, I think. Keith was also something of a genius. Apparently he had been tested and had an IQ that was off the charts. You could tell that he was different – he was precociously articulate, very nerdy in his mismatched t-shirts and shorts and seemed stilted and slightly off-kilter in his social interactions.

The thing about kids like Keith is that they're hard to take in large doses. We would have been fine with him if he wasn't literally always there. We felt sorry for him, but after a while, we also felt sorry for ourselves. Which brings me to the BB gun incident.

The BB Gun Incident

I don't remember how or why my brothers ended up with a BB air rifle, but somehow they acquired one while we were living in Hawaii. I suppose it was just another plaything. I don't remember any of us thinking of it as a "weapon", per se. In fact, I'm not sure what exactly my brothers shot with it – Targets? Birds? Squirrels?

One of the things we soon discovered about air rifles is that even without BB's in it you can pump it up and get quite a whistle of wind when you cock and shoot it. Mike had playfully "shot" my younger brothers any number of times, pretending all the while to have loaded it with actual BB's.

On this particular afternoon my youngest brother, six-year old Ku, and several other boys were sitting on the lanai, idly joking around when Ku, thinking the air rifle was empty, pumped it up and playfully shot Keith in the back. Only the rifle wasn't empty and after the popping sound, Keith arched his back and screamed.

By the time the rest of us came out to see what the commotion was about, Keith was jumping around trying to touch the spot on his back, where his t-shirt was now showing a tiny stain of blood. Ku had shot Keith! Ku was as stunned as Keith.

My mother took Keith into the bathroom to have a closer look at the wound. She knew she had to get him to the hospital to have him checked but couldn't reach his mother by phone. She stopped at his house on the way, but wasn't surprised that no one was there. She left a note and continued on. At the emergency room they x-rayed him and removed the BB and told her it had just missed his lungs. Eventually, the police tracked down Keith's mother but by then it was all over.

We didn't see Keith for a few days, but then he started showing up at our house again. We left Hawaii shortly afterwards and lost track of him, but he became a part of our family lore, nonetheless.

Penny, the Nanny

My parents needed to go to Washington, D.C. before my dad returned to Bangkok. They needed to find someone to come and stay with us, to run the house, taxi everyone to school and activities for a week or two while they were gone.

My mother started interviewing nannies and we ended up with Penny, a young British woman in her 20's working her way around the world. She may have been trained as a nurse, too, although I'm fuzzy on the details. What I do remember was that she had a great accent and was easy-going and fun.

Her one big contribution to the family was her recipe for Shepherd's Pie. It became a family favorite for years afterwards. I had the romantic idea that it came out of her childhood in some pastoral British township, but I'm sure I made that up in my overactive imagination. Probably she just looked it up in a good cookbook under what to cook for a crowd.

Winter Surf at Waimea

In December, before we headed back to Bangkok, we heard over the radio that a storm out at sea was expected to result in a huge storm surf along the northern shore of Oahu – at Sunset Beach and Waimea. That sounded like something worth seeing. The flat surf of Waimea during the summer was all we had known and we wanted to see what a storm surf looked like.

We headed across the island to the north shore. In the car, we teased each other about who would be too afraid to even get in the water. When we parked and walked over to the beach, we could see the long board surfers out in the distance, but closer in, the water was full of body surfers and boogie boarders. The surf was bigger than we had seen before, and it seemed like the biggest waves were every three or four, in a set. Mike and Jerry and I all dove in and caught a few waves. When I came up beyond the break, I was astounded at the strength of the surf. Normally, the ocean felt relatively calm between waves. But this surf felt like the churning of a washing machine.

It occurred to me as I treaded water just beyond the break that maybe this wasn't such a good idea, after all. I was a strong swimmer and a decent body surfer, but these waves were strong. It's not until you got caught in the curl that you realize you might be up against something bigger and stronger than you had anticipated. That's what happened to me.

Hoping to get back on shore quickly, I caught a wave, then as I felt the swell of the next wave, I turned to dive under it but I wasn't quick enough and suddenly the surge of the wave drove me forward towards shore. It broke and I was thrown up and over, then tumbled in the surf over and over again, until I no longer knew which way was up or down. I was out of breath and clawing at the churning water trying to break to the surface. The gritty sand scraped my arms and shins as I flailed in the wave's grip. Then suddenly, I felt the solidity of the beach beneath a knee and I sucked in air. I coughed and sputtered, wiping the sand and salt water from my eyes, pulling the wet strands of my hair back away from my face. "Look out!" I heard someone yell and I scrambled in panic to my feet.

I still couldn't see, but knew another wave was just behind me ready to swallow me up. I heard the roar of it breaking as I struggled to get away. The wave surged around my legs and knocked me down again, but at least I was crawling in the right direction, towards higher land, away from the breaking surf. If I didn't get dragged into the next undertow of the ebbing wave, I would be OK, I told myself. At the edge of the breakwater, I collapsed in a heap, trying to calm my racing heart and catch my breath. I knew that I had nearly drowned.

My brother, Pat, was jumping in the surf, laughing with the excitement of the big waves. He had no idea what I had just endured. He pointed at the next wave. "Look how big that one is!" he yelled gleefully, running down to meet it. Before I could warn him, he dove in and rode it up the beach.

I sat, still stunned by my experience and watched the surf for a several moments. "Hey, come on in, Reen!" Jerry yelled, bobbing in the surf from beyond the break.

I shook my head, smiled weakly, and waved. I was done for the day; that I knew.

I got up and walked a few feet up the beach to where my mother was sitting, ostensibly reading a paperback, but peering at the water anxiously every few moments. She glanced up, "How was it?" she asked, then she shook her head. "I don't like it when it's like this," she nodded at the ocean.

I agreed. "It's pretty strong. The waves are really huge."

She glanced at the beach, counting children, I realized. Her brow furrowed. "Where's Pat?" she asked.

I looked over to where he had been a short while ago. "He was over there body-surfing," I pointed at the spot I had last seen him.

She stood up and shaded her eyes, even though she was wearing sunglasses. "I don't see him," she said, worry coming into her voice.

I stood up and walked towards the surf. I vividly remembered my experience of being caught in the curl and I knew that the same thing could be happening to him. I glanced around, staring with a new intentness at the breakwater swirling and surging up from the last breaking wave.

Then I caught sight of him. He was all arms and legs, struggling to get out of the grip of the surf around him. He got to his knees, fell, and then got to his knees again, bracing with obvious effort against the ebbing surf. He held on and finally stood up, swaying and then came trudging towards us, coughing and shaking his head.

"I nearly drowned," he croaked.

I nodded. "I got caught in it, too," I said.

We sat next to each other, hugging our knees, towels draped around our shoulders, mesmerized by the waves breaking in front of us. We sat that way for a long, long time.

A week later, we heard that the "real" storm surf had arrived. Denny was home for a short visit and we went to Waimea again, but this time there were police, ambulances, lifesaving equipment and warnings about getting too close to the surf. No one needed to tell me to stay out of the water.

The waves were twice the size of the ones the previous week, towering walls of water, breaking huge and powerfully, the sound was a roar in our ears. A few people dared to get wet and tempt fate in the breakwater that came up and over the sandy beach, almost to the coral cliffs along the road. The beach, where we had sat just a week before was very nearly submerged in pounding surf.

We stood for maybe an hour or more, enthralled by the power and fury before us. We could not believe what we were seeing. We could see a scattering of intrepid long board surfers in the distance, but no one – not surfer, not swimmer, not body boarder – was in the mean water churning along the beach.

I had dreams – sometimes nightmares – about those waves for years. Eventually, perhaps ten years later, I learned to force my dream self to go out and attempt to swim in the big waves. Usually, I woke up in a panic long before I got near the surf. However, the night I dreamed that I swam in them was the night the nightmares stopped.

Return to Bangkok

In December, my mother suggested that Mike and I might want to stay on in Honolulu in order to graduate from Kalani. But honestly? Neither of us wanted to do that. He had a girlfriend in Bangkok and we both were anxious to get back to our friends. So eventually my mother gave up the idea.

I guess my mother was thinking it would be nice to save us one more change of schools, or maybe she was trying to save herself and my father from the aggravation of having to deal with Mike when he returned to his old life and lifestyle in Bangkok. He had been on his best behavior while we were in the States for home leave, but I know my mother was worried that things might get out of hand once we were back overseas and he again had easy access to drugs and alcohol.

But return we did. That Christmas of 1967 we flew to Japan and then to Hong Kong where we met my father on Christmas Eve. The flight into Hong Kong on that Christmas Eve was memorable because as we approached the Hong Kong airport for landing, the pilot happened to still be back in the coach section, just a few rows from us on the nearly empty flight chatting up a pretty young woman passenger. The cockpit had to request his presence so that we could land. All was very relaxed and jolly, seeing as it was Christmas, but at the time, I was horrified, not realizing that the copilot could easily have landed the plane, had it been necessary. Still, I thought things were maybe a little too relaxed.

Chapter 10   Bangkok, Thailand (1967 - 1968)

The Sullivan Kids, circa 1967

Ages of the Sullivan Children upon arrival in December, 1967 back in Bangkok, Thailand:

Dennis (Denny), age 20 (in the Marines, in California)

Michael (Mike), age 18, high school senior

Maureen (Reen, Reeny), age 17, high school senior

Robert (Jerry), age 14, high school freshman

Patrick (Pat), age 12,

James (Jamie), age 11

Christopher (Ku or Chris), age 8

Welcome (Back) to Bangkok – Dec. 1967 to Dec. 1968

One of the things about living in a diplomatic or military family is that it's made very clear early on that having the family on an overseas post is a privilege, not a right. Everything the dependents do reflects on the diplomat or military officer, not to mention, on the entire American community. So, when a teenager got into trouble overseas, it was sometimes reported to the U.S. Ambassador and the ambassador would then meet with the troublemaker's parents, basically calling them on the carpet to explain their son or daughter's misdeeds. A really big transgression could even jeopardize the father's career.

What sorts of things would get you "on the Ambassador's List"? Usually major infractions like getting publicly drunk, buying drugs, beating up a local, or being caught in a raid by the MP's at an off-limits establishment. Sometimes your name would go "on the list" simply by your being reported to have been in a place you shouldn't have been. That's what happened to all three of us – Mike, Jerry, and I – the first night we returned to Bangkok from Hawaii a few days after Christmas in 1967.

It was an impromptu welcome back party at a nightclub called The Trolley (the place was done up to look like the inside of a trolley car, complete with leather straps hanging from the ceiling – I think I still have one packed away somewhere). Unfortunately, the CID agents (Criminal Investigation Division of the US Treasury) happened to be there that night looking into suspected drug-trafficking, and consequently, they were taking down names. And guess whose names were on every person's lips that night? The three Sullivan teens being welcomed back – Mike, Jerry and Maureen! My poor parents. They grounded all three of us (in our family it was called "being put on restriction") and so we weren't allowed to go out on New Years Eve, which I suppose was just as well.

Maybe it wasn't an auspicious start, but we were thrilled to be back in Bangkok, among our friends. For Mike and me, it meant graduating with our class, the 1968 ISB senior class.

Our Bangsue house

Our second house in Bangkok wasn't quite as far away from everything as the Bangkabua house had been, and it was at least 100 years more modern. We still lived within a walled compound with a gate, of course, but this house was more contemporary. When you came in the front door, the living room was to the left and the dining room to the right. Beyond that was the kitchen, but I have almost no memory of what it looked like, which, I suppose, means I rarely went into it.

Upstairs, the stairway opened into an area with a pool table and the four bedrooms were off this area. To the left of the stairs was my room, next in a clockwise direction, was my parents' master bedroom suite with its own bathroom, then came the family bathroom for the rest of us, next was Mike and Jerry's bedroom, and opposite mine, on the other side of the stairwell, was the little kids' bedroom (for Pat, Jamie and Chris). The family area upstairs also had a door to an open-air patio where my parents would sometimes have cocktails in the evening before dinner. I never had a strong feeling for this house, neither liking nor disliking it, probably because I was so involved with high school and myself, that I don't remember spending much time in it except to eat and sleep. Still, it was a comfortable place in a slightly more convenient location.

Jamie, Pat & Ku at Bangsue house, (with Rebel, the German shepherd), 1967

Life in Bangkok, The Second Time Around

We had been gone for about seven months on our home leave including our one semester sojourn in Honolulu. Although in Bangkok we noticed there were a few new kids who had arrived at the beginning of the school year, overall we didn't seem to miss a beat as we rejoined our high school class in January. It was great having friends from the previous year who welcomed our return. We immediately got back into our routine of running around Bangkok with our friends, going to the Teen Club and other haunts on the weekends and generally having a great time.

There was the occasional bomb scare at the school that basically required us to stand around in the parking lot while the buildings were swept for explosives. It was a reminder that all was not particularly well in the world around us. A bigger reminder took place at the end of January (1968): the Tet Offensive, when the North Vietnamese swept into the capital, Saigon, for the first time. It started at Chinese New Years (e.g., "Tet" in Vietnam) which that year took place at the end of January.

I recently found a short paragraph from an old diary that mentioned the Tet Offensive. The parents of one of my friends had been in Saigon over the Tet holiday and she was extremely worried at school for two long days because she still hadn't heard from them. Luckily, they returned safe and sound. But they weren't the only ones who were caught in Saigon as it suddenly came under attack. Many of the "Saigon Wives" had gone to Saigon the previous weekend to visit their husbands and had to be evacuated out. Ironically, for some it was their second time being evacuated from that country!

*[**Note on the term "Saigon Wives"**: This is what the American community called the dependents of men working in Vietnam. Generally, they were military officers' wives or wives of the diplomatic corps. Most had been living in Saigon when the war started and as it became increasingly dangerous and the American School was closed, the dependent wives and children were evacuated to Bangkok "for the duration".*

Some returned to the U.S. rather than live in Bangkok without their husbands, but a number of them settled in Bangkok with the hopes that they would at least get to see their husbands occasionally, on brief visits back and forth. Of course, after the Tet Offensive (January, 1968), most of those weekend visits were stopped, and I think the men began receiving "hardship pay" for living and working in a war zone.]

Mike's Car Accident April, 1968

My parents were never sure how to handle Mike, or even if it were possible at this precarious stage in his life. He was a rebellious teenager to begin with, and his drinking and drug use added new extremes to his personality. There seemed to be the "good" Mike and the "bad" Mike. The Mike we talked to when he was sober was always contrite about his transgressions.

Looking back, he had always been that way, even when he was younger and would get into fist fights or whatever trouble, and afterwards he was always very, very sorry. Mike was a smart guy, intelligent and normally very caring, but he also knew how to manipulate my parents, my brothers, and me.

Mike was also a clotheshorse and had a real sense of style, unusual in an 18-year-old boy. He cared about how he looked, his hair had to be just so, and when he got dressed to go out, he made sure that he looked "cool". Unfortunately, Mike thought that to be "cool" meant wearing all black, drinking and using drugs. For other people, that might not have been a problem, but for Mike, alcohol and drugs brought out the "bad" Mike. Today, he would be the subject of an afternoon special on TV, so common is his story, but at the time, and in the situation we were in overseas, it was difficult for my parents to help him.

I was the closest in age to Mike and we were in the same grade and shared many friends, so in many ways, I became his go-between, trying to keep the peace at home. He would act up – get drunk, get stoned, get into fights, cause problems – and I would lie to protect him or to minimize the storms at home. It was not a good situation and by the time June rolled around, I couldn't wait to go away to college.

Mike's partying and bad behavior all came to a head one Saturday night when he and his friend, Jon, were out on the town in my parents' light blue Corvair Monza sports car. They were driving between clubs when a blue Datsun pulled in front of Mike and when he swerved to miss the other car he flipped the Corvair.

When we saw the car the next day, it was still resting on its side up against the telephone pole that had prevented it from flipping completely over on to its roof. Mike had been driving and his friend, Jon, had been in the passenger seat. This was before the days of seat belts, so when the car crashed they were both banged up pretty badly. In the accident, Jon had been thrown against the windshield. With the strange irony of violent accidents, we found his contact lens the next day in the backseat of the car. My mother had a ream of typing paper in the backseat and in the accident it had ripped open and the white paper coated the back of the car. We literally reached in and picked up a contact from the top of one of the sheets!

There's a strange fascination with the mangled remains of accidents that stay with you long after the event. For instance, the gearshift was bent at a 90-degree angle as if Mike had somehow found some superhuman strength and pressed it to the floor. The car windows were all shattered and two of the tires were completely flat.

Another car of American teenagers wasn't far behind Mike when the accident occurred and they immediately pulled over and called an ambulance and tried to help Mike and Jon, as best they could. Mike was unconscious and bloody while Jon had a gash on his forehead from hitting the windshield. Jon was conscious and upon seeing Mike, took his shirt off and wrapped it around Mike's head in an effort to stop some of the bleeding. We were told later that it took 14 minutes for the ambulance to arrive. The MP's (American military police) got there first and as he came to, Mike tried to take a swing at them as they were trying to get him into their vehicle to rush him to the field hospital. I guess he thought he was being arrested.

Finally, they got the two boys to the 5th Army Field Hospital and my parents were notified. The doctors told my mother and father later that Mike had lost an incredible amount of blood and that he owed his life to the fact that the 5th Field Hospital had so many battlefield-experienced doctors on staff that knew precisely what to do and how to do it quickly.

But it was a while before Mike lost his ghostly pallor, not to mention the scars from all the cuts and gashes, and the hundreds of stitches. I'll never forget visiting him the next day when he was lying limply in the hospital bed bandaged and hooked up to a spaghetti mess of tubes. We could barely recognize him and I had never seen him look so small and pitiable.

Mike hated being in the hospital, and as soon as he could get out of bed and walk a few steps without passing out, he talked one of his friends into bringing him some clothes so he could sneak out of the hospital and go home. I think the doctors and staff were glad to be rid of him because they never complained about his sudden departure.

Senior Skip Day

While Mike was recuperating, time was slipping by and we were heading towards our high school graduation, June 3, 1968. One of the traditions at the school was Senior Skip Day, an event that is not officially condoned, but for which the teachers and administration tend to kindly look the other way.

Maureen's Senior Class "milk mug"

My senior class was determined to have a great Skip Day and so we decided to rent a bus and drive down to the beach resort of Pattaya, then rent a couple of fishing boats to spend the day on one of the islands offshore. The class came up with a beer mug fund-raiser (thanks again, Dave Rogan!) to get the money to pay for the trip. When the principal got wind of the beer mugs, he put his foot down, and Dave quickly changed the name to "milk mugs", so that we could continue selling them. The fact that they are decorated with Singha Beer insignias wasn't mentioned. I still have mine.

The trip itself was all that it could be. A bunch of seventeen and eighteen-year-old teens in swimming suits, with coolers full of soft drinks, beer and food, enjoying a day on the fishing boats (we raced them out to the islands), laying on the beach at the island, and falling asleep on the bus on our return. It was a perfect fun finish to our high school career and we have the home-movies to prove it!

If our Senior Skip Day was the social end of the year, our graduation on June 3, 1968 was the scholastic finish line. Graduating overseas is not like graduating any place else, I suspect. When kids overseas "leave home" it's all backwards – we leave our homes and families to GO "home" to the States. Most of us were on planes within a week or two of graduating, flying the 8,263 miles from Bangkok to Los Angeles and points beyond. Well, at any rate, I was.

My mother went as far as Hong Kong with me, where we did some last minute clothes shopping, then she put me on a plane to Honolulu, where I had a night or two to adjust to the time difference, and then on to Los Angeles to spend a week or two with my brother Denny and finally on to Dallas, Texas to spend the rest of the summer with a girl friend from Taipei.

At the end of the summer, I went to visit my grandmother in Omaha, before heading to Missoula, Montana to begin my freshman year at the University of Montana. But that, of course, is a different story altogether.

In fact, what happened next is also an unexpected story, as well. You see, I had a picture that I carried around in my head of my family and their daily life in Bangkok. I left home, but I could picture them in our house going about their usual activities. It was comforting and reassuring to know that even though I wasn't there, they were going about a life that I understood and knew well. But then the unexpected happened: my father was transferred to Addis Ababa, Ethiopia, and by the time my 18th birthday rolled around on December 7th, 1968, they were in Africa, not just a new post in a new place, but they were on a whole new continent.

Chapter 11   Addis Ababa, Ethiopia (1968 – 1972)

The Sullivan Kids, circa 1968

Ages of the Sullivan Children upon arrival in December, 1968 in Addis Ababa, Ethiopia:

Dennis (Denny), age 21 (in the Marines, in California)

Michael (Mike), age 19 (in the Army, in Vietnam)

Maureen, age 18 (freshman, U. of Montana, Missoula, MT)

Robert (Jerry), age 15 (high school sophomore)

Patrick (Pat), age 13

James (Jamie), age 11

Christopher (Ku or Chris), age 8

Surprise Move to Africa

I was a freshman at the University of Montana in Missoula when I received the news from my folks that they would be moving to Addis Ababa, Ethiopia. My mother wrote on October 26, 1968, that the previous Sunday my father had received "a phone call which carried news of big changes in our lives."

The call confirmed that a cable had been received from Washington requesting my father's presence in Ethiopia immediately. It was a big promotion for him (just one level away from the Director's level). He was being named the Special Assistant Director for Industrial Promotion working directly for the Director of the USAID Mission in Ethiopia, Roger Ernst. My father had worked for Mr. Ernst in Taiwan and they had a lot of respect for each other and got along well. My father was excited about the opportunity and cabled back that he could be available the first of December.

When I heard the news I had to look up the location of Ethiopia in an atlas because although I knew it was in Africa, I had no clue as to where on that huge continent it might be.

Sure, I had heard of Emperor Haile Selassie, but beyond that I knew nothing at all about the country. The move was pretty surprising news for several reasons: first, that my family was moving so suddenly and in the middle of a school year, and, second, that my father would actually be posted someplace outside of Asia! Here was a career diplomat with a dozen languages under his belt but NONE were remotely African. It was mystifying.

Leaving Bangkok would be difficult for them, I knew; but not going back to Bangkok was a huge disappointment for me, too. We all loved Bangkok, but for me it was "home" on so many levels. Still, I could understand that the thought of moving someplace so completely different was also an exciting prospect for my father, filled with challenges and opportunities.

I had two phone calls from my parents that school year – the first one was in October when my parents called to confirm that they were moving to Addis Ababa. The other call came on my 18th birthday, December 7th, to tell me that they had arrived in Addis and that, by the way, my youngest brother, Chris, had already managed to break his leg running across the field behind their house. It was nice to see that the more things changed for my family, the more they also seemed to stay the same.

Even so, the idea of my family moving to a new country without me remained unsettling. It was difficult enough to be thousands of miles from home – particularly that first year of college when I was most homesick – only to discover that I could no longer imagine what home looked like anymore nor could I imagine what my family's life there would be like. I never realized until then what a reassurance it was for me to be able to picture their house and know how they spent their days. If I could imagine them going about their everyday tasks – going to work and school, shopping at the PX and Commissary, dealing with power outages or temperamental phone lines, then I didn't miss not being there as much, nor feel that I was missing out on something.

The hardest thing about their move for me was that I could no longer imagine the setting for my family. If I couldn't conjure up "home" in my imagination, then how could I be sure that there was still a place for me there, that there was a home for me to go back to?

My brother, Jerry, had stayed behind in Bangkok for several weeks so he could finish up the fall semester before flying to Addis. He was supposed to fly from Bangkok to Athens and then on to Addis Ababa, but it turned out that there was a problem with his passport – it had been lost!

Apparently, his diplomatic passport containing his new visa had been misrouted when it was sent back to him from Addis. The American Embassy in Bangkok issued him an interim tourist passport so he could travel. However, when he got to Athens to board the Ethiopian Airlines flight for Addis, they wouldn't let him on the plane without the necessary visa, or barring that, he would need proof of an air ticket leaving Ethiopia to qualify for a temporary tourist visa. This was back when countries were afraid of the traveling hippies who might gain entrance to a country with a one way ticket, never to leave again.

Jerry was out of luck. While he sat in Athens – well, actually he spent the time touring the Acropolis and other sites (Sullivans are not much for sitting and waiting around) – my parents rushed around Addis, sending telegrams and tracers on his diplomatic passport and finally arranged for a ticket out of the country (to Nairobi, Kenya) that he could show to the authorities.

In the end, he never had to use the Nairobi air ticket because eventually his passport with the valid visa intact resurfaced and all was made well again. The crisis was averted.

Addis Ababa, Ethiopia, located on the Ethiopian Highlands, altitude 8000 ft. above sea level

The first thing a visitor notices about Addis Ababa is its remarkable climate. It is in Africa, after all, and located just nine degrees north of the equator, a mere 600 or so miles. Being so close to the equator, one expects hot, humid temperatures, like in those jungles of the old Tarzan movies; but that's not at all what one gets.

In fact, in my opinion Addis has nearly perfect temperatures year-round. It can be hot, to be sure, if you're standing in direct sunlight, although the temperature might only be in the mid to upper 80's; but it's strangely cool in the shade or inside buildings, in the 60's, and even cooler in the evenings after the sun goes down. How can this be? The answer is: the altitude. Addis Ababa is located at an altitude of 8,300 feet.

In fact, the altitude is a very big deal. They warn you when you arrive that the altitude can cause physical problems, even for healthy people. Travelers may experience shortness of breath, fatigue, nausea, headaches, and an inability to sleep. Individuals with respiratory or heart conditions are warned to be extra cautious.

It's interesting that nearly everyone reacts to the altitude differently. For me, it appeared to change my body's metabolism. I lost about fifteen pounds in the eight or so weeks I spent in Addis my first summer, all without dieting or without any increase in exercise.

Perhaps it could be explained by my body having to work a little harder at that altitude; I don't know. I didn't have any of the other altitude-related side effects, except that it didn't take much to get tipsy when I had a beer or a mixed drink. Some people reported that particular side effect as one of the "benefits" of the altitude – after all, it made social drinking and partying a whole lot cheaper.

Our First House near the Airport

I never lived in the first house my family rented in Addis. I only saw pictures of it. It was located near the airport on Bole Road – the major thoroughfare between the international airport and downtown Addis Ababa. My brother, Jerry, tells a funny story about the culture shock of his arrival to Addis, several weeks after my parents arrived.

When he finally arrived after his delay in Athens due to the missing passport, my parents picked him up at the airport to bring him home. The drive home took just a few minutes. Poor Jerry was stunned, and maybe even a little depressed to think that this might be all there was to the town – an airport and one long road!

Of course, he hadn't yet seen the rest of the city – and it was a huge capital city, even back in 1968. It wasn't until the next day when they drove him around that he reported feeling greatly relieved. After all, he had been reluctant to leave the bustling city of Bangkok and all his high school friends, his rock band (he played the drums and guitar), his Karate class, and all the other important things that make up a teenager's life. The last thing he wanted was to have to spend his next three years of high school at an isolated outpost living in a house on a single long road to nowhere.

One of the odd things about that first house that my mother wrote me about was that the house came with a donkey! I don't know whether it was indeed part of the house, or if it just wandered into the yard one day and stayed. But it was one of the first indicators of how different – even odd – this new post might prove to be. My mother said that one day she was sitting in the living room reading when the muzzle of a donkey came down and rested on the top of her book. She looked up startled to find that a donkey had come in through an open door and quietly stood in front of her, apparently wanting some attention. I'm not sure if he could be considered a pet, but apparently he thought he was!

I always liked this story about the nameless donkey because it spoke of the strangeness of this new place. And Addis wasn't like anyplace else we had ever lived.

Owning Horses in Addis

One of the novelties of living in Addis for my younger brothers was in owning and riding horses. The Ethiopian horses could be bought for around $30 Ethiopian Dollars (comparable at that time to about USD$8). It cost just $20 a month to feed the three horses my younger brothers eventually acquired. What a deal! All those years I had wanted a horse, prayed for a horse, made deals with God and Santa Claus if only I could have a horse of my own; all for naught. If only we had moved to Ethiopia sooner. Of course, these Ethie ponies weren't thoroughbreds by any stretch of the imagination. They were swaybacked, malnourished nags, at best, but I don't think that mattered one iota to my brothers, who were enthralled with the novelty of it all.

Chris with his horse at the Bole Road house, 1968

My brothers actually rode to school on horseback often, bringing one of the servants along to take the horses home and then to return with the horses to the school at the end of the school day so my brothers could ride home again. No, they didn't have to ride to school; my parents would have driven them in the car, and did so when the weather was lousy, but they preferred to ride, so ride they did. How fun is that?

Of course, it wasn't always "fun". Here's one of the stories from my mother's letter dated Sept. 29, 1969:

Dear Reen,

So I am again slow in writing, but these past two weeks have been wild. First, Pat was coming home on a horse, when an Ethiopian lady jumped in front of him and was knocked down and her water jar was broken. A big crowd collected, within five minutes police came, and I arrived after a wild-eyed zabanya (guard) arrived jabbering, with the only word I could understand being "Pat". I was sure he was dead from the zabanya's looks, but upon arriving I found Pat in a crowd of about 500 who were spitting and pulling and screaming at him, with the woman rolling and moaning on the ground. The policeman spit down the front of my dress when I insisted on him going to the police station so that I could call the American Embassy. Final result: Pat went to the police station, with the horse and the crowd of people, and stayed there until four hours later when the Embassy Consul got him out on Dad's signature.

The woman went to the hospital and she was finally released last Friday. Of course, the cost was on us. There was nothing wrong with her, but a needed vacation and good food, on us, of course. This happened one night at 5:30 with dinner guests arriving at 6:30 and, of course, the whole evening was spent answering the telephone with the latest from the police station, and the dinner guests enjoying the latest eventful news. One of Dad's Ethiopian friends offered to go to the station to help, and enroute ran over a man, so he also was at the hospital, and the station with his own problems. Just another day in the life of the Sullivans. Never calm around here. I am in need of a vacation. Will trade you: you come back and keep house, I will do this year's work for you.

Horses weren't always a good thing, of course, even when they weren't running over pedestrians. Rabies was rampant in Ethiopia and horses were often the animals that contracted it and passed it on to their human owners. My brothers had a friend, a boy of about 13 or 14, who noticed that his horse was unusually jumpy one afternoon. He tried to calm the horse down, only to discover the horse was foaming at the mouth. It had apparently become infected with rabies. The horse was shot and the whole family had to submit to a round of rabies vaccinations – a nasty ordeal involving long needles in the stomach, or so we were told; but that wasn't the end of it. They also had to hire a huge backhoe to dig a hole deep enough to bury the horse so that the hyenas wouldn't dig up the carcass and eat it, thus perpetuating the rabies virus and spreading it still further.

Luckily, we never had to deal with any of that.

Our Second Addis House

House in Addis Ababa, 1969

My family moved into their second house before I arrived the summer of 1969. Because there was no American military base providing base housing in Addis, American families lived in individual family compounds throughout the city. Most of the American families lived in the area near the school, PX, and Commissary, but many lived at the other end of town near the airport, where my family's first house had been located.

This second house was a big contemporary split-level house in a walled and gated compound. Because my father was required to do a great deal of entertaining as a part of his job, they needed a house large enough to accommodate the lifestyle as well as large enough for our family of six.

When you drove up to the house, you tooted the car horn and the zabanya (guard) would come out to swing the gates open to admit you. As you drove up the driveway to the house you had a choice of either going straight into the carport attached to the lower level of the house, or turning to the left where the driveway continued a short distance up to the foot of the steps leading to the front door.

On the lower level of the house there were two rooms and a bathroom. My family initially used them as bedrooms until three years later when Jerry left for college. For the first few years, Jerry was the reigning "king" of the family, which in our family meant that as the oldest child he got his pick of the kids' bedrooms. Jerry chose the large room downstairs. It was originally designed to be a family room of sorts because it was a large space and had a door leading outside. I think he liked the idea of its direct access to the outside, but especially its separation from the rest of the family. The other bedroom downstairs next door to Jerry's became Pat's bedroom and he and Jerry shared the downstairs' bathroom.

front of house in Addis Ababa, 1969

Also on the lower level was a large closet just across from Jerry's bedroom door that Jerry requisitioned as his own and kept locked. In it, he stored all of his precious possessions, including his coin collection, his savings, and anything he didn't want his brothers to touch. Back in Bangkok, Jerry had a locked trunk that served the same purpose. I look back on it now and think of it as just one more indicator of the "large family syndrome". You lose a lot of privacy in a large family and there is a great deal of competition among the siblings and many territorial disputes that seethe under the surface. A family with six boys is like a wolf pack where the alpha dogs vie for dominance. Locking and hiding your stuff is one way to cope; particularly when you aren't the oldest, biggest or strongest. On the other hand, it might just be a personality thing. In our family, Jerry was considered a bit of a miser and he always took great care of his stuff – everything he owned looked shiny new, whether he'd had it for a day or a year. He's still like that – and I don't say it as a negative because it's served him well. After all, he's ended up independently wealthy, and spent many years living on a bluff overlooking an expanse of the Pacific Ocean on the island of Hawaii. It's probably not a fluke.

Upstairs in the Addis house, was a master bedroom suite with a master bathroom, plus two smaller bedrooms and a large family bathroom. My parents had the master bedroom suite, of course, and the other bedrooms were for my brothers, Jamie and Chris. When I came for a visit, my brothers doubled up and one of the bedrooms became mine.

An interesting feature of the house is that all of the windows were protected by huge Italian metal shutters that at night would be slid down on the outside of the glass windows where they would clunk securely into place. These heavy shutters darkened the rooms to pitch black, and were designed for security, as well as to keep out the mosquitoes and other night critters.

Speaking of security, in addition to the shutters, we had a day zabanya (guard) and a night zabanya who patrolled the compound. The day zabanya also opened the gate for cars and worked as gardener. The only day zabanya for many of the years we lived in Addis was "Old One Eye", or at least, that's what we called him. I don't recall what his real name was. He was an old soldier, who fought against the Italians in "The War" (Second Italy-Abyssinian War, May 1935 – Oct., 1936). He lost an eye in his service to the Emperor, and still proudly wore his ragged old uniform complete with medal, making a point to salute my father when he honked at the gate each evening. He opened the gate for the rest of us, too, but we were lucky to get a nod of the head, much less a salute.

Rebel, the Alsatian, 1969

The night zabanya's job was to walk around the compound at least once or twice an hour all night long. My mother caught the night zabanya sleeping on the job once, and from then on, he was required to tap his nightstick against the wall so we could hear him as he made his rounds. The night zabanya used to bring our pet Alsatian (a larger version of a German shepherd), named Rebel, with him on his rounds, too. Rebel was his security, I guess.

As for the rest of the house: From the foyer of the front door, on the left was a hallway that led to the bedrooms; to the right were a couple of steps that led up to the living room. The living room was huge and had a large fieldstone fireplace that was the main source of heat in the house. The servants would light the fire each morning before the family was up to take the chill out of the house, and it would be lit again in the evenings when the sun went down.

living room in Addis house, 1969

There was a tiny den/TV room off the living room, and a covered balcony that wrapped around the house outside the living room. To the left of the living room was the dining area where our big round dining table sat. To the left of the dining table was a swinging door that led into the kitchen. The kitchen was large with many cabinets up and down, a gas stove and oven, a large refrigerator and a double sink.

We also had a water filtration system set up in one corner. We boiled all the drinking and cooking water, and then filtered it into huge containers. The prevalence of cholera, typhoid, and particularly amoeba dysentery in the country made the extra precaution of boiling all our drinking water mandatory. While we may have been inoculated against most diseases, the only protection against amoeba dysentery was precaution.

Even so, I managed to contract it while in Addis on one of my visits home. It's an awful illness. Your temperature spikes and you start hallucinating weird fever dreams, then dehydration sets in due to the unrelenting diarrhea and vomiting. No matter how much water you sip (and believe me, you don't feel like drinking or eating anything!), you can't keep any of it down. I can readily understand why it kills babies and people in less than great shape. Thank goodness for antibiotics.

From the doorway of the kitchen there were a few steps down to the front door foyer on the left or to the back door on the right. Out back were the servants' quarters – two small rooms and a tiny bathroom. We kept our freezer in one of the small rooms, along with the bag of horse feed. The other room was used by one of the servants.

Field Mice

The bag of horse feed reminds me of one horrific event involving field mice. It was my brother Pat's job to feed the horses, whose stables were on the other side of the back wall of the compound. One afternoon he went out to feed the horses, as usual, but when he reached in and opened the bag of horse feed, he surprised a family of fat field mice who sprang out at him. His horrified screams as he danced around, swatting at the leaping rodents would have been hilarious, if Pat hadn't been so completely traumatized. Yes, we did laugh about it later, and obviously, we haven't forgotten the event, but I admit that it still makes my skin crawl.

The truth is that field mice were everywhere. I suppose in the ecological scheme of thing, when they cleared the land to build the house, they didn't tell the local families of field mice what they were planning for the neighborhood. Perhaps the mice thought the house had been built just for them?

Personally, I was terrified of them. Yes, I admit it. I'm one of those females who climbs on top of chairs and tables when a mouse scurries across the floor. I can't explain it because I don't tend to be nearly as frightened of snakes and spiders as I am of mice. What I discovered, to my horror, in the house in Addis is that after we turned out the lights and went to bed at night, the mice came out and took over the place. It was a lesson learned not to walk around in the dark in the house, not if you didn't want something small and furry racing across your instep. (Shudder)

The mice didn't confine themselves to the unoccupied areas of the house either. Oh no. One night, I heard scratching under my bed. I finally got up enough nerve to look under the bed, and I was surprised when there was nothing there. I climbed into bed again and then heard the scratching again coming from beneath the bed.

When I pulled the bed away from the wall to investigate further, I discovered a tiny hole in the side of the box spring and a huge mouse peering at me from inside the hole. I watched as he then squeezed out through the hole. To say that I flew from the room would be an understatement; but I'm pretty certain my feet never touched the floor. I slammed the bedroom door behind me, thinking to trap the mouse in the bedroom, at least. But it was late and I was tired so I went in search of someone to help me.

Pat, after his scare with the horse feedbag, flatly refused to come near the room, but my younger brother, Jamie, age 12, said he was game. He found a broom and set off into my bedroom. I could hear him swatting the broom and hollering, and laughing, too, for probably fifteen minutes and then it was quiet. Jamie came out and reported he had trapped the mouse in the closet and locked the closet door. That should keep the mouse confined until morning when one of the servants could come and kill it, he told me.

It wasn't an ideal solution, but it was better than having the rodent running around my room, or worse, inside the box spring of my bed! All night I could hear the desperate scratching coming from the closet, but Jamie was right, the locked closet door kept it in. However, the next morning when one of the servants opened the closet door, we discovered the mouse had nearly scratched completely through the thick wooden door during the night. A little longer, and he might have chewed his way to freedom.

Family Pets in Ethiopia

We had lots of pets while living in Addis Ababa, including three dogs. There was Rebel, the Alsatian shepherd mentioned before, as well as Gemo, a black male miniature poodle, and Gigi, a brown female miniature poodle. And because of the poodles, we ended up with lots of puppies when Gigi had several litters.

Gemo & Gigi near the front door of the house, 1969

We also had the horses, and of course, the tortoise, who was 'sort of' a pet (more about him later).

Mom's tortoise making his rounds in the yard

My First Visit to Ethiopia

The summer after my freshman year at University of Montana, I talked my best friend, Chris, into accompanying me home for the summer, by way of Europe. Need I add that it didn't take much convincing? Who wouldn't want a trip through Europe, with a bonus couple of weeks in the mysterious 'Land of Prester John' on the Horn of Africa?

I had been lucky in finding a good college friend in Chris. She was my next-door neighbor on the 10th floor of Jesse Hall, the freshman dorm at the university. Chris and her parents practically adopted me over the school year, warmly opening their Boise, Idaho home to me for vacations and holidays. I'm sure they felt a little sorry for me, the foreign kid who couldn't go home for holidays, but I appreciated their welcoming attitude and feel lucky to have found them. Chris and I have been friends ever since. Like I said, I was the fortunate one.

In 1968 I was such a foreign American after arriving in the U.S. from Bangkok that I spent most of my freshman year trying to figure out how to fit in. I learned, as all "overseas brats" eventually do, that while you can talk about your experiences of being raised overseas, you shouldn't expect others to understand. Some think you are just some rich kid bragging about all your world travels; others truly suspect that you are only nominally an American and should be treated politely, but at a distance, as they do with the Foreign Exchange students at the school. Things are changing now, I believe, because the world is indeed shrinking thanks to global communications, but back then, having a background like mine was a handicap to hide or at least minimize as best I could. I became a chameleon, learning my American culture just as I had absorbed the Korean, Chinese, Filipino, and Thai cultures as a child. You learn to adapt, and luckily, with my background I was, indeed, very good at adapting.

So Chris and I set off on our trip, meeting in New York City and taking a meandering trip through the major capitals of Europe. We visited the great museums and more churches than I knew existed, went on wine tasting tours in Germany, got chased by drunken sailors in Venice, and had a lot of hilarious adventures (some funnier in hindsight than at the time). Chris was an art major and her father was one of the leading architects in the Pacific Northwest, so I had the advantage of traveling with a knowledgeable art critic. She was a great person to travel with because she already knew quite a bit about the art, sculpture and architecture we were seeing, and between us we had a fair amount of history and literature knowledge. Still, we both wished that we had brought a history book along with us on the trip to check the facts and refresh our memories on the details. I think now of how lucky travelers are with an Internet search just a few keystrokes away! It would have been heaven to get answers to the holes in our memories instead of trying jog each other's memories like a trivia contest gone amuck.

We traveled by plane, train, and even managed to deviously rent a car for a day in Switzerland to see the Alps up close and personal (we were under the legal age for an international driver's license or for renting a car, but apparently we were appealing enough to talk someone into renting to us. Of course, using our parents' American Express cards probably helped.). The trip through Europe was great fun and it concluded with a long overnight flight from Athens to Addis Ababa, my new home.

The Kingdom of Ethiopia

Addis Ababa is located on a grassland plateau at the foot of Mount Entoto (9800 ft.). The site for the city was selected by Empress Taytu Betul and it was founded in 1886 by her husband, Emperor Menelik II. At the time (1969) it had a population of around 2.7 million. The city is a crowded mix of people from all the regions of Ethiopia, a country that has approximately 80 nationalities speaking 80 different languages. All three major world religions are practiced – Christianity, Islam, and even Judaism, a religion that is represented by the Falashas who are purported to be the lost tribe of Israel.

The Amhara are one of the largest ethnic groups, at least in the Ethiopian Highlands region of the country. The predominant religion of the Amhara is Coptic Christianity. The unique attributes and the dominance of the religion in the lives of the people, as is the case in many areas of the world, give the country its distinctive flavor. Coptic

Christianity seems medieval to us Westerners, perhaps even biblical, at times. The pomp and circumstance of its rituals haven't changed much from the early days of Christianity, when the Eastern Coptics split from the Roman church. Part of the reason that things didn't change much in Ethiopia, or Abyssinia, as it was originally called, was because it was so isolated for centuries from what was happening in the rest of the known world. The Highlands provided the kingdom with a natural rock fortress, not easy to get to, and there was little incentive to seek the world out when the emperors realized that keeping foreigners out might prove beneficial to their longevity. So with the high altitudes and the incredibly rugged terrain, the peoples of Ethiopia were cut off, by choice and by nature, from the rest of the world.

Coptic priests at Timkat (Epiphany) celebration

There are fascinating legends that rose out of the mysterious land, as well – that the Queen of Sheba was from Abyssinia and that she traveled to Jerusalem to visit and apparently become impregnated by King Solomon. She returned home to produce a son, Menelik I, who founded the dynasty upon which all rulers – right down to Haile Selassie, so they say – were heir.

There were other tales that are fascinating to contemplate, regardless of whether they are true. The one I liked the best was that the Ark of the Covenant was spirited away from Jerusalem by Menelik (the son of King Solomon and the Queen of Sheba) and brought for safekeeping to Ethiopia. It is said that it was originally hidden away in a secluded church on an island in Lake Tana, the source of the Blue Nile. Later it was moved to the Chapel of the Tablet at the Church of Our Lady Mary of Zion in Axum, an ancient city in northern Ethiopia named after the Kingdom of Aksum, which was a naval and trading power that ruled the region from about 400 BC until the middle of the 10th century. The kingdom was occasionally referred to in medieval writings as "Ethiopia", which is how Abyssinia came to be called "Ethiopia". And, by the way, the Ark is purportedly still there!

The Coptic Christian church rules much of the daily life of the Ethiopians. There are a confounding number of holy days, and countless fast days. In fact, the Coptic Christian laity is expected to fast 165 days per year, including every Wednesday and Friday as well as the two months that include Lent and the Easter season. That's a lot of missed meals! The religion, in fact, is similar to the Orthodox Judaism in its adherence to Old Testament practices, like strict dietary rules, the covering of a woman's head, removing shoes upon entering a church, and many others. It was fascinating to discover the variety and weight of these centuries' old traditions and to see the ancient practices mix so seamlessly, and sometimes, not so seamlessly, with the modern.

H.I.M. Emperor Haile Selassie, King of Kings, Lord of Lords, Conquering Lion of the Tribe of Judah, Elect of God and Power of the Trinity

Emperor Haile Selassie was still in power during the first years my family was in Ethiopia. We learned to admire many things about H.I.M. (His Imperial Majesty) – certainly his dedication to removing the Italians from his country during the 1930's as he took to the world stage and he spoke so eloquently before the League of Nations and finally found success in getting the Italians out of his country during the early days of World War II. After the war, he worked valiantly trying to guide his medieval country into the 20th century. He set up schools and founded colleges in an attempt to increase literacy, he sent deserving students to Russia and the U.S. for advanced studies and training, he built a modern city with multi-storied buildings and paved roads, and invited help from the West. My father, working for the Agency for International Development, was one of those called to help. His job in Ethiopia was to help set up Private Enterprise, getting interested companies in the U.S. to set up manufacturing, agricultural, and even low-income housing projects in Ethiopia.

On the downside, I don't think that Haile Selassie was ever really interested in setting up a Western-style democracy in his country. Yes, he wanted his country to develop, to be successful, to take its place as a leader among the newly independent African nations, but he didn't want it to change that much. He had some vested interest in the aristocracy and in the intricate and strangling land ownership patterns (basically the Coptic church and the aristocracy owned all the land, and the people were considered tenants – and perhaps peasants or serfs would be a more apt description).

One of the problems that my father described one night as we sat around our round dining table was Ethiopia's recent development of a "middle class". You would think that would be a good thing, wouldn't you? This growing middle class was made up of young Ethiopians who didn't belong to any of the traditional classes in society – they weren't part of the aristocracy, they weren't leaders of the church, they weren't tenant farmers. Instead, they were returning college students, some with advanced technical degrees, and they were small business owners, who ran the many new shops and businesses in the thriving capital. Many had graduated from the local university or returned from studies abroad only to find that, to their dismay, in Ethiopia there were very few middle class jobs. This left a whole segment of the population – a very educated and vocal segment – feeling cheated and in turmoil, and demanding change.

Last, there was the succession problem. This was the late 1960's and early 1970's and the Emperor was getting older (he was 77 in 1969), his son, Crown Prince Asfaw Wossen, was in ill health, and his grandson was a teen and not ready to take over the reins of power. What would happen if Haile Selassie suddenly dropped dead? Who would succeed him?

And, there were the rumblings of ferment about the need for land reform. The Emperor's power base, the aristocracy, was dependent on the tithes they collected from their tenants. But where's the incentive to work harder and produce more when you didn't own the land and wouldn't be able to keep the proceeds? When the harvest was good, you paid more; when the harvest was poor, as it often was, you starved but still owed the landlord.

Summer of 1969 in Addis

Chris and I landed early one July morning in Addis and after getting through security at Bole International Airport, we were wrapped in my family's embrace. For me, it had been over a year since I had last seen any of my family. My younger brothers had all grown taller – I was shorter than or eye-to-eye with all except my youngest brother, Chris (nicknamed "Ku" as we still called him then). They looked at me and said they thought I had changed too – not really taller, but perhaps slimmer, and my hair was a lot darker than any of them remembered. The sun-bleached blonde highlights of my tropical childhood were gone now after spending the past nine months in Montana. I like to think that my newfound college maturity showed, too (although, oddly, no one mentioned it).

My family can be a little overwhelming to the uninitiated – and Chris only had one brother, not like my six, four of whom were at the airport that morning. Little did Chris know that the real test of acceptance would come at dinner that night. Dinner is special for the Sullivans. It was a family tradition to spend time with each other around the table each night, so although all of us are fast eaters, we don't eat-and-run. Instead, we stick around and talk, sometimes for an hour or more. My father would discuss current events or things he had seen or done in his job, my brothers would bring up the latest happenings at the American Community School that they all attended, my mother would talk about her job running the Commissary, or her play group, the school board, or women's club, or whatever activity, party or event she was currently involved in.

That night, as we sat around the infamous round table, the cook laid out the serving dishes on the lazy Susan at the center. Initially, things were calm as each person served himself or herself from the serving dishes. My friend, Chris, watched for a minute or two then jumped right in, reaching out and holding the lazy Susan in place with her left hand while she calmly served herself with her right hand. My brothers looked on in surprise. She was the first guest who had done it "right" – most rookies have a very hard time adjusting to our lazy Susan. For one thing, they don't realize that it needs to be a two-handed job – one to hold it in place, so that others won't begin spinning it while you're serving yourself.

We have had some spectacular accidents – some like the famous beans-in-the-lap accident in the Philippines, but most of the time it's less dramatic, although it can be equally hilarious. Like once, when the guest lifted the spoon from the serving dish but didn't act quickly enough to actually scoop anything up before the dish spun away and he was left holding an empty spoon in the air. Another visitor went to put the ice tea carafe back on the lazy Susan only to mow down everything else as the lazy Susan began to move before he released hia hold of the carafe.

But Chris adapted quickly. In fact, I knew she would be fine when a little later, she caught hold of the lazy Susan at the same time as my little brother, Ku. There was a short tug of war when she eyed him and very calmly said, "Let go, Ku". (She had already acquired her great "teacher's voice"). In surprise, he did. Then we all laughed. It doesn't take much to fit into my family and my friend, Chris, managed to figure out the key in record time: Be firm, be bold, and don't back down.

Shopping at the Mercato

My parents wanted to make sure we had a great time for the few weeks that Chris would be there, and for the several weeks more that I would remain until returning to Montana for school in late September. Besides touring the city and seeing the local sights, they took us souvenir shopping at the Mercato, an open-air market downtown. It was filled with every sort of item, including souvenirs that were consummately African, in nature. For instance, we were offered the skins of endangered animals, monkey-tail flyswatters, giraffe-hair bracelets, carved ivory tusks, huge Ostrich eggs, among other things. There were also carved wooden stools, baskets of every design, and of course, there were the famous crosses. Although the Coptic crosses are not mass-produced, they are ubiquitous. Each is slightly different from any other, with intricate metalwork designs, scalloped edges, and exquisite balance. If you wanted to buy something uniquely Ethiopian and beautiful, a Coptic cross was a good choice.

Women vegetable sellers at Mercado open markets, Addis Ababa, 1970

We attracted a lot of attention, of course, as we walked through the market. Beginning with the swarm of little boys demanding money to "watch the car". I'm sure it was the first time in her life that Chris had ever been harassed by beggars and lepers; it was the first time in a very long time for me, as well. The last country I had lived in overseas was Thailand and that country had a Buddhist belief in the meritorious deed of dispensing charity that did much to keep the destitute off the streets. While one was occasionally accosted by bands of little Thai boys, these Ethiopian poor people – ragged women, bloated-bellied children, legless men – were by far the worst off I had ever seen.

Camping at Lake Langano

My mother wanted us to see a bit of the country outside of Addis, too, and so they took us camping while Chris was there. This was my first camping trip to Lake Langano, and over the next few years I went on dozens more. Our camping trips, to Lake Langano in particular,

Flat tire in the rain on the way to Lake Langano, camping trip, 1969

became one of my favorite memories of the country. That was true for the rest of my family, as well. In fact, based on the letters I received from my mother over the next few years, it seems they went camping at least once a month for most of the time they lived in Ethiopia; if not to Lake Langano, then to Lake Awasa, the Awash Game Park, or to Sodere Hot Springs, among other spots.

Getting to Lake Langano in 1969 took a bit of planning – not just for the expected, but for a whole range of the unexpected. We carried all our potable water, food, and camping gear, of course, but we also carried "just in case" extras – like additional fan belts for the car and cans of brake fluid. You just never knew what might happen, and once you left the relative safety and convenience of Addis, it was a long drive – or bus trip back – with little or no reliable repair services along the way.

On that first camping trip, we managed to suffer only a single flat tire on the way down. We were caravanning in two station wagons, and within moments of stopping the cars, we were surrounded by spectators – these were Gallas or more correctly, Oromos – one of the southern ethnic groups in Ethiopia.

These people were darker than the Amhara and had more Negroid features. They were shy of us, but also very curious. A few of the men carried tall sticks; several of the women had infants on their backs. The little girls were miniatures of their mothers, with colorful shawls and multiple strands of beads and metal necklaces around their necks. A few had decorated gourds hanging from their belts. All the women were also wearing a lot of jewelry – huge chunky brass armbands on their upper arms, beaded leather shawls, long dangling silver earrings. These were not people who kept their bounty locked away in a jewelry box; they wore their wealth proudly as it was a sign of social status in their culture. Their hair was matted with rancid butter (a hair product you don't want to be downwind of) with their hair tightly twisted and intricately woven. Interestingly enough, they didn't like being downwind of us either – they thought we smelled oddly unpleasant to their noses, too. Touché.

We bought a few of the brass armbands from them. In the seven months they had been living in Ethiopia, my brothers had already picked up a store of basic Amharic phrases and my father was fast becoming fluent in the language, so between that and a lot of sign language and gesturing we were able to do some rudimentary bartering. Once they realized we wanted to trade them Ethiopian currency for their jewelry, they pried off the armbands and bracelets from their arms and happily handed them over, grinning and bowing their gratitude.

It was raining lightly and my mother was moving among us handing out Hershey Kisses from her coat pocket. Chris and I both thought this was quite funny, but oddly touching. My mother was just doing her part to keep everyone's spirits up. Finally, the tire was changed, the jack was put away and we were on our way again. We arrived at Lake Langano in about two hours, arriving mid-afternoon.

Putting up tents, boys vs. girls, Lake Langano, 1969

This was before my parents bought the family its own tent,

so we had to borrow camping gear from the American Embassy – several old but sturdy canvas tents. With my friend Chris on my side, we decided to challenge the boys to a race to put up the tents - girls against the boys. (Need I add that the girls won handily? Girl Scouts Rule!)

Camping in Ethiopia isn't quite like camping anywhere else in the world. During those early years, there were no campground showers, or other established facilities, so instead, we bathed in the lake using Ivory soap bars (chosen because they float). We discovered the lake was mineral water. This was lucky, because many of the lakes and rivers in East Africa are infested with a nasty parasite called Schistosomiasis, also known as bilharzias, which is a disease caused by parasitic worms that live in freshwater lakes and rivers in Africa, but they aren't found in mineral water lakes.

Another odd feature of Lake Langano was the huge volcanic pumice rocks littering the beach that looked like they might weigh a ton, but when you picked them up were as light as feathers, and some of them even floated!

Lake Langano beach, 1969

We didn't have a "normal" camping experience by any stretch of the imagination. For one thing, we not only had all the normal camping gear, but we brought along a servant/zabanya (guard) to do the heavy lifting, chop wood for the campfire, and keep an eye on the campsite. Our camp zabanya (guard) was our servant named Arage.

Arage

Arage was a cheerful, strong, and helpful young man, in his mid-20's (as near as we could figure). He was originally from the southern part of the country. He didn't speak any English when my mother hired him, so we never were able to get a complete history on him. My mother was convinced that he was fresh out of the bush when he arrived at our gate. He had a huge smile on his face, was eager and willing to work hard, but knew nothing of housework, cooking or cleaning, so at first, she hired him as an outside zabanya. It wasn't long before he realized the pecking order of the servants, which meant that being an inside servant was more prestigious than being an outside worker. He asked my mother if he could work inside. "I work hard!" he promised, charming her with his huge toothy grin. She believed him, and although she knew he could learn everything there was to know about cleaning, she also knew that she couldn't let him work inside until he began to bathe regularly. She explained it to him, as best she could, handing him a bar of soap and explaining the bathing process with mime and lots of repetitions until she thought he understood. It turned out that he did.

A while later she heard him hollering from the back cement area in front of the servants' quarters. "Ma-dam!" "Ma-dam!" "Na!" ("Come!"), he yelled. She ran to the back door and looked out. There was Arage, stark naked, standing in a metal washbasin, sopping wet and covered with soapy suds. "I take bath!" he said with enormous pride. All you could see, she later reported with a laugh, were the whites of his eyes and his huge toothy grin.

My brothers made it their mission – and entertainment, I might add – to teach Arage "good" English. He was an earnest student. Generally, they taught him English phrases. Some were helpful, like "please", "thank you", "yes, sir", and "no, madam". And some were just for their own amusement, like "I love you, goddamit", "Out of sight!", and the ever hilarious "I'm from California, cool, man, cool!". Arage, after all, had no idea what he was saying, and they convinced him that these were pleasantries in English that meant innocuous things like "Please let me help you." "I'm happy to have been of assistance." Things like that.

The entertainment value backfired on my brothers one night when my mother was having a party for the Ambassador and his wife, when Arage opened their car door, bowed low and said, "I love you, goddamit!" and followed it with "I'm-from-Cal-ee-for-nee-ya, cool, man, cool!" My mother had the devil of a time explaining how Arage came to learn his "interesting" version of English.

Moonwalk – Apollo 11, July 20, 1969

Our first Lake Langano camping trip took place the weekend of July 18th during the summer of 1969. On Sunday night, July 20, 1969, the First Moon Walk took place with Neil Armstrong announcing: "Tranquility Base. The Eagle Has Landed". That happened at 4:17

First camping trip to Lake Langano: Jerry (on top), Maureen, Chris Cline, and David Ernst

p.m., EDT, but for us it was 7 hours later, at 10:17 p.m. local time. One of the really cool things about this coincidence of events was that when Neil Armstrong and Buzz Aldrin were landing the Eagle on the moon, it was nighttime in Ethiopia and we were lying on our backs on the hood of the station wagon staring up at that very same moon. It gave me goose bumps to know that the moon we were looking at had two Americans in a small spacecraft sitting on it at that very moment. We were listening to Voice of the Gospel, the only English-speaking radio station we could pick up on the car radio and we were fortunate enough to hear the event as it took place, in English. What an incredible memory! I had been overseas for so many of the "where-were-you-when" moments that people ask about (Kennedy's assassination, etc.), it's amazing to me that for the first time, by being overseas, I was actually in the best place to experience the event.

My father had to go back to Addis for work on Monday, the 21st, but the rest of us stayed at Lake Langano. When he arrived at work that day he told us later that he was amazed and deeply touched by the literally dozens of Ethiopians who came up to him on the street in Addis to congratulate him for being American, the country that took "one small step for man, one giant leap for mankind". It's hard to appreciate what a powerful and positive event it was, not just for America, but indeed, for the entire world.

Speaking of missing momentous events, a month later Woodstock took place back in the U.S., and yeah, I missed it; I was still in Ethiopia. Would I have been able to go had I been in the U.S.? Probably not since I went to school in Montana, not anywhere near upper New York State. So it was just as well that, instead, I was in a place I grew to love: Ethiopia.

Hippos in Lake Langano

There were all sorts of wild animals in the Rift Valley bush around Lake Langano. At night, you could hear wild sounds in the dark – particularly the hyenas and their weird barking laugh. But the strangest was the occasional report of hippo sightings. Here's a note from one of my mother's letters, dated Oct. 11, 1971:

Dear Maureen,

How about a hippo in Lake Langano!! Well, there was this weekend. About 11 p.m. on Sunday night (over the long Columbus Day weekend) after the lights went out, I was checking on the kids and all of a sudden I heard the long spurting noise of something emerging from the lake, and a sort of roaring sound. Pat Haggerty (Note: family friend – Len, her husband, worked with my father at USAID) jumped into the air scared to death, and then the Dutch family near the beach came running saying a hippo was in the lake. So all of us got the flashlights and went to the beach. He was there, and we followed him all the way down to the bend. Of course, the next day people were a bit hesitant about swimming, but they finally did. We had a marvelous weekend, and the new tent is really nice."

Dating in Addis

The American community in Addis was very tight back in 1969. It's probably that way now, as it is in most small posts. Americans stick together and provide a community for each other. That's true for the adults and it's also true for the kids. Wherever in the world they are, teenagers find other teenagers, young adults find other young adults, and so on. After living in Addis for six months, my brother, Jerry, had already made many friends, and one of them, Tam, had an older brother, Gray, who had recently returned home to Ethiopia.

Gray and Tam's father was a pilot for Ethiopian Airlines. The boys had been sent to British boarding school in Nairobi, Kenya, and they had a different upbringing than my brothers and I had had. Americans overseas are not all the same. There are missionary families who have a different overseas experience than do the diplomats' families like mine, than do the military families, than do the private Americans working on contract for international companies or for universities or for government agencies.

Ethiopian Airlines was originally the stepchild of TWA. It contracted with TWA to provide American pilots to fly their jets, train their pilots, and fly along side them until they had enough experience to eventually replace their Americans mentors. Tam and Gray's parents and other Ethiopian Airline contract workers came over to Addis in the early 1950's and because there were no English-speaking schools at the time, they sent their children to boarding schools in

Kenya. Once the American Community School was established in Addis many of them went to school there.

Need I say that there aren't a lot of college-aged girls to date in Addis? So when an American girl arrived in town, even just visiting for a few weeks, she became fair game for the Peace Corps volunteers, the Marine Guards at the Embassy, or any other unattached guy in his early 20's who happened to be living in Addis. When my friend, Chris, and I arrived, Gray, Tam, Jerry and the rest of their friends, made it a point to take us to the few local nightclubs and to show us a good time.

By the time that Chris left a few weeks later, I was dating Gray. For the next month, we went everywhere together – to the movie theaters, even if the films shown were years old and already being rerun on TV back in the States; to the nightclubs to dance to music already six months to a year old; and to house parties.

Speaking of movies, I was amazed to discover that there was actually a drive-in theater in Addis! The films themselves were ancient – I think we saw an old Clint Eastwood spaghetti western one of the nights – but the really charming thing about the drive-in was that a waiter came to your car window and took your order. Did you want a beer or a mixed drink? No problem. What about popcorn? It arrived on a silver platter – one big pile of salted white popped popcorn! Amazing.

So what did someone like Gray do for work in Addis Ababa, Ethiopia? Gray had left college in the states and returned home a few months before I arrived. He looked around for a job and managed to find an interesting one: he became an apprentice White Hunter.

Gray Goodman, apprentice White Hunter, Omo River valley, Ethiopia, 1969

I thought at the time, (and still do) that being a White Hunter had to be the most romantic occupation possible. I was an English major, after all, and had read Hemingway's *The Snows of Kilimanjaro*, I had seen Humphrey Bogart and Katherine Hepburn in *The African Queen*, and read Karen Blixen's account of life in Kenya, and all of Robert Ruark's books. Gray was all that, and more. He worked for some of the best and probably the last of the big game hunters in Ethiopia, including Karl Luthy and Ted Shatto. I learned a lot about African wildlife from him and through him I began to understand how Africa could change a person and get under your skin, if you are open to it.

There is a joke that I have heard pretty much universally among the Americans and other ex-pats living in Africa; the punch line has to do with "being on Africa time". It's usually said in a derogatory way, as a put-down. It's an obvious generalization to say that Africans don't "get" the importance of being on time or adhering to schedules. It took me a while to realize that perhaps, in fact, the reverse is true: that we don't "get" the value of ignoring time; that time has little relevance to what's really important in life. It's ironic that these days, Americans talk about "being in the zone" and the timeless feeling when immersed in a pleasurable pursuit or task, but isn't that just living on "African time"?

In addition to dating in Addis, Gray showed me a bit of the country, as well. We went camping at Lake Langano and took a memorable car trip to Awash Game Park during a very muddy Rainy Season. That trip, it was Gray and me in the front seat of the borrowed station wagon with our brothers, Jerry and Tam, in the backseat. The four of us headed out of Addis on our way to Awash Game Park, perhaps a four-hour drive south.

The trip down was blessedly uneventful until we got to Awash. This was summer and it was the rainy season. There aren't traditional Western Hemisphere seasons in the Horn of Africa – Winter, Spring, Summer, Fall – instead there are really just three seasons: the Dry season, the Little Rains and the Big Rains. Or at least, that was the way it used to be before a number of multi-year droughts wreaked havoc on the cycle.

Anyway, in the late 1960's, the rains seemed more predictable. In June, July and August, the country would have the Big Rains – where we would be inundated with huge amounts of rain every single day and when it wasn't raining, it was cloudy. This was good for the land and its agriculture, but not quite as good for those of us visiting during the summer months.

The "little rains" came in January and February. I can't speak about them, because I never managed to be in Ethiopia during those months of the year. I will say, though, that the dry season (during the Fall and Spring months) was spectacular – deep blue skies and bright sunny days; every single day.

Jerry and Tam Goodman, car stuck in the mud, Awash Game Park, Ethiopia, 1969

So our trip to Awash took place during the summer rainy season. We didn't have much rain on the trip, but when we turned off the main road to head into the game park, we hit muddy tracks, and then deeper mud with barely any tracks, and finally all mud and no tracks. In all that muck, the station wagon eventually got stuck. We spent hours pushing, spinning the tires, and trying to rock the car out of the mud only to move a few feet and sink in even deeper.

Just before sundown, a Land Rover appeared. We thought we had been saved. A Land Rover, we knew, would have four-wheel drive and possibly a winch. As a matter of fact, it had both, but unfortunately, the driver was a tad overconfident and didn't switch over to four-wheel drive until after he also became stuck in his own muddy patch. To make a long story short, the Rover couldn't get out either. They sent word to the game camp for help and we ended up sleeping in the car.

The night we spent in the car was pretty amazing, in retrospect. The stars were bright and so huge they practically hung from the curtain of black sky over the Rift Valley around us. Periodically, Gray would turn on the headlights and we would marvel at the dozens upon dozens of eyes reflected in the light. We were surrounded by animals in the dark – herds of waterbucks, giraffe, gazelle, a lone lion, possibly a hippo even – all traveling in the darkness to the nearest salt lick or water hole. It was an incredible sight – bright eyes and moving dark silhouettes – and one I'll never forget.

Help arrived in the morning in the form of a second Land Rover and without further ado, they winched both the first Land Rover and our station wagon from the muck. It wasn't long before we were on our way again.

That day, we drove around the game park and saw more animals, and on the way back, we found something really amazing resting in the center of the dirt road: one huge tortoise. Apparently, Gray and Tam had promised my mother that they would bring her a tortoise if they ever came across one. This, they decided, was the one. Tam got out and sat on it and we all agreed that it was indeed "the right one". We loaded it into the back of the vehicle and brought it back to Addis.

Tam on the tortoise, Awash Game Park, Ethiopia, 1969

In Addis, we presented the tortoise to my mother, who then let it go in the yard at the house, where it remained for the next several years. The only mishap was a year later the tortoise was run over in our driveway. Not to worry. My mother picked him up, put him under some bushes in the garden, and lovingly cared for him, feeding him dog food and salad greens for about a month as his shell slowly healed. A year later, you could still see where the shell had been cracked, but it had completely healed over, and the tortoise continued to make his rounds of the compound, inch-by-inch, foot-by-foot, year-by-year.

At the end of the summer, in September, I returned to college and conducted a frustrating long-distance correspondence relationship with Gray. It brings to mind the old adage, "Out of sight, out of mind." I should have known better.

Still, as I got back into the routine of school again, I was already looking forward to the following summer because the next year was another home leave summer and it was the home leave we would go around-the-world; again.

Chapter 12   Home Leave – Summer of 1970

The summer of 1970, my parents decided that the whole family would meet in L.A. in June and then we would to go to Honolulu to spend a few weeks together in our house in Hawaii – our first ever family reunion. My brother, Denny, and his wife, Sandee, would fly out from southern California. My brother Mike thought he could arrange an R&R from Vietnam and would also meet us in Hawaii. I flew to L.A. from Montana after my final exams were over.

Over that school year, Gray and I had been corresponding and it turned out that he was going to be in Los Angeles at about the same time, so we arranged to meet there a couple of days before my parents arrived from New York. He and I had a good time seeing Disneyland together, but, by the time my folks arrived, he made himself scarce and I didn't see him again until later in the fall in Addis.

Hawaii Reunion Summer of 1970

My brother, Mike, was near the end of his first tour in Vietnam and he was eligible for some R&R in Hawaii while we were there. My parents, and brothers Jerry, Pat, Jamie and Ku, and I moved into our house overlooking Diamond Head and Waikiki and waited for the rest of the family to assemble.

Denny and Sandee arrived, as planned, but no Mike. We waited. When he still didn't arrive, my parents got in touch with the American Red Cross. Getting very worried at the silence, after several days and

Family reunion, Lurline Drive house, Honolulu, Hawaii, 1970

telegrams back and forth, we finally got word that he was in the hospital in Vietnam. On his last combat mission before his R&R, he had been hurt jumping out of a helicopter – apparently he was injured by the jump from the helicopter, not by bullets or bombs. That was an incredible relief after days of not knowing.

So the rest of the family, all except Mike, had our first family reunion. It was great being together, but a little bittersweet to be missing a member.

Trip through Asia

Denny and Sandee returned to L.A. and the rest of us spent several weeks in Honolulu before leaving for the trip back to Ethiopia. Our first stop was Guam to see my mother's sister, Fern, and my Uncle Philip. Then it was off for a long-anticipated trip through the Orient, visiting Hong Kong, Taipei, and Bangkok, before returning to Addis via Nairobi.

One of the interesting things about our trip through Asia on our return to Ethiopia was in getting the opportunity to revisit places we had previously lived.

In Taipei, we drove around our old neighborhood in Yang Ming Shan (Grass Mountain). It was all very familiar, but had grown a bit older in the six years since we had lived there. The trees we had planted in our yard were taller and fuller and my mother's garden had blossomed with its vibrant rose bushes and perennials along the walkway and around the edges of the house. It was like viewing your home in the midst of a dream – it looks the same, but you know it's not really the same because everything else, including you, has changed.

Hong Kong was as exciting as ever with all the bustle of a thriving commercial Chinese city. There were more tall skyscrapers, but the shops in Kowloon and the Star Ferry across the harbor to Hong Kong Island all were very familiar. We had never lived in Hong Kong, only visited it many times over the years, so we didn't have the same sense of the changes.

Returning to Bangkok, though, was much more deeply felt, as it was a place we had loved, and it had only been a lapse of two years since we had left it; not a very long time. In fact, I found several friends from my graduating class who happened to be in Bangkok for the summer visiting their parents, and I felt like I was living vicariously. They were having the experience I had thought I would have when I left Bangkok in June of 1968. At the time, I had assumed that I would be back in June of 1969, coming home and reuniting with many of my high school friends. We had planned to have great reunions as we returned from far-flung colleges. Now it was August of 1970, two years after graduation, and most of my friends weren't in Bangkok that summer because their fathers' tours were up and they had moved on to some other country or back to the States. So I was happy to have found even a few familiar faces.

It's odd to return to a place of your past. It's like time-elapsed photography with the changes seeming jerky and sudden. But it's also satisfying for someone like me who has more memories than tangible evidence of my past. To go back and try to make contact with your former self is a rewarding, if disconcerting, experience.

It's also instructive. You soon realize that your memories are of the people you shared the time and place with, not just of the place. Without the people – your friends, your family, your community – a place is just a place and it loses much of its cachet. I think that's why I always used to say my home wasn't a place, it was wherever my family was; and I still believe that to be the truest definition of "home," even today. I hope my own children and their children feel the same way.

After Bangkok, we had a long flight to Nairobi that involved a change of planes in Bombay (Mumbai). We left Bangkok late in the evening and arrived in Bombay in the early hours – one or two in the morning. There is something eerie about that hour of the night, even if you are standing in a brightly lit transit lounge at an international airport. The fluorescent lights seem to cast a weird greenish glow on everyone and there are the ever-present stale odors of foreign food and unwashed bodies.

For some reason we had to go through Indian Customs – I no longer remember why. To do that, we had to collect our suitcases and then check in for the connecting flight to Nairobi, Kenya. The problem was that two of our suitcases were missing – my father's suitcase and one of my mother's suitcases. It was unfortunate because it was my father's only suitcase containing all his clothes, whereas my mother had her clothes packed across several suitcases. Where she might be missing a blouse or a particular dress, my father didn't even have a change of underwear!

He couldn't believe that two suitcases out of 14 could possibly be missing. Did they not get on the flight in Bangkok? Or had the missing luggage been overlooked in the cargo hold by the baggage handlers? They offered to let him go take a look in the baggage hold of the plane and my father jumped at the chance to see for himself. He climbed aboard, ripping the seam in the seat of his pants as he stretched up through the cargo door, cursing his bad luck. He was in the belly of the plane for a long time. When we saw him again, he looked grim. No suitcases were discovered, so obviously they weren't on the plane. With nothing more to be done, we boarded the next flight and headed to Nairobi.

Nairobi, Kenya

Arriving in Nairobi was exciting. Here was a new place for us to see, a thriving African capital. We landed at the airport under the East African sunny blue skies. The rainy season was over and the flowers were in bloom throughout the city. Flowering vines of bougainvillea hung from walls, orchids and rose bushes were lush with colorful flowers. It was one of those cities and times of year when you just wanted to stop and breathe in all the sweet aromas.

After settling into the hotel and getting a good night's sleep, my parents got in touch with some old friends and we were immediately invited to their house for the afternoon and dinner. Their home was in the Highlands, a district just outside Nairobi. My poor father had nothing to change into. My mother washed his one pair of underwear the night before but with the heat and humidity it was still damp the next morning. She sewed up the ripped seam in his pants and did the best she could to iron his one pair of slacks so he would be presentable, but he finally decided to wear them without underwear, rather than risk an embarrassing damp stain from the wet underwear. Who would know, after all?

My Father and the Army Ants

We arrived at our friends' house and it was a lovely, very British large estate surrounded by formal gardens, that the British were so clever at creating wherever in the world they colonized. After a tour of the house, they asked if we wanted a tour of the gardens and we readily agreed. We walked along the well laid out pathways and exclaimed at the beautiful roses, orchids, and other flowers and trees.

Then it happened. A line of red army ants crossed the footpath. My father was second in line and I was third as we unknowingly interrupted the ants' progress. Within seconds, all hell broke loose. My father froze then he swatted at the leg of his pants. I don't think he knew yet what was happening. Then I felt the crawling sensation, too, followed by the fiery stinging bites up and down my leg. I couldn't believe how fast those insects were! They climb from your foot to your waist within seconds, and you have stinging bites all along the way.

Our gracious hostess turned and instantly realized what had happened. "Army Ants!" she exclaimed. "Quick! You have to drop your pants, Gene, and pick them off."

But my father wasn't listening; instead he had turned and run for the bushes. I, on the other hand, didn't have to be told twice. I quickly unzipped my pants and shimmied out of them in seconds. Next, I yanked the whole pant leg inside out and to my horror saw dozens upon dozens of ants swarming over the material. I dropped the pants and glanced down at my legs. I could already feel the stings on my leg turning into small welts. They were around my ankles, at the backs of my knees, on my thighs. Everyone gathered around to pick at my legs and swat at any visible crawling ants.

Once I seemed to be free of the pests, we picked them off my pants, squishing them before flicking them off with a finger. Brushing at them didn't work. They clung to the fabric and to my skin like glue. You had to literally pick them off, one by one.

Later, I asked Dad why he didn't drop his pants and get help picking the ants off like I did. He blushed and had a funny look on his face. My mother answered for him, "Because he didn't have any underwear on." We all laughed. Apparently, modesty is the last to go!

Chapter 13   Addis Ababa, Ethiopia (1970 – 1972)

The Sullivan Kids, circa 1970

Ages of the Sullivan children in the Fall of 1970 in Addis Ababa, Ethiopia:

Dennis (Denny), age 23 (in the Marines, in California)

Michael (Mike), age 21 (in the Army, in Vietnam)

Maureen, age 19 (taking a semester off before starting junior year at Boston University)

Robert (Jerry), age 17 (high school junior)

Patrick (Pat), age 15 (high school freshman)

James (Jamie), age 13

Christopher (Ku or Chris), age 10

Addis, Fall of 1970

We arrived back in Addis and I had been expecting – silly me! – that Gray would be at the airport anxiously awaiting my arrival. He wasn't. That should have told me all I needed to know, but I was insanely optimistic and it took quite a while for it to finally sink in that it was over.

Those four months in Addis turned out to be an interesting, although completely unanticipated time in my life. I had taken the semester off because I wanted to see more of Ethiopia while spending a lot of time with Gray. In the end, I got half of what I wanted.

Trips around Ethiopia

With or without Gray, I was thrilled to be back in Ethiopia and I wanted to make the most of it. I traveled with my family and with friends of my family to as much of Ethiopia as I could manage in the short four months I was there. Whenever a trip was planned, I was ready to hop in the car or on a plane to go.

Of course, we went on several family camping trips to Lake Awasa, Lake Langano, the Awash Game Park and Sodere Resort. It amazes me how my family took to camping in Africa. We had never done any camping in Asia at all, but in Ethiopia, we went at least once a month and ended up owning our own tent and quite a bit of camping gear.

Lalibela church, 1970

In addition to camping, I managed to visit the Blue Nile Falls on the road the Bahir Dar, and took trips to Dire Dawa, the dusty market town on the edge of the desert; the biblical-looking Harar with its Hyena Man who fed wild hyenas at the city gate each night; Axum, the original capital dating back to 100 BC with its ancient obelisks; and of course, the rock-hewn churches of Lalibela.

On one memorable road trip to Harar over the mountains and down off the highland plateau, we stopped at the famous Coptic church at Kulubi. There is an intriguing superstition surrounding this particular church. It is the church of Michael, the Archangel and is said to be the church of wishes. The superstition is that if you go there in good faith and make a wish, it will come true, but once granted, you must repay it by revisiting the church within a year to thank God for your good fortune. Beware the person who neglects to repay the favor! There were a number of cautionary tales filled with terrible accidents and Job-like runs of bad luck. But as is the way with these things, they tended to be stories about friends-of-friends and were hard to verify. Still, if my wish is ever granted, I'll gladly go back to show my appreciation. Who wouldn't?

Hyena Man of Harrar, 1970

Kulubi Church, 1970

Plays, Addis Style

One of my mother's passions has always been the theater. But plays in Addis weren't performed like plays anywhere else. My mother had been involved in theater groups in Korea and she kept up her interest throughout the years we were living overseas. She'd had some drama club experience in high school and college, but to be honest, in the off-off-Broadway theater groups available overseas, a person only needed the willingness to volunteer his or her talents and time, and in my mother's case, they got a bonus in her ability to organize and lead people.

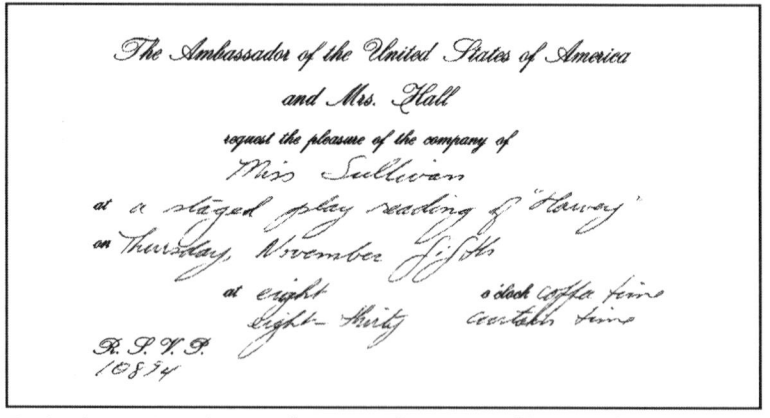

Invitation to American Embassy performance of "Harvey", Nov. 5, 1970

    Once she found a few interested people who thought putting on a play would be fun, she was off to the races. First they would decide on the play they wanted to do, then my mother would write to publishers in the U.S. for copies of the script. She didn't want to pay performance fees, royalties, and all the other expenses of putting on a full-boat theatrical production, so she called these productions "readings" with limited props, costumes and sets.

    With the people, script, and play practices in motion, the next step was for my mother to cajole the Ambassador into allowing the group to use the Ambassador's Residence as the theater venue for a night or two. Then as word got around, everyone would vie for invitations, including some of the Ethiopian royal family, foreign dignitaries and important local political personages. For the foreign community, it was a night out and a novel cultural event to look forward to. For the American community, it was a chance to dress up and enjoy an evening's entertainment at the Ambassador's home. For the actors, it was a chance to let their hair down and act out of character for a change.

There is something really unique about being a part of a theatrical group. A camaraderie and affection grows in the group as they get together to practice lines, brainstorm and prepare for the presentation, and the bonds of friendship that result sometimes last for years, if not decades. It's a win-win situation – the audience gets a night out to enjoy their friends doing something outlandish, while the actors get a chance to stretch themselves. There is no downside, except maybe stage fright, nerves and the occasional mishap.

My father didn't view himself as "an actor" and would never have volunteered had my mother not coerced him into it. The first time, for a play called *Bus Stop*, she convinced him to "just take a small part so that he could enjoy the fun of being a part of the production without having the pressure of a leading role". She needn't have worried because as it turned out, he was a natural ham and enjoyed the experience tremendously, so much so that he was practically the first to volunteer for every production thereafter.

My mother was usually the director and sometimes took an acting part, as well. There may have been others more qualified to direct these productions, but she had the edge because she was actually willing to organize the whole thing, took the headaches in stride, and was able to manage it all to its successful conclusion.

She was particularly good at paying attention to the important little details, like printing up formal Embassy invitations for the plays, and making sure there was plenty of food and drinks at the post-production party. The night of the production was always an enjoyable evening and it gave the community something to talk about, focus on and to share for weeks before and after the event. In Addis, her group did a number of shows: *Bus Stop, Harvey, Dial "M" for Murder*, and even *The Sound of Music*.

The Sound of Music was the biggest production they had attempted and it turned out to be a spectacular presentation with talented singers. Because of the size of the cast and the interest in the play, they discovered they needed a bigger venue with more seats and a larger stage. They ended up at the Ethiopian music school. Of course, there were the inevitable mishaps on opening night. Here's my mother's description from the 1971 Christmas letter:

With a cast of 64, Hope and Gene directed and produced a favorite. We were delighted when we sold out all performances, receiving raves. The last night we even had children sitting on the floor and Ethiopians bringing their own chairs rather than miss the production. Addis does not have a theatre, and is starved for entertainment. Of course, we had many "tragedies" or at least, near tragedies. The first night at 6:45 with a curtain call for 7:30, all power in the area went off. We put makeup on by candlelight, dressed the stage of the Government-sponsored music school with candles, and planned a Shakespearean Theatre presentation. The director, Hope, ignored the pleas and moans of the sound man, who said his tape recorder would not work with candlepower. But one minute before curtain, on the downbeat of the overture, the lights came on. Gene had called the Power Board at the Ministry, and managed to convince them to restore power. This happened two of the three nights; the third night the Royal Family was present.

Cast of "The Sound of Music" (brother Jamie is second from the left with his arms in the air). Jamie played the part of the oldest Trapp boy, Friedrich.

Turkey Soup

At Thanksgiving, we always had a big celebration and invited many of my parents' friends. My mother liked to invite some of the families or Peace Corps volunteers who didn't have access to the Commissary and its seasonal supply of Thanksgiving turkeys. Americans who find themselves overseas at the end of November, for some reason really miss the celebration of an American Thanksgiving more than other holidays. Maybe it's the sentimentality of families being together and missing the camaraderie of an extended family and neighbors.

Thanksgiving Dinner, Addis house, 1970 Diana Manchak and Jerry on left

This particular holiday we invited the American school superintendent, Dr. Lutz, and his family, along with several other close friends. We ended up with a large crowd for dinner. There were the seven of us, plus several friends of my brothers, and a number of other friends of my parents, and the Lutz family. All went well until at the end of the evening, Dr. Lutz said he would "love" to take some leftovers home and somehow, he ended up taking home nearly all of the leftovers. No one is quite sure how he managed it.

The next day, there wasn't enough turkey to make sandwiches, but we did try to make turkey soup with the scrapes of bones that were left. Funny thing about that. My mother and I were in the kitchen, boiling away the bones, liver, and innards of the turkey to make the turkey broth. We added the vegetables and were on our way to a great turkey soup. However, at the end when we were ready to pour in the egg noodles we upended the box only to discover that the pasta was infested with tiny black bugs that were now swirling in our soup. Ugh. We scooped out as many of them as we could. I looked at my mother, "What do we do?" I asked.

She shrugged, "They look like pepper. No one will ever know the difference."

I laughed, "Yeah, but we will know."

We served the soup for dinner that night and everyone ate heartily. I confess I didn't take much and ate it sparingly. My brothers asked why I was acting so weird. "I'm not that hungry, I guess," I replied with a shrug, not able to make eye contact with my mother. But she was right. They never knew.

My 20th Birthday

On December 7th, shortly after Thanksgiving, I celebrated my 20th birthday. It was the first time in three years that I had been home to celebrate my birthday. The last time had been when I turned 17 in Honolulu shortly before returning to Bangkok. My family sang "Happy Birthday", I made a wish and blew out the candles, and we ate cake, just like we had done when I was a little kid. It was a wonderful way to end my teen years. It's hard to believe that when I turned 13 in 1963, I was in the 8th grade in Taipei, Taiwan and here I was turning 20, a junior in college, and celebrating in Addis Ababa, Ethiopia. So much had happened in the intervening seven years and so many changes were just ahead.

Maureen's 20th birthday, 1970

My Last Family Trip

The last trip I took while I was in Ethiopia was to Asmara, Eritrea in December just before Christmas. My father, mother and I flew on Ethiopian Airlines to Asmara, about 400 miles north of Addis, and we spent several wonderful days Christmas shopping at the American PX at Kagnew Air Station as well as seeing the city.

Asmara was quite a contrast from Addis. The Italian influence on the architecture of its buildings and the laid-back nonchalance of its people were remarkably different from the more staid Amhara traditions of the Ethiopian Highlands. I was glad for the opportunity to experience both.

In retrospect, I was also glad to have that short time alone with my parents, although I didn't appreciate it at the time. It turned out to be the last trip I would take with my father and I'm glad to have those warm memories.

Back to the States

During that fall in Addis, I had transferred from the University of Montana to Boston University at my father's suggestion, and after getting accepted, I made plans to fly to Boston in January.

When I left, I was happily looking forward to a new chapter of my life, to spending my last two years of college in Boston on my father's home turf.

On the day of my departure, we were up and at the airport early. Flights from Addis to Rome left at 6:30 a.m. and we were at the airport an hour and half before the flight time so that I could go through Ethiopian Customs and security. My father got special permission to escort me through customs and to stay in the transit lounge with me.

It was early and we just stood together not talking. When my flight was called, he turned and gave me a tight hug and told me to enjoy Boston, and of course, to do well in school.

I nodded and said "goodbye" feeling a little choked up at the thought of leaving. I headed towards the gate with the other passengers to walk out onto the tarmac to the airplane stairway. Before going up the stairs, I turned and scanned the crowd for my father. I saw him grinning at me from behind the glass. I waved and smiled and he waved back. That was the last time I saw my father alive.

A year later he contracted Black Water Fever, a fatal form of malaria, on a business trip to Dire Dawa. My mother said initially they thought he had come down with the flu, but when his fever refused to break he was flown to the military hospital at Kagnew Air Station in Asmara, Eritrea. He died the next day, on January 21, 1972.

A Death in the Family

A sudden death in the family is devastating no matter when or what the circumstances. It's the swift change in your life plans that makes it so hard to come to terms with. There's just no way to prepare yourself. And then there's the deep, deep hole in the family that the person leaves in his wake.

Like most people who go through a sudden death, we played the 'What If' game. What if they had diagnosed the malaria immediately? Could he have survived? What if they could have airlifted the dialysis machine from Germany? Would that have saved him? But, in the end, you realize, it's a moot point. He's gone and it's too late. Life must go on.

A memorial service was held in Addis before my mother left for the States. My mother told us later that it seemed like half the city turned up and people stood in the aisles and crowded the doorways at the church.

My brothers Denny and Jerry, and I flew to Omaha to meet my mother who had accompanied my father's casket back to the States for the wake and funeral services. Because my younger brothers had also been exposed to this virulent form of malaria, it was recommended that they remain behind in Ethiopia. My brother, Mike, was located by the Red Cross and airlifted out of Vietnam on emergency leave to the States. He arrived in San Francisco, literally from the battlefield with hand grenades still hanging from his belt. In their hurry to get him back to the States, they had neglected to take any of the combat paraphernalia away from him. He was a mess, but he was there.

For me, the Spring semester at B.U. had just started and I had to get permission from my professors to miss upcoming classes. I had to go to each professor and explain that my father had died and that I would be gone for a week to attend the services. It was very hard and I remember having to steel myself not to cry.

"How did he die?" they would ask solicitously. I would cringe at the question because I knew they were expecting me to say a heart attack or car accident, but instead I would have to reply, "He died of malaria." It sounded like some maudlin tale from WWII, from some Pacific island like Midway, Wake, or Bataan. But in 1972? How many Americans died of malaria in 1972? It was surreal.

We had dinner with my mother's sister, my Aunt Inez, the night before my mother and my father's body were due to arrive in Omaha. Denny, Jerry, Mike and I were sitting around the table, subdued but still glad to see each other. Mike was sitting in his brand new ill-fitting civilian clothes not saying a word. I'm not sure whether he realized this wasn't a dream, or nightmare, perhaps. He was quiet for several seconds and when I glanced down the table at him I realized that he had fallen asleep, literally with a fork full of mashed potatoes halfway to his mouth. It was bizarre. But everything seemed a little bizarre just then.

My father had a wonderful mischievous sense of humor and in those dark hours in the icy chill of Omaha in mid-winter, we very much needed to be reminded of it. And, indeed, he did manage to amuse us one more time the morning of the funeral as we were heading to the church where the funeral mass was to be held.

It was the morning of Wednesday, February 2nd and the roads were a mess, snow-covered and slick. We were late getting to the funeral home; so late that just as we pulled up the hearse was pulling away and getting on the highway. We looked at each other in surprise as we watched the hearse drive off without us. "Where is Dad going?" Denny asked with a smirk and we all laughed. It was so typical that he had waited just so long and then decided to go on ahead without us. Heck, he probably thought he had our passports in his pocket.

We felt his presence that evening, as well, when we huddled around the TV set in my mother's hotel room to watch the Military Draft

Lottery. The days of the year (e.g., numbers 1 to 366) were written on slips of paper and the slips were then put into plastic capsules. The capsules were mixed and then dumped into a deep glass jar from which they were drawn one at a time, like a huge bingo game.

The 1972 lottery was for boys born in 1953 and they would be drafted based on their birthdays. Jerry was a freshman at Georgetown University and would be turning 19 the following week, on February 10th, so we were anxious to find out his draft number. As the dates were pulled, we sighed in relief – his number was 361 – we decided my father must have had something to do with Jerry's luck. Ironically, Denny and Mike, who were both already in the service and not affected by the lottery drawing, would have had numbers 4 and 5, based on their birthdays!

Although my father's wake and funeral services were in Omaha that February, his burial wasn't scheduled until later that summer, in July of 1972, at Punchbowl, the National Veterans Cemetery of the Pacific, in Honolulu.

My father had dearly loved Hawaii and there wasn't a better place in the world for him to finally be laid to rest; the fact that the cemetery would be Punchbowl, a beautiful and serene spot overlooking Honolulu and the blue Pacific, was a bonus.

That summer, I flew to Addis from Boston and stayed with my younger brothers (Pat, Jamie and Chris) while my mother, Denny, Mike and Jerry met in Honolulu for the burial service.

They had wanted a very private burial, but at Punchbowl that isn't always possible because it is a popular tourist destination particularly for families of WWII soldiers killed in the Pacific fighting. So on that July day, many tourists were milling around. Jerry told me later that he felt uncomfortable having to go through this somber ceremony with so many pitying and curious eyes upon them.

But then something amazing happened. Just as the burial ceremony was about to begin, it started to rain – a light tropical downpour that cleared the area of tourists and left my brothers and mother in peace to bury my father in his final resting place. Naturally, we assumed he had managed to arrange that privacy for them, somehow.

Chapter 14 Epilogue
Fall of 1972, Boston University, Senior Year

It was November, 1972, the bleakest month in New England. I looked down at the soggy streets of Boston from my third-floor walk-up. The colorful foliage was gone; there were just muddy piles of misshapen leaves that have turned black and mushy in the gutters along the city streets.

My apartment was located on Beacon Street. Not the elite Beacon Hill area, but rather past Back Bay in the poor student area along the edge of the Fens. It was a quick walk to B.U. and my classes and the rent was affordable.

My father had been dead for eleven months and I was no longer sure about school, my liberal arts degree, and what in the world I would be doing a year from then. I hadn't heard from Gray in months and I was pretty sure that it was over but that he just hadn't gotten around to telling me yet.

I sighed as I thumbed idly through the mail that I brought up the three flights of stairs from my mailbox in the vestibule near the front door. I noticed that there was no letter from my mother and I was disappointed. I craved the connection with my family still in Ethiopia.

She had been writing often since I left Addis in September. I knew it was probably because she needed someone to talk to about her adjustment to being a widow, facing life alone for the first time in 26 years. I wasn't sure that I was up to being her sounding board, though. I was still feeling very raw myself about my father's death and still found myself choked up and teary-eyed at odd times and places.

There were lots of huge decisions my mother had to make, but she had at least been fortunate that she hadn't had to face a move back to the States on top of everything else. She had her own job running the American Commissary in Addis when my father died. Because of her good relations with the Embassy and the Ambassador himself, she and my younger brothers had been permitted to stay.

That was very unusual. Normally, when someone dies at an overseas post, the whole family is shipped immediately back to the States. I'm glad she stayed in Addis, for my own selfish reasons. For me, it meant I would be able to return to Ethiopia.

I looked through the circulars and the bank statement when I noticed a small postcard from the university. I turned it over and realized that it was an invitation to a get-together at the Student Union for the next weekend. I flipped the card over to read the return address for the first time. It was from the B.U. Foreign Exchange Student group. Apparently, I was being invited to join their club. No doubt they selected me based on my Addis Ababa, Ethiopia home address. Immediately, it took me back to my freshman year in Montana.

It had been four years since I arrived in the U.S. from Bangkok. I was a bit older and wiser and I had learned to adjust to life in the United States. I had changed. For one thing, I wasn't as quick to mention my background any more. Of course, I was always thrilled when I met someone whose father was in the military, or who had spent a few years abroad. I relaxed and felt an instant connection, like we belonged to the same secret society and our overseas childhoods was our secret handshake.

But those meetings were few and far between. The rest of the time, my childhood overseas, the exotic experiences, weird pets, and my wonderful wild family were my secret other life that I had learned to share only with my closest friends.

It takes a while for acquaintances to realize that my reserve is a kind of shyness and that I'm wary of telling too much too soon. I don't want to scare their friendship away by emphasizing our differences rather than the things we might have in common. I had learned to talk more about our dogs and less about our monkey, more about my mother's cooking, and less about having a cook, more about my family, less about its location.

I waved the postcard in the air, thinking. "Well, why not?" It could be fun. Maybe I would meet some Ethiopian students and I could make them feel less strange by saying "Tenastaling" and mentioning the hyenas that wandered the dark streets of Addis. I smiled and tucked the card into my shoulder bag.

The End of a Chapter; Not the End of the Story

It would be unkind to end the story here. Time heals, but it's a slow slog getting through the days and weeks and months that provide the necessary salve. It's true that you never get over the death of someone close to you, but life goes on and being good troopers, my family carried on, too.

We each learned to arrange our life without Dad. But without my father, who were we now? It required a redefinition of our whole family lifestyle. We wouldn't be the family of a diplomat any longer. There would be no more overseas posts to look forward to; life as we had lived it up to then was over.

I can't speak for my brothers, but it was a while before I stopped feeling cheated and let go of the assumptions and expectations I had had about our family's future. Eventually I was able to appreciate what my father was and to let go of all the things he could never now become.

What I have come to realize is that although my father was a patriot and a diplomat for his country, I think deep down he was more of a Catholic missionary at heart. He truly believed that a rich nation like ours could make a bigger difference by sharing its good fortune with the rest of the world than by exploiting it. The more that you are given, the more that is expected of you. And the more you give, the more that is returned to you.

To be effective overseas, it was up to us – the visitor and guest – to learn the foreign language and respect the local culture. My father had been committed to helping in Korea, in Taiwan, in the Philippines, in Thailand, and in Ethiopia; he had been proud to be a part of the effort. We in turn were proud of him. And perhaps, in the end, that is enough.

Aftermath: Our lives and fortunes, 1972 – 2010

My mother stayed on in Ethiopia for another three years, working for the American Commissary. Remaining in Addis was a blessing. It meant my younger brothers could begin to heal without having to switch schools, leave their friends, and face a huge transition to American life all at once.

Two years after my father's death, my mother married an American Army pilot in Ethiopia and she started a new and different life. They returned to the United States in 1975.

My brothers and I carried on, as well. I graduated from Boston University in 1973, worked in a travel agency and then for a Congressman in Washington, DC. I met my future husband on Capitol Hill and we moved to New Hampshire, his home state, where we married and have lived ever since. I got my MBA from Simmons College in 1980 and worked as a software trainer and computer consultant for several years. I'm currently a technical writer for an international trade software company by day and a novelist by night. I have two daughters – the older one is a filmmaker, the younger, a student attending college in Lugano, Switzerland.

Denny, age 10 in 1957 when we first went overseas, was the big brother of the family. Being the first-born, he was the first to try new things and because he was the oldest was given a lot of responsibility and privileges that the rest of us could only envy. He was a good-looking, gregarious boy, a good athlete and seemed utterly fearless to his six-year-old little sister. At school, he was always a part of the "cool" group and the "sports jocks", and he reveled in being the center of attention.

In 1972 when my father died, Denny was 25, married to Sandee, out of the Marines and living in Los Angeles. He got his B.A. after getting out of the service and had a long career in Sales at various companies. Before he passed away in February, 2010, Denny lived in southern California and was a successful insurance salesman and financial planner. He has a daughter and two grandsons who live in

Sydney, Australia; and he has a son who recently returned from an around-the-world trek and now lives in northern California. His ashes are buried along side my father at Punchbowl Cemetery in Honolulu.

In 1957 when we first went overseas, **Mike**, age 8, was Denny's opposite. He was Trouble with a capital "T" from a very early age. He was mischievous, strong, and smart, but plagued with an undiagnosed reading problem that sometimes made him feel that just keeping up was a struggle. He also grew up in Denny's shadow — a tough act to follow, to be sure — but he had a surprising goodness in him that was his saving grace on more than one occasion. He empathized with the underdog and lived by his own code of ethics, even when he was getting into trouble. I remember him once saying that he would rather "do" something than to "read" about it, that he would prefer to make his own mistakes; and another time he said that he planned to become a priest just before he died so that no matter what he did in this life — and he planned to do a lot — he would be assured of getting into heaven. You couldn't fault him for his strategy; however, he hasn't started studying for the priesthood yet.

In 1972, Mike was in Vietnam. He served two tours in Vietnam with the US Army before returning to a civilian life of college and marriage. He is married and lives in Florida, owns a landscaping business and devotes many volunteer hours to the local VA hospital helping returning vets. He has a son and a daughter.

Jerry, age 6 when we went overseas, was the high achiever of the family, although it was a while before the rest of us appreciated how determined he was. As a young child, he was fun and smart and probably got away with more than any one in the family simply by being the "middle child". My parents had their hands full with guiding the oldest and nurturing the youngest. It left Jerry with plenty of freedom in his middle spot to maneuver "just under the radar".

Jerry graduated from the American Community School in Addis in 1971. He was a freshman at Georgetown University the January my father died. He completed his B.A. then went on to Thunderbird, the elite master's global business program in Arizona, where he obtained his MBA. Today he is an independent stock trader, living out his dreams on a bluff on the big island of Hawaii in a house overlooking the Pacific Ocean. He's married and has two stepdaughters.

In 1957, **Pat**, age 2, was a toddler when we moved to Korea. In a very real sense, he, Jamie and Chris were raised entirely overseas. They responded more easily to the Korean spoken by the amahs that took care of them, than to English. Pat was always a sweet-natured child and brother. I have often thought that he was my mother's favorite, but then, he was so nice, funny and caring, how could he not be? Now, looking back, I suspect that we were all her favorites but for different reasons — Denny was the oldest and a charmer. Mike had his deep goodness and struggle. I was the only girl. Jerry had his intellect and leadership, Pat, his sweetness. Jamie was her quiet genius and steadfast. Chris was the lovable baby of the family.

In 1972, Pat was a sophomore in high school in Addis Ababa. He was 16 when my father died. He had started taking flying lessons the summer prior to my father's death and continued taking lessons and received his private pilot's license while still in Ethiopia. He has some amazing stories of doing his solo flights over the deserts of eastern Ethiopia. He graduated from the American Community School in Addis in 1974 and attended Embry-Riddle Aeronautical University. Today he is a United Airlines captain. He is married and has a young son. He also lives on the big island of Hawaii next door to Jerry.

Jamie, born within the first month of our arrival in Korea in 1957, doesn't remember much of his early years overseas. I guess for him and for Chris there was no other "normal" American lifestyle. Jamie had a high IQ and as with many bright kids, you would never have known it. He daydreamed his way through early elementary school and got middling grades. And he was socially awkward until he found his footing in junior high and high school. It couldn't have been easy being the sixth child, the fifth son, and a bit shy in a family as boisterous as ours. I think he found himself either ignored or the favorite victim of teasing by his older brothers.

In 1972 when my father died, Jamie was a freshman in high school in Addis Ababa. He left Ethiopia in 1974 to attend Marion Military Institute in Marion, Alabama for his final two years of high school. From there he went on to Texas A&M and then into the Air Force and had a 25 year military career. He served at many bases around the U.S., including a two year stint at the Pentagon, a year with Air Force

One during the Clinton administration, and ended his career with the rank of colonel. He is currently a pilot for American Eagle and lives in New Hampshire. He has two sons.

The youngest, **Chris**, was born during our second tour in Korea. As such, he missed out on our first two houses in Seoul and our early introduction to living overseas. He was born on the military base in January of 1960 and only spent two years in Korea before we moved on to Taipei. Chris was the baby of the family, an easy-going, happy child. Although for a while he was tagged with the epithet "Voice of America" because he had a tendency to broadcast family confidences, not realizing that some things are meant to stay within the family. But, when you're the youngest, you can get away with such things.

In 1972, Chris had turned 12 years old the week before my father died. Chris graduated from high school and college in the U.S. Today, he owns a home security company in the Chattanooga suburbs, is married and has two stepsons who now work with him in his business.

So we all turned out fine and my father would have been proud. It's not the story I thought I would be telling, but it is my story.

The End

In Memoriam

In the past thirteen years since this book was originally published, we've lost a few members of the Sullivan family.

Dennis (Denny) died in California in February of 2010.

Michael (Mike) died in Florida in April of 2011.

My mother, **Hope** (or ***Grandma Hope*** as her grandchildren affectionately called her) died a week short of her 91st birthday in February of 2017.

Eugene F. Sullivan was added to the U.S. State Dept. Memorial Plaque in May, 2011.

Family gathered in the lobby of the US State Dept in Washington, DC for the Plaque Ceremony

Chapter 15   Appendix: My Mother's Christmas Letters

The following pages include many of the annual Christmas letters my mother used to write to her family and friends back in the States, and around the world.

Christmas 1958
1958 Greetings from Korea
(Annyong hasimnika)

This seasonal greeting marks the anniversary of the second Xmas in Korea for the Sullivan family. Since the time of our last annual epistle to friends and relatives, we have just about run the gamut of strange, colorful, wonderful, and not so wonderful experiences.

The four oldest children, including Dennis (11), Michael (9), Maureen (8), and Jerry (5) have adjusted pretty well to Korea and to the daily routine of activities at the Sacred Heart School for foreign children. In fact, they have adjusted to school better than the nuns have adjusted to them. The study of French and Korean is included in their curriculum in addition to the three R's. Extra curricular activities include Boy Scouts, Cub Scouts, Brownies, piano lessons (for Hope too), dancing lessons, bike riding, and the usual seasonal sports.

The two youngest children, including Patrick (3) and Jamie (1) have also adjusted well to Korean living. Pat goes to nursery school every day and Jamie still rides around on the mama-san's back, although he is getting more and more proficient at running after his brothers and sister.

According to the mama-san, Jamie is already speaking Korean. However, we maintain that it is Americanized (mi-guk) baby talk. The OEC personnel chief recently remarked that the most amazing sight that she has been so far in Korea was when our mama-san went to her office to get a pass carrying Jamie on her back. Jamie now goes many places with the mama-san, including the dentist, the market, and in Korean hap-sungs (jitney bus) in Korean fashion on the back.

Mamma and Pappa Sullivan too have become accustomed to and in some instances fond of such mundane facets of Korean life and culture as kimchi, endol (hot) floors, kisaeng parties, Buddhist temples, folk songs and dances, papa and mama-sans, waterfalls, pagodas, fishing boats, and last but not least that clever, tantalizing, frustrating, incongruous Hangul language. This transition has been successfully achieved partly as a result of making the many field trips required to implement the ICA-OEC (Office of the Economic Coordinator) program of developing and improving Korean industries, but mostly as a result of taking Royal Asiatic Society (R.A.S.) tours all over Korea. The latter have included three and sometimes four day trips to such areas as Kyunggi & Taegu in the Southeast, Mokpo and Yosu in the southwest, Yangyang, Kangnung and the gorgeous mountains and sandy beaches of Kangwon-Do in the northwest, and last but not least the incomparable volcanic island of Cheju (Quelpart Island) which is about 100 miles southwest of the Korean mainland and about 300 miles east of Shanghai. The latter trip was made on an ROK Navy Destroyer –Escort as a courtesy of President Syngman Rhee to stimulate the tourist business in Korea.

Our tours with the R.A.S. have helped us learn and understand a culture quite different from ours. A year ago if one had told us we would be vitally interested in some ruins of a Buddhist temple from the Yi dynasty period, we would have laughed. But we are now enjoying each trip to a new or old temple so much that our reaction has changed from "What! Another temple?" to "When do we go?"

Gene's work takes him and sometimes Hope too, all over the country as Korea's industrialization program continues to make good progress. Although there still is a lot of work to be done in making more efficient use of the raw materials and resources available in the country, the number of new smoking chimneys is on the increase.

Hope too adjusted so well that the OEC personnel section has requested that she as past president of the OEC Women's Club, give a repeat performance (3rd time) at the OEC Orientation Course for new arrivals. This course is mandatory for both employees and dependents. Her job is to show women how they can actually enjoy their tour here. She is living proof that you can raise a healthy family (ours have all been well); mingle with the people; eat their food (even kimchi); shop in their markets; ride their taxis; enjoy their folk songs & dances and adjust to such pleasures as cold houses, cold or no water, intermittent electricity, faulty phones, no transportation other than self-locomotion when you need it most and the usual language barriers.

This year found us faced with moving into the American Community in the Itaewon Section of Seoul. We all hated to leave our Japanese-Korean house on the economy, but it hasn't kept us from pursuing our investigating and curiosity led way of life.

We are planning a trip home next summer. You notice I say "trip" because we are planning on returning to Korea. We are tentatively planning out our time, we will visit Gene's parents in Boston, finish all business and reconnecting with friends in Washington and Rockville, and visit in Nebraska and in Colorado on the way to the West Coast and then by ship back to Korea. All are warned now of our coming in July and August. See you soon!

Love to all: Gene, Hope, Dennis, Mike, Maureen, Jerry, Pat, and Jamie.

Christmas 1960
Greetings from Korea – Again!!

This will probably be our last Christmas message from the land of Kimchi and Rice, Mama-sans, and A-frames, Hangul phrases and Student Demonstrations. Our three and a half years here have been extremely challenging, eventful, and personally rewarding. Our tour of duty in Korea on the mainland of northeast Asia, has given us a chance to take a long comprehensive look at many facets of the Far East geopolitical and socioeconomic situation. Specifically, it has given us a vivid close-up picture of the Korean people enmeshed in a frustrating day-to-day struggle to survive and advance in an impatient world that is reluctant to wait for Korea to emerge from its current dilemmas.

This past year was indeed a memorable one for the Sullivan clan. It not only initiated a new decade, but it marked the arrival of Christopher Eugene Sullivan, Chris for short (he is now 11 months old); another promotion for Gene; a new school year for Dennis 13, Mike 11, Maureen 10, Jerry 7, and Pat 5, and Jamie 3; and many new activities for Hope. Gene and Hope traveled to Japan, Taiwan, and Hong Kong last spring, and this fall Gene went to the United Nations sponsored Pulp and Paper Conference in Tokyo on TDY (Temporary Duty), and I joined him there for an impromptu but refreshing vacation. Denny also went to Japan this year for a couple of weeks with the Boy Scouts. In addition, Denny, Mike, Maureen, and Jerry joined us on hikes and tours to the four corners of South Korea, including Cheju-do, the main island off the south coast. We go practically every weekend exploring some new area.

Here are a few remarks by and concerning some of the other members of the Sullivan Family:

I, Jerry, had special swimming lessons this summer. I jumped into the deep end of the pool from the diving board. I play cowboys every day, and love to fly kites, and make airplanes. I will be eight in two months. I went to Pohang on a train, and I went to sleep in a box (berth, Japanese style) on the train. I went to a big beach and I got lots of seashells.

I, Maureen, joined the softball team last summer, and I had swimming lessons. We went on a trip to Pohang on a train. When we got off, we got on a bus, and then went to a Korean school to eat lunch. I joined the Girl Scouts and we are having lots of fun. I have been taking Ballet Dancing lessons this year. Our teacher is Mr. Lim, and he went to school in France.

This year I, Mike, went to Cheju Island. We stayed with the Columbian Fathers for two weeks. We had fun there. We went to Cheju City. When we rang the bell in the city hall, the bell pulled me up and I almost hit my head. My brother held me by the feet. All the Korean children laughed at me and we tickled them. I became a Boy Scout this year. I am already a second class. We went on a camp-out, and I got poison sumac. The Korean man who looked for the site said that it was a friendly plant, so we camped in the middle of a lot of Sumac. All the boys, 22 of us, got swollen all over. The army has gotten us a new Scout Master now.

This year I did many things. (Dennis) At the beginning of the year, I went to Cheju-do. Last summer, I was captain of the Little League Baseball team. When the season was over, I was awarded the "Most Valuable Player" of my team award. I have a plaque with my name and the year on it. During the middle of the summer my Boy Scout troop was invited to go to the National Jubilee camp-out in Japan. While we were there, we climbed Mt. Fuji-san all 12,395 feet of her. I remember so well because we had sore feet for a week. Also because I and two other boys were awarded the Man of the Mountain certificate. The next great shock was when school started. WHAT A RUMBLE!

This year Gene moved into the front office of the Industry Division in the capacity of Deputy Industry Officer. The responsibilities involved naturally are more demanding, and much more time is spent at the office. Away from the office Gene is on the Board of Governors for the Seoul Youth Activities Association. This association governs all activities for children on the Army post. There are 627 in elementary and high school. This includes a youth canteen, all sport

Memories of an Overseas Childhood 223

activities for all seasons, scouting, and special parties on holidays, i.e., Halloween, Christmas, Easter, etc.

The fulfillment of obligations as parents keeps both Daddy and Momma hopping. Naturally, we do things purely for our own pleasure too. In this line, Hope keeps busy. This year she has 16 Girl Scouts in her troop. As a Christmas project, they with another troop made decorations for two hospitals. Hope is involved in Boy Scouts too, like any other mother – furnishing food for overnights, and cleaning up dirty clothes and dishes on their return. She still has her Orientation lecture (for USOM) once every third month for the new arrivals to our post. Added to this is a follow up Tour Group once a month to help acquaint the ladies with various factories, shopping areas, and sightseeing areas. She serves on several committees for the Royal Asiatic Society, one of which is the RAS Tour Group. This committee serves also as an advisor to the ROK Ministry of Transportation and hopes to help the Koreans establish some Western tourism practices. Representatives from Northwest Airlines, shipping (Pacific Far East Lines) and businessmen are also members of this group. One sideline in this capacity is a cooking lesson she gives to the cooks at the railway station, one morning every two weeks. These cooks travel on trains, and prepare the food in all Government Hotels. She teaches them Western style cooking. What fun she has in their tremendous kitchen with fifteen Korean-speaking students. They had great fun making Tomato aspic, and Upside Down Cake last week. You should have seen the expressions when Hope insisted that they turn the cake upside down immediately upon removal from the oven. "Ruin the cake," they said, "TSK TSK TSK."

Hope is also the PIO (Publicity) chairman of the Red Cross in Korea, serves on the Tour Committee of the USO, occasionally does Gray Lady work, gets involved in bazaars given by the USOM, Catholic Women's and YWCA clubs, and works at the International Social Service once a week. This organization is worldwide and handles many of the foreign baby adoptions into the United States, as well as feeding and helping families in time of need.

If this schedule isn't full enough, she has also taken a fling in acting. She has a part in "Auntie Mame" (Norah, the maid), which will be presented the week of Dec. 12. Rehearsals are in full swing now.

Last summer, Gene and Hope took golf lessons, along with Dennis. Hope came in fifth in the fall tournament (women's division) but the one who will be the good golfer is Dennis. We have all three improved considerably and now enjoy the relaxation of the game of golf.

If you have the impression that life in Korea is active and busy, you are quite right. We wouldn't have it otherwise. Since many of our activities are shared with Koreans, we have a chance to learn much about them and they in turn about us and America.

That's all for now,

Christmas Greetings

from Eugene F. Sullivan Family

Memories of an Overseas Childhood 225

South Korea, 1961

Christmas 1962

Merry Christmas 1962 from the Sullivan's!

Greetings from Taiwan, the land of pedicabs, and peddlers, firecrackers and festivals, water buffalo and dragon boats, slit skirts and Chinese Operas, typhoons and earthquakes. After five wonderful years in Korea we are all quite happy to be able to become acquainted with our Chinese neighbors. Our first impression of Taipei was of a modern, orderly, and thriving community. The markets have plenty of food and are very clean compared to many foreign markets. Fish is good and plentiful: fruits, papaya, pineapple, bananas, oranges, tangerines, melons, are in large supply. Foods are quite inexpensive. It is an island with a 3-crop year and the mountainous terrain is heavily vegetated, the temperature rarely goes below 50 degrees during the winter month of January, but it has heavy rain and fog. People do swim the year round however as there are warm and balmy days interspersed with the rainy cool winter days.

Our departure from Korea on May 25th of this year and our subsequent sea voyage home on the USS President Cleveland via Yokohama and Honolulu gave us a trunk load of memorable and mostly happy experiences. Speaking of trunks, we must have left at least a physical vacuum every time me moved our 23 suitcases, bags, boxes, and footlockers from taxis to motels to taxis to planes, etc. Everyone seemed quite happy to see us and I'm sure they were probably even happier after we had gone. In Tokyo we needed three taxis for the nine persons and 23 bags. Enroute to Yokohama we hired a car, crammed bags inside and on top, and found it much too crowded for us, so we rode the train while the car with bags drove the 40 miles to Yokohama. At each stop in the States people meeting us would arrive with several cars, and Hope would have the distressing job of sorting children and bags, and counting and wondering if Jamie had gotten into that car that just left, and saying 'no, he isn't mine, let him go' to a child someone had decided belonged to us. Gene feels that he is qualified for a job as a Professional Tour Guide after three months of handling the logistic problems for a family of nine, and traveling with 23 pieces of baggage from Korea to Japan to Honolulu, San Francisco, Omaha, Washington D.C., Rehoboth Beach, Del., Washington D.C. Omaha, San Francisco. Honolulu, Japan and Taipei. WHEW!

Logistic problems consisted of Passport, Customs immigration papers in triplicate (or more) multiplied by nine for nine different countries enroute; finding that the Bridal Suite was the only room large enough to accommodate all of us in Hotels, finding lost children when they decided something looked interesting someplace removed from the group, knowing just where we were going to be hungry and need to eat so as to make a reservation, etc, etc., etc.

By far his biggest problem was re arranging reservations and tickets when Hope decided she liked this place so much that they would all stay a couple days longer.

According to an impromptu consensus, here are some of the things that really looked good to the Sullivan's on home leave: drive in restaurants, banana splits and movies, escalators and elevators, subways and super highways, shopping centers, multi story Department Stores, Dairy Queen and Howard Johnson's, motels with swimming pools, T.V., and miniature Golf, electronic eye doors, and above all the ABSENCE of bicycles and oxen from the main streets.

Our arrival in Taipei auspiciously followed on the heels of Typhoon Wanda, and was followed soon after by Typhoon Amy which inundated the PX and Commissary warehouses and resulted in a series of "Typhoon Sales". Haig and Haig Scotch $1.10, Old Grand Dad $1.05, Gordon's Gin $0.40 per bottle. Fortunately our stone house on Grass Mountain easily withstood the strongest of Amy's gales, and other than mopping water from around windows, Gene says at least 30 to 40 buckets, we spent a 24 hour holiday behind Typhoon shutters. Taiwan receives an average of 12 typhoons a season with at least two doing large scale damage. It also records about 3200 earthquakes a year, with at least 1000 strong enough for a person to feel the room roll and rock and see the light fixtures and pictures sway.

The children are all happy in school with over 1900 students, 96 percent of whom are American. The 10,000 strong American community on the island consists of Army, Navy, Air Force personnel, Civilian Communications people, and AID and Embassy personnel. Both Gene and Hope are taking Chinese; Gene in an advanced refresher course, and Hope in the Beginners class.

A Chinese French poodle and a Siamese cat have increased our group of nine, along with a terrific Chinese cook, his wife, his baby, his baby's baby amah, our baby amah, our wash amah, and yard man. One thing we promise is that there is always someone home, and Taiwan is a lovely stopover enroute to anyplace. We look forward to welcoming you in TAIPEI.

Gene, Hope, Dennis, Michael, Maureen Jerry, Pat, Jamie and Chris

Christmas 1963
GREETINGS FROM TAIPEI, TAIWAN
Dec., 1963

From Gene, Hope, Dennis, a handsome sixteen-and-a-half-year old who reminds all that is old enough to drive; Michael, a fourteen-year-old campaign manager for anyone who happens to be running for an office at school; Maureen, a quiet, beautiful, delightful-sense-of-humor blonde thirteen-year-old; Jerry, a ten-and-a-half-year-old comedian and student; Patrick, eight-year-old quiet, sweet, loving imp; Jamie, a noisy, busy rough rugged independent six-year-old; and Chris, the spoiled delight of the family but a four-year-old who runs the family.

The year of 1963 marked another milestone in the life and travels of the Sullivan family in the Far East. To recapitulate briefly, the family highlights of the year, and the lowlights too, they were inaugurated rather auspiciously by Gene and Hope, Denny, Mike and Maureen celebrating the New Year Holidays in Hong Kong. In this part of the world New Year is greeted with firecrackers and sky rockets, and hilarity – twice – once on January 11, and again on the Lunar Calendar New Year Day which comes six weeks later. Needless to say all came home happier but poorer, and the three children utterly fascinated with Hong Kong.

When Hope returned to the U.S. for a long postponed but necessary operation in February, Gene continued on admirably as majordomo and baby-amah supervisor number one for almost eight weeks. Meanwhile, Hope had a chance to visit or call many of you while recuperating in the U.S. After a couple of weeks in the hospital in San Francisco, she had a joyful and an unforgettable experience of sharing daily life with her sister and brother-in-law, the Lomaxes of San Manteo, California for a few weeks while awaiting travel clearance orders from the doctor. Hope claims that she has never had it so good.

The summer season here starts earlier and lasts longer than in the United States. While Denny was busy working as a lifeguard at the Officers' Club, the rest of the family went on weekly picnic trips to the local beaches along the north coast – they are almost as lovely and beautiful as Hawaii – or watched Michael playing baseball in the Pony League. The other children participated in the Taipei American School summer and recreation program. Maureen attended mainly to continue her Chinese language studies. All the children are taking Chinese, but Maureen is by far the best, with almost perfect pronunciation and is also learning to read and to write. The summer season ended unofficially with the advent of the first couple of typhoons. You all probably read or heard about flood damage in Taipei as a result of Typhoon Gloria. We fortunately suffered no damage personally, but the PX, Commissary, and Officers' Club, as well as many, many Chinese families and 300 American families did suffer with an average of 16 feet of floodwater for 24 hours. The support activities, movies, library, commissary, bowling alleys, etc., were all out of business for one month while cleaning up. The School had 8000 books under water, and many of us helped with the physical scrubbing up both of the school, desks, books, before school was able to reopen. It is horrible to wade about in ten inches of slimy mud while trying to wash and scrape off mud without adequate water pressure. The School library is almost ready to reopen with newly bound books.

After the kids were well advanced into the new school year, Hope and Gene went to Japan and Korea for a 2-½ week vacation via military planes (most of the trip). Everyone in Korea greeted us and made us feel at home. We could see many changes in Korea since leaving 18 months ago, mostly in the physical improvements in Seoul in the traffic, roads, parks, etc. Japan is busily building and preparing for the 1964 Olympics. Tokyo, the world's largest city, as modern as New York, and as thrilling as Paris, is 80 percent under reconstruction – or so it seems. If you have to wait in traffic for your meals, for your hotel, for anything, the excuse is always the same – "We are getting ready for the Olympics."

Upon their return, Hope again plunged back into her extra-curricular activities including the Vice President of the PTA, which includes also the membership chairman of the PTA, Chairman of the USAID Welcome Committee, Vice President of the Grass Mountain Community Center, replacing Gene, Secretary of the USAID Women's Club, Chairman of the Christmas Party for the orphans at Yi Kwang Orphanage (367 Chinese children), as well as her "fun" activities of golf, bowling, mahjong, bridge, etc. She has given up Girl Scouts, Boy Scouts, Cub Scouts for the first time in 20 years. Naturally, she still has the duties of mother, chauffeur, chaperone, referee, teacher (homework), planner, comforter, disciplinarian, friend, locator of lost objects, and all the other minor duties expected when you have a household that includes seven children, two dogs, five birds, five servants, and visiting friends. Which reminds us that we should mention that our terrific cook, Yong, and his wife, Yuki, are still making life wonderfully pleasant. Gene is the one who receives the royal treatment – in this part of the world he is lord and master – (and take it from me, says Hope, he is getting harder to live with all the time.)

Although the USAID program here is gradually phasing out, Gene is earning his promotion as Industry Officer by assisting in the implementation of the US financed survey and evaluation of Taiwan's pulp and paper, iron and steel, and fertilizer industries. He recently escorted the pulp and paper team (headed by the Director of Kimberly-Clark Paper Co – "Kleenex") around the island visiting paper mills and dining with the Provincial Governor (similar to having dinner with the Governor of New York). Next month, if will probably be a repeat with the Kaiser Steel team as Gene again serves as escorting officer for the visitors.

Next summer, we'll be returning to the U.S. for home leave. We have been told that we will be returning to Taiwan with Gene being one of the last to leave as AID phases out its Taiwan program. Hope, Denny, Mike, Maureen, Jerry, and Pat will leave for the States boarding the President Roosevelt in Hong Kong July 30. After a stop of a few days in Japan, and then Hawaii to enroll the children for one semester of school, they will continue to Omaha via Disneyland. Gene will join them there bringing Chris and Jamie on the plane with him. (How Hope managed to persuade Gene to travel with the two youngest children is a well-kept secret!!!). After a short visit in the

East, Hope will take the Children to Honolulu for school while Gene does TDY in Washington before joining the family for his vacation, between 9 a.m. and 3 p.m.. We hope that many of you will plan to visit Hawaii and the Sullivan's during our stay there.

See you all soon,

Merry Christmas from the nine traveling SULLIVAN'S

Christmas 1964
1964 Welcome from the Philippines!

The year of 1964 is closing, and again the Sullivans wish you Merry Christmas and Happy New Year from Manila. This has been an eventful and challenging year for us. We have moved to a new country, the Philippines, our oldest son has left the nest, and our youngest son has started school.

With the completion of a two-year tour in Taipei, Taiwan, and the phasing out of our USAID mission there, we moved to Manila in August. Though we were unhappy to leave the beautiful island of Taiwan and the many Chinese friends that we made while stationed there, we are always eager to explore our horizons. We left an oriental culture and foreign speaking people to investigate a western-oriented civilization and English speaking people. Manila is as modern as New York City and as exotic as Hollywood – at least on the surface. The houses in the higher income class areas are "stateside". When leaving these housing areas, you see and taste slum conditions similar to India. The provinces still retain their Spanish, Chinese, Filipino flavor, and conditions are poor. People there live in Nipa huts, a grass hut made from palm leaves, that stands on stilts.

Many of the people understand democracy as we define it, and are fighting to be recognized in the free world. We are here, helping to increase food production with modern methods, to improve health and sanitation by better education, and to industrialize their economy. Gene is here specifically to assist in establishing and advising the Economic Development Foundation, which is a private non-profit, non-political service organization dedicated to the development of private enterprise. It is being sponsored and supported by the local business community and USAID. Gene is finding it a time consuming, challenging and interesting job.

An area 150 miles north of Manila is where we escape the heat. This is mountainous Baguio, with cool breezes, temperature in the

50, 60, 70's, and a lovely resort town where we go to relax and play golf. After several consecutive days on the hilly course, your legs ache and the score is sometimes horrible, and you decide that Baguio is a recreation area, not a golf course. Of course, for you non-golfers Baguio is the area where the famous wood items are carved that are exported from the Philippines, and there is much good shopping there.

Now that we have established a routine, Hope is again enjoying hot weather year round on the golf course. If you can imagine shopping, wrapping and writing Christmas cards in the 80 to 90 degree heat, or in our air-conditioned bedroom, then you can imagine the climate here. And this is the cool season: We know it because the Filipinos are wearing sweaters, and the newspapers have announced a big cold wave just because the temperatures dropped to 70 degrees at night. Hope is already involved in the Women's Club, is Housing Chairman for the mission to aid the new personnel to find housing, is helping wrap 90,000 Christmas packages for the President's wife's project for charity as a team captain, and is on the dance committee to plan all the high school dances for the year.

The children love the schools in which they are enrolled, except that they are now struggling with Spanish as the required language instead of Chinese. They can say at least "Good Morning" and can count in five languages now, and the older four are developing more fluency in the languages they have been required to take each school year. Maureen is a freshman in high school, Jerry a sixth grader, Pat and Jamie are second and first graders in the American School. Chris is attending a private Kindergarten, and Michael is in a private Boys School and is the only American in his class. Dennis spent a month with us before leaving for Kentucky Military Institute in Lyndon, Kentucky in September. He also loves his school, but has had a minor adjustment living with boys all the same age instead of with little brothers who demanded his full attention. He did spend his summer teaching the two youngest to swim while working as a lifeguard, and now all the children can swim and dive. He also played varsity football at school and received his letter as well as an award for the best player of the year. He will spend his first Christmas away from home with Taipei friends now in the Washington, DC area.

Part of the fun of leaving a mission for the new post is the farewell parties that are given for you. This starts about three or four weeks before departure and continues until friends wave a fond farewell from the airport, or until the husband involved drops dead on his feet from work all day and play all night. Three parties in particular were memorable of our departure from Taiwan. A progressive dinner that provided transportation via pedicab between houses. The fun, of course, was the fulfillment of the suppressed desire by all males to be the driver. They found that sitting at the desk does not develop leg muscles. Pedicabs, in case you are not familiar with this mode of transportation, is a carriage behind a bike in which one or two or even three passengers may ride. On another occasion, we had a night tour of Taipei using this same transportation, and eight of us had "Roman chariot races" around town. A third night we had a swimming party at the Grand Hotel, where we swallowed half of the pool during a rough water polo game, men vs. women. I won't say who won, but we were nearly half drowned.

Upon arrival in Manila, we were established in three huge rooms in the Manila Hotel, until we found a house to rent. This can be a problem because there are no real estate agents as in the States, and so while parents rode taxis and stopped whenever they saw a "for rent" sign, children made friends with the staff at the hotel. It does come as a shock when you find your seven-year-old acting as the new elevator boy when you go down to breakfast some mornings. Another day we returned to find Chris missing, and after looking all over the hotel, we finally located him asleep in a room several doors down the hallway. He had been helping the room boy polish the floors and had decided on a nap. When Dad wanted to know why someone had eaten and charged $25.00 for lunch, the answer was the teenagers had asked some friends for lunch to "our house". But the best story of all is the evening that Denny was pinch-hitting as "father" in the dining room and a tourist asked him what they (all seven) were doing in Manila. The answer: "Oh, we got tired of our parents so we are making a world tour." So you see that the Sullivans haven't changed, just have grown one year older, and are counting the days until the President Roosevelt sails from Manila on May 23, 1965 with all of us coming to visit many of you on our home leave.

Mabuhay or Best Wishes from Manila, and see you all soon –

Gene, Hope, Michael, Maureen, Jerry, Patrick, James and Christopher – and Dennis from the States

New address effective January 1, 1965 –

Mr. & Mrs. E.F. Sullivan, USAID, APO San Francisco 96528

Christmas 1964, Taipei, Taiwan

Christmas 1965
1965 MUBUHAY FROM THE PHILIPPINES

DURING this past summer of 1965 we had the good fortune of seeing and talking to some of you, though usually too briefly, on our recent home leave trek across the United States. This trek began on May 7 after Gene and Hope returned from a two week conference in Taiwan – we returned to Manila for two days to pick up the children – and 8 Sullivan's and 23 pieces of luggage boarded the Pan Am Jet at Manila International airport for the Unites States. First stop GUAM, and many persons including the Air Line wondered WHY GUAM? For two days. But the visit with a sister and brother-in-law made the stop imperative, in spite of the snafu that we caused the airline in finding us accommodations in the tight housing problem on Guam. It hasn't really recovered from the Typhoon that blew everything away a couple of years ago. But we deplaned and put the customs into an uproar with our 23 bags in their small crowded Quonset hut, so much so we had to return later to pick them up. The two days were delightful and we discovered charm that the tourist is going to love in a few years. The only really bad thing that happened on Guam was the dollar Hope lost to that 'cheating?' brother-in-law on the gold course. Next port of call was our beloved Hawaii and the balmy shores of Waikiki where we all rapidly readjusted to the life in America minus the sounds of the musical horns of the jeepneys and taxis in Manila.

OUR arrival in the 50-degree smoggy weather of Los Angeles in no way dampened our spirits nor our desire to begin the three-day visit of Disneyland. Needless to say this visit more than exceeded our expectations and will probably warrant another visit in the future, if the children have anything to say about it. The speed of the traffic was the main irritant on the whole trip, and in Los Angeles we had our first taste of it. Gene kept passing the turnoffs, because the signs just went by too fast.

SHORT visits in Boston for Gene and the children, and Kentucky for Hope to visit Dennis and Kentucky Military Institute preceded our stay in New York City. The children covered every corner of the World's Trade Fair and the sights of the Great Big City, and they had a delightful time with the Room Service at the hotel while dad and mom were out on the town for a bit of night life. The temperatures were still on the cool side and after the hot humid climate to which we have adjusted we were all freezing cold most of the time.

IN WASHINGTON we didn't have the time to see as many of our old friends as we had planned nor as many as we would have liked to visit; nor were we able to get to Vermont and Connecticut as we had originally planned. Hope was busy sorting and discarding the household effects which have been in storage for the past eight years and which we have been able to live without quite comfortably. Meantime, Gene was on consultation at the Philippine desk in USAID headquarters in the new State Department Building. The new highways almost wore off some of the tires on the car as Hope went from Virginia to Maryland on the highway once five times in one day. Denny joined us in the middle of our stay in Washington, after Maureen, Hope, and Mike flew to Kentucky for the last-week-of-school festivities, and Maureen attended her first formal dance, the Junior and Senior Military Ball. After short visits in Omaha which was a rush of family visits and activities, and San Francisco, to see our favorite Big American City, we finally arrived back in Honolulu to spend our home leave in our house on Upper Maunalani Heights overlooking Diamond Head. Gene and all the children except Denny stayed for about seven weeks and then headed back to Manila to register the children in school, which began on July 26. Picnicking on the northern beaches of Oahu, surfing off Waikiki, drinking cocktails on top of the Ilikai, watching the Trans-Pacific Sailing regatta and watching the glorious sunsets from our big new sun deck ("lanai" in Honolulu) were among the pleasant highlights of Gene and the children's brief stay in Honolulu. For Hope, since she stayed on after their return, the pleasures continued for two and a half months longer. Also the work then started as she painted the whole house inside and out during her stay. Except for the pictures that son Dennis (he stayed on also until his school started) took of her on the movie film while crawling into a bedroom window, and the fall from the tall, tall ladder and the paint all over her as a result of the fall, she enjoyed the job, and is very proud of the results. Many job offers *have come in because of this, too, but duty calls elsewhere. It didn't keep her from shopping the big beautiful stores, nor from visiting the beaches, nor from having constant company. Some very good friends from Taiwan visited and during their stay Hope visited Maui with them. This island is even more beautiful than Oahu and also slower developing than Oahu hence the charm of old Hawaii remains. Hope's mother and niece also flew out from Omaha for a visit. They also fell in love with the islands, in fact, Hope had to put her mother on the plane for Omaha only an hour before she took off for Manila. Of course, the life in Hawaii is slower than on the Mainland, and the attitude of "why do today what can wait until tomorrow.....or next week....or next month....plunkety plunk on the guitar" prevails in all aspects of life. In true Hawaiian fashion we all assumed this routine, so much so in fact that when a niece stopped over for a week enroute to Guam for the summer she missed her plane by 24 hours and had to remain for a week longer until she was able to board a plane on a standby basis. Hope returned to Manila after spending a few days on Guam with her sister, and her brother-in-law finally forgave her for the slip-up on his daughter's failure to arrive on time. (She still believes that he just didn't like getting up for the 5:05 a.m. plane arrival time.) Capsule opinion of the States by the family: Dad "there must be an easier way", Maureen "where is the blue grass here in Kentucky?" Pat "those aren't slot machines, Jamie, that is our parking meter", Mike "I hate Honolulu, Disneyland, World's Fair, Washington, friends we have to visit" (etc. or whatever we were doing at the time. Later he had nothing but admiration for each place and person), Chris "where are we going today?" Jerry "did he say Manila was just outside of Cuba?" Jamie "not another airplane, and where did I put my shoes?" Hope "freeways...Do we HAVE to enter them at sixty miles an hour?"*

MANILA AND the Philippines are still hot and quasi-Americano. They speak in English, but don't understand English. They love our money and help but don't like the Americans particularly. They mimic everything western, but adapt it to their own ways. The country had an election this year with a new President Marcos, the victor. However, this took four weeks to establish, and the campaigning took one year, and a tremendous amount of money. The voters in many cases voted under stress, and with bribes of money, threats or beatings. To collect they had to present a carbon copy of the ticket to prove that they had voted the way they had been told. Some voted several times, many of them at least twice. Beatings and shootings were not unusual, but in spite of all of this, this country is the closest to being Our type of democracy in the Asian world.

It is a cosmopolitan city, with modern nightclubs and restaurants, magnificent golf and tennis and polo clubs, fancy homes and parties. However, this is for the chosen few, the average income of the Filipino last year was only $110. On a trip to the southernmost island of Mindanao with Gene this past fall, the real life of the Philippines was introduced to Hope. The city of Davao reminded her of many of the Chinese cities that she has known, with the dust, the ever-present numberless populace, noise, and confusion. The electricity is sporadic, and fluctuates constantly. The women must carry their water, and the sanitary conditions are not any more developed than in other Asian countries. The roads are reminiscent of the early twenties in the States, and it is not unusual to spend the night in the jeep, about the only means of transportation, (other than caribou or water buffalo), if one is caught in a rainstorm. The bridges are rickety and dangerous, the roads dusty and bumpy, and some of the bridges so bad that you walk across ahead of the jeep just to be sure that you make it without a swim in the river. Lack of good transportation and lack of a communication network is one reason the election results took so long. But the Philippine Islands are beautiful, green, lush, and tropical with many beautiful ocean and mountain scenes, very friendly people, and the promise of tremendous economic development. The handicraft is exceptionally good, especially the wood products and carvings, the hand embroideries, and the rattan products.

THE SCHOOLS here are very good and Mike attends a Philippine Boys School, and some of his experiences are delightful, but that would take another long letter to describe. The other children attend the American school, and it is a top-notch American curriculum school. It was conceived and initiated and still controlled after 30 years by the large business community here in Manila, hence is not a military dependent school similar to the previous ones that our children have attended. They have all the stateside activities that *accompany school, and they are all active in them. They are required to take Spanish from the second grade upward, and so the children are learning another new foreign language.*

HOPE IS still involved in her various and many activities, school PTA and board meetings, women's clubs, charity events, floor shows for the dances the Embassy gives, theater groups, shopping in the many farmer and open markets, learning the Philippine dances, etc. Gene keeps busy with the Economic Development Foundation, which is a privately endowed consultant firm for the Industry here in the Philippines. He is hoping to set up an Export Promotion Center this coming year for the Department of Commerce and Industry. His job here is a bit more advanced in technical advice since the economy here is more advanced and developed than in some of the former countries in which we have lived and worked.

WE WILL be thinking of all of you while we enjoy Christmas with the temperature in the high 80's or in the 90's, and while the Christmas spirit and Christmas carols are celebrated to the fullest we will wish we had a real true-to-life Christmas tree, and not the painted tree branches or the simulated silver tree that we substitute for the pine tree of the States. And so for another year Gene, Hope, Dennis, 18, Mike, 16, Maureen 15, Jerry, 13, Patrick, 10, James, 8, and Chris, 6, all wish you the very best of the Holiday Season and good wishes for the coming year.

Christmas picture for 1965 - taken in Hawaii, summer of 1965

Christmas 1966

The tinsel glitters in the sunshine; the red and green balls bounce gently in the warm balmy air, and the candy canes are taped to a palm tree, but this is the season of Christmas. The Sullivans are celebrating this season in an atmosphere far different from our Christian Customs, as Buddhism prevails. The many people that populate this part of the world are never quiet, and the sounds that are so familiar to our pattern of life, would fascinate those who would spend a night with us. The noodle man with his clacking sticks, the night watchman that rings his bell on his hourly rounds outside the gate, the clanging gong from the Wat (temple), the ice cream boy shouting his presence, the charcoal man who is vaguely similar to the chimney-sweep of Dickens' time, (he sells the charcoal with which everyone cooks their food), the dogs barking, the geese honking, the ducks quacking, the millions of laughing children, and the subdued roar of the gossiping neighbors as they conduct their daily exchange of news as the work day is ending and they are again all sharing a common room. The frogs that sound similar to a distant jet taking off, and if you listen carefully the millions of insects and animal life that start their roaming as the twilight sets in. Life has not changed here for several hundreds of years, and the pattern is only rarely disturbed by the few modern additions such as a far off police or fire siren. THIS IS LIFE IN BANGKOK, THAILAND.

At the end of 10 years in the Orient, broken by a two-year tour in the pseudo-western Philippines, we are nostalgically thinking of snow at Christmas, and the rush and excitement of the Christmas Season at home. That is Mother and Dad are, the Children do not remember much of the Stateside Christmas Season. We hope that in the new year we will again be living for a short period in the States while Dad takes some advanced executive training.

This past year has been exciting and interesting, starting with Dennis saying good-bye to the family and returning to Kentucky and school after a Christmas vacation. Early spring was routine, if anything in our lives could be routine, to be broken by a request of a

TDY (temporary duty) for Gene to the Bangkok Mission. Following his return to Manila we started the tension producing diet of cables. "Can Sullivan come?" "When?" etc. etc. until the climax of "Sullivan reports May 26". When this news came we again started the usual procedures: selling, sorting, packing, and the inevitable round of farewell parties.

Our final farewell to friends in Manila was a planned May 4th Aloha Party; with 85 invited guests (all of whom accepted) an outside-in-the-yard-sitting-on-the-ground Hawaiian style luau was the answer. The 200 giant banana leaves and the 5 bushels of flowers were delivered the day of the party, and arranged in the yard. Of course this part of the world has a dry and a rainy season, and this rainy season was due in June. But at 6 p.m. the heavens opened up and the dam broke, after all it hadn't rained for the past 6 months, and there was 6 inches of rain in the yard. With everyone pitching in, including the early arriving guests, we moved all the furniture into the garage, and rearranged our jungle scene inside, and had a marvelous time.

Enroute to Bangkok, we descended upon Hong Kong, our "Super Basket Shopping Center" in Asia. For 8 wonderful days we rode the tram to the peak, wandered about Chinatown, (yes, there is a Chinatown in HK since it is a British colony), and we bargained with the Chinese merchants. He considers this a big part of the sale, and we enjoy this pleasure so much, and have become habitual users of the system, that occasionally have found ourselves trying to bargain in the big stores in the States, to no avail, I might add.

Of course, our many friends in HK helped to make this a very enjoyable vacation, and on our last night with the plane scheduled to leave at 9:30, we were surprised to learn at a party we were attending, that the plane had been rescheduled without our knowledge, for an hour earlier departure. We all rushed to the hotel, where we found sleepy-eyed children watching television in their underwear. (Saving the clean travel clothes until the last minute.) By throwing clothes on children irrespective of colors or sizes, rushing down to the lobby and into the 3 awaiting cars with the 9 bellboys hurry-scurry behind us carrying 30 suitcases and hand carries, with a telephone call to alert the Airline that we were coming, checking the luggage in (it was only 110 pounds overweight), we arrived breathlessly on board only 10 minutes late. We barely had time to fasten the seatbelts when we were airborne, but the airline treats us as a tour group when we travel, and which airline likes to take off half empty?

Arrival in the middle of the night, in a new city in the Orient, is probably the best way to assimilate the feel for an area. It comes to life after dark when the families are all together after a day of hard work of minimum survival. Dad and Mother noticed many changes in Bangkok, which they had visiting in 1959. The many klongs (canals) had been covered over, there are a few main ones remaining, and were now roads, more lights, more buildings, but wide-eyed and fascinated, the children kept remarking on things that reminded them of Korea and Taiwan.

The following morning marked the beginning of house hunting, and happily the Erawan Hotel has a swimming pool, where the children fast became friends with Thai attendant and started to learn their first Thai words. Mother spent hours in the hot car (95 in the shade) looking for housing. The Thai custom is to live, sleep, eat, study, and play in the same room. Most houses have but two bedrooms, and each day the real estate agent would assure Mother that today she would see only 4 or 5-bedroom houses, and proceed to show her smaller ones. Their explanation each time around would be "But Madam, these are really big rooms." It soon began to be a pattern to find a sink, shiny and new, built into the middle of the living-dining-kitchen room. But after seeing some 48 houses someone told us of a big solid teak old-style Thai house, and after negotiations and signing the lease, we all moved into it in the unheard of 8 days after arrival. Most families stay in the hotel at least the 3-month maximum the mission allows. This huge house has 5 bedrooms, living room, dining room, 4 bathrooms (with 1890 plumbing), reception hall, and family room; the compound is completely walled, ½ acre of lush tropical landscape, meaning more green than color. This also means frogs, snakes, mosquitoes, and ants, ants, and more ants, and to this we have added 2 dogs, 7 ducks, 3 geese, 1 monkey, and at least six children. We had air –conditioners installed to find the landlord didn't understand much about electricity, and that with a current of only sufficient to carry light bulbs, adding refrigerator and fans, we have to count what is running or we are plunged into darkness. This is fun since we must then call the repairman from the electric company. By yelling into the phone, "Farang, Faj Fa, Sya, Sam Nyg, Ha Ongkarak Soi, rew, rew," a man arrives to fix the sick electricity, and then we find the electricity silently waiting for us to plug one too many into the socket again. This is not the only exciting event, which could and does happen daily. The water pump was first installed to deliver water to the 19th floor, but we have but 2, so water pipes burst under the pressure. Even now we are never sure when the pipes will growl and quit leaving the unfortunate one soapy. But we have all adjusted to the Mai Pen Rai (It makes no matter) attitude of the Thai people.

The children attend the International School, where children of 47 nationalities mingle with one another and learn their ABC's in the English Language. All are delighted with the high grades they are making. Many social events along with sporting events keep them busy after school hours. Maureen's favorite is the Foreign Affairs Club, a spirited group who partake of the Cosmopolitan atmosphere of Bangkok. All Embassies, including the Communist countries, along with SEATO, UN, WHO, ECAFE, FAO, UNESCO, UNICEF and others are represented here. Mike has grown up and is interested in girls and sports; Jerry is President of his class, and a drummer in a combo. He arrived in Bangkok, and found the electric guitar players flooding the market, so he negotiated with a local Chinese merchant for a set of drums. (Lately we have been leaving out the earplugs during the practice sessions.) Pat and Jamie are playing Little League baseball, and Chris is delighted that he now can read all the books he has been hoarding for 6 years.

During the summer vacation we haunted the tourist treasures of Thailand. We visiting all the famous and not so famous temples, River Kwai, Floating Market, Thieves Market, Sunday Market, Snake Farm (large collection of snakes where they extract venom for serums), Thai museum, and Zoo, where you may have elephant rides on Sunday. When we weren't learning about the marvelous area in which we reside we played golf and swam.

The political situation here is touchy, and there are many evidences of the fact that this area is on FIRE. We are geographically very close to Vietnam, only 1-½ hours by jet to Saigon. There are daily reports of fighting and infiltration from the borders of Cambodia and Burma; and there are many R&R U.S. Military, but technically we are not at war in Thailand. We feel no more uneasy here than we did during our years in Korea. We are very conscious of the fact that we are needed to hold back the surging wave of Communism and feel concerned about our sometimes stumbling efforts to counteract the influence from the north and northeast. We always have hope and confidence that we shall win; many times we wish our friends in the States could better understand our neighbors here in Asia.

This year Hope started working at USOM, with the children all in school and the house empty, she decided to contribute. As a Research Assistant she is currently setting up a Technical Research Library for USOM Bangkok. By surveying, reading, abstracting the files (since 1950), she will be the most knowledgeable person on USOM Bangkok in Thailand when she completes her task. She hasn't lost her identity in the Dependent Wives group, as she is coordinating the Christmas program for the American Women's Club, serves as a member of the Welcome Committee of USOM Wives Club, PTA, Chaperones for high school dances, will soon be teaching high school students to fox trot instead of monkey as the chairman of the Dance Committee, and participating member in the Women's Golf Association at the Royal Sports Club. Life is full.

The year ends with Thanksgiving on the beach at Pattaya, a resort 100 miles south of Bangkok on the Gulf of Siam; it is only 15 miles from Sataheep, largest airbase in Far East. It wasn't the New England Traditional dinner, but we did have the turkey, dressing, cranberry, and pumpkin pie. The most perfect part was sitting under a swaying palm tree watching the sun sinking lower and lower as it burnt the puffy clouds into a riot of red, orange, and pink. Also as the year ends Dennis, who has been visiting for the past month, returns to the States to report to the Marines. After boot camp in California, he will attend Aviation Electronics course for a couple of years. Proud as we are of him, it is hard to realize that Gene and Hope are parents of a Marine.

MAY GOD BLESS AND KEEP YOU IN GOOD HEALTH. MERRY CHRISTMAS AND A HAPPY NEW YEAR.

Gene and Hope, Dennis, 19, Michael, 17, Maureen, 16, Jerry, 14, Patrick, 11, James 9, Chris, 6.

Christmas 1967
Welcome again from Thailand!

One startling result of our eleven year odyssey in the Far East was effectively demonstrated during our recent home leave in Honolulu by 8-year old Chris watching the people in the corner house getting ready to move and astutely remarked: "Those people are only moving to another house in Honolulu because they don't have all the lift vans and water-proof packing papers that we have when we move."

The first few months of 1967 were devoted to just such logistic preparations for the Sullivan family's assault on Europe culminating in a final forty day whirlwind automobile trip which spanned the mainland of the United States. In mid-June, after Gene had departed via the Pacific Ocean for consultation in AID/Washington and a 7-week intensive course in International Marketing at Harvard Business School, Hope led the Sullivan expedition by train from Bangkok down the 3000 mile length of the Thai-Malaysia peninsula to Singapore, with brief three-day stop-offs at Penang and Kuala Lumpur. Although the three-day train trip was advertised to include air conditioned staterooms, the only air available was that coming through the open windows which was greatly conditioned by the soot and smoke from the coal engine, and the red dust from the road bed. By the time that the train had reached the Malaysian border, all the Sullivans were the same color as the local inhabitants after leaning out the window to wave at the children and saffron-robed Buddhist monks who use the railroad tracks as a path from village to village. This Disneyland-like train ride through the dense tropical jungles was one of the early highlights of the trip.

In Singapore, the traveling seven -- Hope, Mike 18, Maureen 16, Jerry 14, Patrick 12, James 10 and Chris 8 – found that the Suez Canal was closed due to the Middle East hostilities and the Italian liner on which they had been booked for a one-month trip to Venice was re-scheduled to a six-week trip around Africa. The delight of adding a few African ports to their itinerary unfortunately was overweighed by the necessity of arriving in the United States by the middle of August. Hope then spent a frantic three days changing all seven reservations in Europe and flew with the children to Rome via Bombay. Only a travel agent knows the headaches involved in such a change.

Rome was "out of sight" from the moment they arrived in the wee hours of the morning, and the Italian people treated them family like visiting royalty when they heard that Hope had so many boys with her. It was obvious to all that this was not a typical American family touring their country. With guidebooks in hand, Hope served as tour guide not only to her own brood but several tourists who also joined the group. Ham that she is, Hope often deviated from the book in giving delightful little homey touches about this statue or that building. In fact, that quaint couple from Podunk, Idaho were quite surprised to learn that Julius Caesar always wore pink underwear "because that pretty guide with those children said so."

In Geneva, the 4th of July was spent with the large American community enjoying the traditional display of fireworks following a full day of games and races and picnic. Hope rented a yellow Mercedes and drove through the small villages bordering Lake Geneva, then up to Strasbourg, where they stayed overnight in a small hotel built originally in 1400; and because of ghosts or simply lack of funds apparently still had the air or smell of antiquity about it. Then on to Frankfurt, where after two days of sightseeing, they boarded a plane for London.

In London, the family had the fun of adding to Maureen's wardrobe at the mod-mini skirt shops since her suitcase disappeared enroute and did not catch up with them until they arrived in Boston. Imagine a girl arriving in London with no luggage! After three days of sightseeing, they all expressed amazement of not seeing very many people over 40 walking the streets of London. It truly seems to be a city where young people have completely taken over.

In summarizing the trip through Europe, all were in agreement that a return trip is absolutely essential. Maureen wants to go back to Germany and visit the castles and stay overnight in several of *them that have been converted into youth hostels. Mike wants to go back to Rome and see more of the Museums, fountains and statuary (pretty girls too). Jerry wants to go back and visit a street of shops in a small village along the Rhine River. Patrick wants to go back and use the paddle boats on Lake Geneva. James wants to revisit the zoo in Frankfurt. Chris wants to go back and see everything he missed when he would fall asleep usually with his head on the table during dinner, which was served European style at 9:30 each night. Hope wants to return and see what goes on in Europe at night when you are traveling with a husband instead of six children.*

The second part of our trip started off by flying from London to Boston, where we met Gene who was just completing his studies at Harvard. After a week of visiting relatives, sightseeing and watching the Boston Red Sox win some exciting ball games on their road to the pennant, we drove to New York and took the kids to see "Hello Dolly" which they enjoyed heartily. (They saw "Fiddler on the Roof" in London); then on to Washington, DC and Memphis, Tenn. where we visited Denny aged 20. He recently completed advanced electronic studies in the Marine Corps school in Memphis graduating 10th in a class of 145. He is now being transferred to El Toro Marine Base in California for helicopter radar training.

We finally arrived in Omaha in mid-August for the long-awaited Corkin family reunion or tribal conclave to be exact. It was the first time in 8 years that all five of the Corkin sisters and their respective families were able to be present in Omaha at the same time. Since there were 39 of us to be housed and fed, we took over one of the nearby motels. It was a good opportunity for the traveling Sullivans to get re-acquainted with their traveling cousins.

The Sullivan wagon then headed west to Denver on Route 6 and up to Boulder, Colorado where we stayed overnight in a motel in the foothills of the Rockies that Gene and Hope remember so well since they were married there in the University chapel on May 4, 1946. While walking around the campus, the teenage Sullivans thought that Mom and Dad were "simply gross" in showing them the bench near the lake where Gene proposed, and the younger Sullivans made one couple occupying the bench break into hysterical laughter by telling them "they had better be careful, since look what happened to their parents after they sat on that bench."

After a brief stop off in Colorado Springs to talk to the Registrar of Colorado College about the possibility of Mike and Maureen going there in the fall of 1968, we traveled on to New Mexico, the Grand Canyon and Las Vegas, where Hope doubled the $20 that Gene limited her to and then on to Los Angeles where we boarded a plane for Honolulu and home leave for Gene and I and school for the children.

In November, Gene returned alone to Bangkok to start his new assignment as Resident USOM Advisor to the Ministry of Industry. He has found us a new house and servants so 1968 will see us back in Thailand again. Christmas will find us celebrating in Hong Kong where we will meet Gene and travel back to Bangkok – thus completing about 28,000 miles of round-the-world and other travel.

So another year has passed, and the extended stay in the United States for the Sullivans, for the first time in 12 years, was very enjoyable, but each of the Sullivans is happy to return to their adopted "home" in the Far East.

To those of our friends whom we didn't have the necessary hours to visit, please forgive us. We promise that next time you will be first on our list.

Merry Christmas and a Happy New Year

Memories of an Overseas Childhood 253

Christmas 1967

Photo taken Omaha picnic, summer of 1967

Christmas 1968
1968 The Year of "UP UP AND AWAY" for the Sullivans

We started the year with travel from Hawaii back to Bangkok, and after a wonderful few days in our most loved city of the Orient, Hong Kong, we returned to the routine of another tour in Thailand.

Hope was involved in several very interesting and time-consuming jobs, which enabled her to learn a tremendous amount about the life, country and politics of Thailand. She coordinated the Asian Agricultural Cooperative Conference with 125 representatives from 11 countries of the Far East. This enabled her to supervise the 10 American secretaries and the 30 Thais which recorded the proceedings and also act as nursemaid, confidant to the delegates. Following the conference she edited and laid the mats for the published conference proceedings. And until you edit 11 versions of the foreign interpretations of the English language reports, you do not know what ramifications editing can take. Following this she coordinated the Northeast Agribusiness Team, a group of business men from the U.S. who came to investigate the possibilities of establishing a Farm Marketing Service Center in Northeast Thailand. After helping them with their on-the-spot investigation, as well as providing and setting up appointments with the important persons with whom they spoke, and giving them background reports, she wrote the evaluation of their report study, and followed this with a summary handbook which will be published for use by potential investors in this area of Thailand. Every minute was profitable and enjoyable, even though it did not leave much time for other activities. In spite of this, she was the President of the USOM Women's Club and helped the membership grow from a few members to 200 active members.

Gene began the new year in his new assignment as USOM Advisor to the Ministry of Industry. This meant leaving his new air-conditioned office in the USOM building for a large, spacious, old un-air-conditioned office in the Ministry. In spite of the inconvenience,

Gene has made some lifelong friends there. His day started early in the morning, and lasted late into the night, as the Thais love parties, and after dinner always went out dancing. He assisted the Ministry in taking a more imaginative and aggressive attitude toward the industrialization of Thailand. He is quite happy in his new job and the results are starting to speak for themselves.

Hope's job took her on several trips around the Far East and particularly to the Northeast of Thailand. Gene's job took him on a conference to Taiwan, in addition to the field tripping within Thailand, and this trip to Taipei brought a renewal of friendships made during our tour in Taiwan. Several Hong Kong trips for shopping and business were scattered throughout the year.

And then June arrived, and we had two seniors graduate, Mike and Maureen. The spring was spent wondering which college would accept and which would send refusals. But finally that tense waiting was over, and after 10 days in Hong Kong Hope helped choose a woolen wardrobe for Maureen, who had lived in the tropics the past seven years, and was now enroute to University of Montana at Missoula, Montana. When the School of Journalism accepted her, she had no further interest in the other schools that had accepted her. From the ecstatic letters and the midterm grades, she made the right choice.

Again in August, ---- Up Up and Away, this time for Michael, wrapped up in the confusion of the contemporary 18 year old boy – service or college. He was kissed and bid farewell by two parents who thought he was heading to college. Four days later a cable was received informing two startled parents that he was reporting for duty at Ft. Ord, California, hoping for Jump School and the Green Berets. He is now in Georgia taking Jump School and Airborne Training.

Also in August, this time via train, Jerry visited friends in Kuala Lumpur, Malaysia for six weeks. It was during this period that Hope all of a sudden realized that she was having the at-home-family-group dissolve and disperse. Gene was in Taiwan, Jerry in Malaysia, Maureen and Mike both off to the States, Dennis still in the Marines, and the three younger boys off spending a weekend with friends.

Hope – alone in the house, sat down to the big round table which had at one point in this family had sat nine for ever meal, and now she was all alone. What a quiet lonely experience, and the clatter of the fork and knife on the plate was too much, the hunger disappeared.

Then comes September and another big event in the Sullivan's life. Gene and Hope were about to join the "in-law group". Not feeling much older than college kids themselves this took some adjustment. After Dad was reminded that he was a year younger than son Dennis, when he decided on marriage, and that he was in the service, and that he had college to finish, and that he had been successful, he started to brag about the "most wonderful girl in the world", Sandee, the girl his son had chosen. She is a girl Dennis has known since Taiwan days, in fact, she was the first girl he had ever been serious about, and it has been on-again-off-again for several years. So the month of September was spent in letters back and forth about plans, and wedding dates, and early next year, 15th of February we will have a new daughter. We have waited for 22 years for another daughter. Dennis is still stationed at El Toro California Marine Base, an Avionics Specialist, which the Marines keep pulling out of units heading for Vietnam, as he is the only one qualified on the West Coast. He has one more year and will then return to college.

Again it was time to start thinking of Xmas letters and gifts, which have a 15 November deadline in the Far East. Hope had just sighed – the last slipcover was installed on the chairs, the house was in good condition, organized, and nothing but relaxation until home leave, which is due in June 1970. Foreign Service people always know that transfers can occur, but the Sullivans were very much settled in Bangkok. The cable arrived requesting Gene in Addis Ababa, Ethiopia. A promotion and a job every man dreams of, one where you get to set up your own program, the jobs and the problems which also go with it. How could we turn it down? 8 days later, unheard of in the State Department, travel orders were in hand, packing days were chosen, lift vans packed and sent, and on the 29th of November the family again "up-up-and-away" to Athens for five days to get the necessary visas for Ethiopia, and then on to the royal welcome by the Mission in Ethiopia.

So this Xmas letter also is a bit sad, it ends our chapter in the Far East. Now we must learn a new culture. But the excitement of travel to far away lands is still with us, and we are looking forward to being "experts" on Africa. Of course, Ethiopia is the "plum" of African assignments. The climate ideal, 8200 feet, brisk cool air, with fireplaces necessary each night, and temperatures a beautiful sunny 80 degrees during the day. In fact, the tourist bureau of Ethiopia publicizes "13 Months of Sunshine". The geography is the most beautiful in Africa, covering mountains, beautiful canyons, likened to the Grand Canyon, deserts, lowlands and seasides.

Pat and Jerry are now Karate experts, Jerry with his black belt and Pat with his brown belt. Jerry plans on teaching a class in Africa, to supplement his income. He still plays the guitar and drums, and hopes to form a new combo in Addis. He is a sophomore in High School, and is fast growing toward the day when he too will be leaving the nest.

Jamie and Chris are both at the fun age, just past babyhood, but not yet a teenage problem. They are active in baseball, scouts, and swimming, in addition to school.

As you can see this has been a year of Up Up and Away-y-y-y-y for the Sullivans. We are looking forward to a calmer 1969, that is after Hope heads home for a wedding in February. We wish all of you as joyous and happy a Holiday Season and the coming year as the past exciting year has been for us.

Gene, Hope, Jerry, Pat, Jamie, and Chris from Addis Ababa Ethiopia; Maureen from the University of Montana, Missoula, Montana; Michael from Ft. Benning Georgia; and Dennis from El Toro, California.

Christmas 1969

Christmas 1969 – ADDIS ABABA
Hope Gene Pat Chris Jerry Maureen Jamie

THE RESTLESS HORSES TIED TO THE HITCHINGPOST OF THE SCHOOL WERE BECOMING *impatient for their riders – and soon the boys came noisily rushing out, giving their books to the zabanya-groom waiting with their horses, and challenging each other to a race for home. Weekends of camping – carrying all of the needed items – the shrieking of the hyenas breaking the quiet calm of the crystal clear starlit nights – herds of donkeys and cattle, and in some places, camels, interfere with modern day traffic – dust and six inch cracks in the ground, caused by the sunshine from the cloudless blue sky making each day the same during the dry season, changes only during the four months of rain, when a knee-deep sticky mud demands rubber boots and raincoats and the necessity of staying on the blacktop roads or having a car sink into the depths –happy restless people, dark in color from the Arabic, Egyptian, and Abyssinian ancestry are ever present and are always surrounding you. Flowers are in profusion, larger than you expect – birds, beautiful in plumage. THIS IS ETHIOPIA!*

After one year we are coming to love the crisp beauty of its physical geography, the delightful temperatures of 60 – 80 degrees during the day, and the 40 – 50 during the night. The 8000-9000 foot altitude makes pleasant living for most of us. Yes, there are beggars, lepers, and the deformed, maimed and lazy, very much in evidence; however, the majority of the Ethiopians are agitating for progress. One of the oldest free cultures in the world, which claims descending from the Queen of Sheba and King Solomon, have in the last 100 years allowed the outside world to come in, and in the past 40 years are rapidly joining the modern world. His Imperial Majesty Haile Selassie I celebrated his 39th coronation anniversary this year as monarch. Much of this progress is due to his leadership.

The Sullivans, in particular, have four boys living at home in Addis Ababa. Jerry now a Junior in High School, Patrick a Seventh grader, James, a Sixth grader, and Christopher, a Fourth grader. During this past year Dennis was married to a marvelous girl, Sandee, and they live in Los Angeles while he finishes up his last eight months in the Marines. Michael is stationed with the Army at Ft. Benning, Georgia, and Maureen is a sophomore at the University of Montana at Missoula in the School of Journalism.

Gene has been very busy this past year setting up a Private Enterprise Division within the USAID Mission and assisting Roger Ernst, the Mission Director, in promoting and encouraging U.S. investments in Ethiopia. Gene has traveled with potential investors over most of the country by Jeep, Land Rover, and the Mission's single-engine Cessna, and is now planning an overland camera safari trip to Nairobi (with Hope tagging along, of course). He also is working closely with the Ethiopian Chamber of Commerce and the Ethiopian Investment Committee in drafting a new Investment Code and in establishing an Investment and Export Promotion Center, which will be designed to assist all local and foreign businessmen. He will be even busier in the new year, but is quite optimistic and happy about this challenging assignment.

Hope complains she is so busy that she doesn't have time to write a letter of resignation, but thoroughly enjoys the many activities in which she is involved. As treasurer of the YWCA she is helping to put up a building in the slowly developing organization (at least within Ethiopia). As Vice President of the International Women's Club she is helping various organizations needing charity within Ethiopia, and in the pleasant atmosphere of a group of women representing 39 countries throughout the world. One of the fun things that she has done is to teach women of 20 different nationalities to make Thai silk flowers, which were then sold at a Bazaar. A weekly responsibility is the editing of the "Lion", which is the U.S. Mission newspaper. This is sent to about 3500 persons living in Addis, and is one job, which she is enjoying the most of all. Of course, there are the various 570 volunteers from the community to work for the Red Cross Bazaar to be held in December. The children also come up with activities, which take supervision, time and energy.

Jerry, now six feet tall, the President of the Junior Class has his black belt in Karate, and as an instructor is teaching a daily class. He also is in demand as a drummer, and plays in a combo, but also played drums for a theatre production of "The Fantasticks". This experience has inspired him to take further lessons in the symphony drums. He is looking forward to next year and the challenge of meeting the world, and is now looking for and making his plans for his choice of college.

Pat spends all his free time with, for, and on horses. Our stable has five, not the big beautiful Stateside animal, but challenging none the less. He has found that the horses require constant and dedicated care, the feeding, the brushing, the right-balanced diet, the training, the stable, all are work, and he loves every minute. He has a "communication" that few persons possess. Of course, he has a certain odor about him! And occasionally he forgets (?) to close his door (his room opens immediately onto the driveway) and Hope will find a horse standing in the hallway looking at her – this has happened a couple of times, and it takes two houseboys to eject the animal and to clean up.

Jamie and Chris don't love the work of the horses, but do ride daily. It is common here for friends to visit each other, using the horse for transportation. It is not uncommon for several visiting horses, with their master playing or doing homework inside the house, to be hitched to the gate at any given time.

Though Addis Ababa is a modern city with a modern jet airport, a Hilton which opened this past August, ten miles into the country you are back in Biblical times. The festivals of the Coptic Church are traditional, colorful and very interesting, and they play an important part in the daily life. This summer while Maureen visited from college for eight weeks we traveled outside of the city a great deal.

The Rift Valley is a series of lakes, each more beautiful than the last. Travel here is reminiscent of Pioneer days. In preparation for a week's camping trip, it is necessary to camp as hotels are virtually non-existent except in 3 or 4 larger "cities", involves detailed planning. The vehicle must be in top condition, as it is required to travel on gravelly pot-holed roads-----or less (meaning none). You can travel for a hundred miles without a village. All contingencies—oil, spare tires, repair kits, tool kits-- must be carried. It also helps if you are a mechanic as mechanics are scarce. Meals have to be planned, food purchased and stored efficiently. Water must be carried, and of course, the stove and charcoal. Tents, sleeping bags, cots, and washbasins, all must be taken.

Our first experience at camping, after a reluctant Gene finally gave in to the pressure of the boys, took us to Lake Langano, a four-hour drive but only 120 miles southwest of Addis. Leaving the altitude of Addis for the pleasant 3500-feet makes it worthwhile, but it is an exhilarating experience to "go back to nature". On this first trip, the seven Sullivans, three friends, boys, 1 friend, girl, and the zabanya crowded into two cars with all of the camping equipment. The boys challenged the girls to a race in pitching the tents. After an hour, in which several lost their tempers, several tents collapsed though they looked fine, and much laughter, the girls won and had a perfect-pitched tent. The boys never did manage to make a "taut ship". Needless to say, during this activity Gene snoozed in the sun, his excuse "I've never camped before and I don't like camping." He had more excuses as evening came, dinner was over and the fire died down – the pup tent for Gene and Hope did not look like his bedroom. But the sounds of the wild animals, snapping twigs, crawly night creatures drove him to bed. Hope is still laughing about his query "What do I do now?" when he bumped his head on the far end of the tent when crawling into his sleeping bag. In trying to put his head by the tent flap, and turning around inside of the tent he sprung the leg of his cot. He was so disgusted he slept on a V-shaped cot all night.

But we have now become experienced, have a camp set up rapidly and reluctantly break camp each time. Even Gene, though this is not his favorite sport relaxation, is enjoying it more each time. Our bathtub is the Lake and each morning in the snappy air, all race for the lake, where much splashing warms the body. The sun is hot during the day, (we have an Equatorial sun) but the nights are crisp. Ivory soap is a necessity, it floats hence you don't lose it. The smell of coffee and bacon mixed with charcoal smoke, guarantees everyone eats four times more than in the confines of the dining room. Hope is the Chief Cook, but Arage, the zabanya, is the dishwasher.

The days are spent hiking, bird watching, reading, and in general discovery of the marvels of nature.

Lake Abeyata is a bird sanctuary, where we have discovered many new varieties of birds, to us at least. The sight of 100-200 flamingos taking flight is an unforgettable sight. Can you see Gene and Hope BIRD WATCHING?

Lake Shalla has many "hot sulfur springs" where the water bubbles up from the ground too hot to touch. This lake is void of humanity and except for the animals and the birds, who resent the occasional camper, it is serene and beautiful.

Awash Park is a game preserve. You camp along a murky jungle river, which boasts of millions of crocodiles. Driving through the park early or late in the day affords you the opportunity of seeing many animals and of course in their native habitat – greater and lesser Kudu, antelope, gazelle, large tortoise, water buck, Oryx, zebra, ostrich, lions, foxes, Dik-Dik, warthog, camels, leopard, mongoose, water buffalo, baboons, monkeys, hippo, guinea hen, and of course the crocs. Driving in this park means Land Rover (or 4-wheel drive) overland driving, dust and sore bottoms from bouncing on a hard seat, but all is worthwhile. The picture of the family this year is taken at Filohwa Springs, four-hours overland into Awash Park, Central Ethiopia. This oasis, amidst miles of volcanic rock, mountain plains filled with animals, has mineral hot springs bubbling from the ground filling a water hole 30 feet deep and bathtub clear, but much hotter, much like a grotto with the profusion of palm trees surrounding the pool.

Blue Nile Falls is north of Addis, a one-day drive. Lake Tana is the source of the Nile River where the Falls pour into the Blue Nile, which provides ¾ of the water of the Nile River. It flows north to Khartoum where it joins the White Nile, flowing from the Sudan and Kenya, and then together they continue to the Mediterranean Sea at Cairo-Alexandria, Egypt. We visited the Blue Nile Gorge during the rainy season where the swollen river was spectacular.

So that is some of Ethiopia, and following a Home Leave in 1970, starting the 20 of May, we shall return to Ethiopia with pleasure. We plan on visiting many of our friends, renewing friendships enroute.

Christmas photo taken in the summer of 1969 at Filowa Hot Springs, Ethiopia

Christmas 1970

It seems like only yesterday when Christmas Greetings were mailed to all of you—such has been the year 1970 for the Sullivans. This year included a trip around the world, and four months away from Ethiopia, since it was a Home Leave Year. Definition of "Home Leave" – That time when one returns to the USA and tries to understand what has happened to fellow Americans during the three-year absence.

New impressions of the USA were formed starting with the shock of prices in New York City during our brief stay of only three days. The general impression of everyone rushing about, we wonder why? everyone in a "Bad News Syndrome", we wonder why? everyone not trusting one another, we wonder why? worry about jobs, food prices, interest rates, integration, schools, new cars, teenage problems, revolts in school and with the students and the teachers, peace marches, inflation, Spiro Agnew and Martha Mitchell, and on and on, we wonder why? Americans have the greatest country in the world, and truly have the highest portion of "Plenty". Living these many years among the "Have Nots," it is hard to understand why so many of the issues are all that important. The most vital thing in this world is health, happiness, and love for one another.

Sullivans' year in a capsule: (would you believe a long capsule?) January through April were very busy with plans for home leave taking the upper most place in their minds. In February, Hope made her debut in her first little theatre production group here in Addis Ababa, as the mother lead in "Barefoot in the Park". Gene made his debut for the first time ever, as the deliveryman, and though he was on stage but a few minutes, and his lines were mainly breathing hard, he was the shining light of the production, his reputation was established. (In April, Hope produced and directed "Bus Stop" with Gene again receiving acclaim as the bus driver, and in November, Gene played the role of the orderly, comic, in "Harvey", again stealing the show. Hope played the female lead, sister to Elwood F. Dowd and his rabbit.)

March and April and the family went camping several times, into the "bush", under the stars; a welcome relief from both the altitude of Addis Ababa and the pressure of daily living in the packed schedule of Addis. The peaceful surroundings soon sooth all feelings of pressure. The lack of traffic, if you don't include the camel trains, the lack of telephones, the lack of smog and air pollution, the lack of running water, not including the running rivers, of no electricity, in other words, pure primitive living, but a blanket of beauty surrounding one makes camping worthwhile. Of course, the sniffing of the animals around the tent, late at night, the hysterical antics if one happens upon a hill of army ants, the curious tribes people who squat down to watch your every move, the momentary panic when the car breaks down, and the car is immediately surrounded by black almost naked, spear carrying people, all add to the flavor, and make one realize they are not camping, USA style.

May started off with packing days, both to store for the summer absence, and for the Air Shipment to Hawaii. May 4th the Junior-Senior Prom, with President of the Junior Class, Jere, in charge of all arrangements. The class had worked hard throughout the year selling hamburgers to the students once a week, and to all ball games on weekends, and these proceeds of over $2000 paid for the plush dance at the New Hilton Hotel in Addis.

The night did not end at the 1:00 a.m. cut-off, as the 60 or so Junior and Senior students proceeded to the Sullivan's for the rest of the night, and the 3:00 a.m. Breakfast. Thanks to good friends helping both to chaperone and also to serve, these gay and happy persons devoured 300 cinnamon rolls, 200 eggs au gratin, a large ham, fruit salad and cake and pot after pot of coffee. At 4:30 a.m., Hope started packing her suitcases in preparation for a 9:30 a.m. departure for Athens, Rome, Tunis, Madrid and Home Leave. After an hour's catnap, the cars arrived to take the Sullivans to the airport along with the 12 remaining friends from the prom. All but Jere waved good-bye to the many friends at the airport, and Hope settled into her seat for the long sleep, seven hours to Rome. An hour later, someone rudely shaking her, "Off the plane, madam, and take all of your hand carries." A glance around was all that was needed to see that the plane was empty and on the ground. Many things flashed through her mind, before it cleared enough to realize that the plane was in Asmara, the first stop, and that Gene and the boys had deplaned, leaving all of the six hand-carries to Hope. Sleepy, tired, angry, Hope gathered all and threatened to never take this airline again, to calling the President of the company to complain. But she struggled down the steps and into the terminal building for a weapons search. This is a part of living where hijacking and bomb scares are common.

This was the pattern at each stop enroute to Rome, and late in the day they were deposited in the middle of the street, across from the small pensione on a side street in Rome. The luggage did cause a traffic jam with seemingly millions of tooting horns and gesturing yelling drivers all telling them what they thought of them, and of course in Italian. Since this experience, Hope has been studying Italian, an hour daily since return from home leave. She will be able to answer the next time. Rome seemed the worst place in the world until the welcome night's sleep, along with the bright sun and friendly people, again all fell in love with Rome. Demonstrations against Vietnam, jammed non-moving traffic, 3-mile walks in cold down-pouring rain, getting lost when a police line could not be crossed, nothing changed their minds about Rome, it captures your heart.

Tunis was the highlight of the brief trip to the USA, and this is probably the best-kept secret from the tourist. The Romans had occupied it in early centuries, and many of their ruins are still there. It is a beautiful blue and white painted city on the Mediterranean Sea. Madrid demands a return for further exploring. The highlight for the Sullivans and Hope, in particular, was the tremendous feeling which overcomes one when standing in the center of the Bull ring, on a day when there is no fight, and the stadium is deserted. It must be something like old Roman days, standing in the pit, waiting for the lions to be released into the same ring with one.

A taste of living in Washington during May and June did not excite them enough to ask for a posting in that city. The redeeming feature was that many friendships were renewed. Headquarters were set up in the Presidential Gardens, a furnished apartment complex that many military use when looking for quarters in that area. It was but 15 minutes from work for Gene, and while he worked the family played, shopping, walking up and down the aisles of the supermarkets buying items which were new since the last home leave.

A couple of trips to New York and Boston, and then heading west for a short family visit in Nebraska, overnight stop in LA where Gene became reacquainted with his new daughter-in-law and on the 24th of June----the land of the balmy breezes sweet and heavy with flower scents, blue skies, and friendly people singing their greetings – arrival in Hawaii. But this time, we did not find these attractions until later in our stay on a visit to Kauai, one of the outer islands. Honolulu is facing a smog pollution problem, the airport is being enlarged to accommodate the 747's and the only family reminder at the airport of the good old days was the water cooler with the pineapple juice, free for the sampling. Which all the Sullivans did, until it was almost empty.

The house was marvelous, though, after the first week of scrubbing, it had been rented to a group of way-out hippies according to the neighbors, but to a very upstanding nice nightclub performer, according to the realty company. Here they settled in to the marvelous routine of being Americans doing their own cleaning, cooking, painting, yard work, and so forth. Each day late in the afternoon, the roaring surf, a cool swim, the smell of steaks cooking, the relaxation of the beach, pulled them to the shore. Sundays they found all beaches very crowded, even the remote ones on the north shore, which they always had felt, they had discovered. The necessity of escape, to find a beach that was "theirs" alone for the day, drove them to the outer islands. Late in the summer, Gene and Hope found just such a place on the very northern-most remote top of Kauai. Now they have their own beach, not with a house as yet, but after living in Ethiopia, and until a house can be built, camping can be a lot of fun.

The summer was waning, and when Jere boarded the plane with a week or so stopover in Bangkok, to return in time for his senior year in Addis, it was a fact that home leave was about over. Jere was very fortunate as this year he stayed on post to finish school, and preceded the family on his return. This gave him a trip around the world on his own, and what 17 year old doesn't dream of such an opportunity?

The excitement of visiting old familiar places in the Orient was the only enticement that made leaving Hawaii possible this time. Guam, another of those secrets which American Tourists have not discovered; Taipei, which is now developed to a Hong Kong of 15 years ago; Hong Kong, a huge British City, and almost as expensive as any other large city; Bangkok, where the traffic has gotten worse, hotels all over the place, the charm of the old canals and samlors gone, now replaced with modern streets and millions of taxicabs. But the charm of the Orient still hangs over these modern developments, and visiting with old friends was enjoyable.

The stopover in Bombay enroute to Nairobi was a two-hour disaster. While Hope and the children waited in the Customs area, Gene was clearing bags and rechecking them for ongoing flight, but in addition, his bags, both of them, were missing on the plane from Bangkok, hence he spent part of his time, crawling through luggage compartments in 104-degree heat, at 2:30 a.m. in the morning, looking for the bags, which never turned up until several days and two countries later. In the process of jumping from the plane's luggage area, his zipper of the trousers broke, and this only added to his frustration. People usually do not clutch their stomachs for two days, but Gene did.

The last stop before arrival back in Ethiopia was in Nairobi, where they visited the Game Park. Their being caged in a Land Rover, driving overland hunting and shooting (with camera) a total of 19 of the 24 varieties of animals were nice enough to show themselves. Seeing how content and calm animals are in their native habitat is quite an experience, and this setting is the most beautiful in the world. Our favorites, a hundred giraffes racing along side the Land Rover, the proud ostrich on the skyline as the sun is setting, a mother lion with her two playful cubs, the grace of the gazelle and the antics of the baboon and monkeys.

The routine since return to Addis Ababa has been very hectic, with many stateside visitors, both official and non-official keeping the party schedule more full than is enjoyable. The boys, Pat, now 15 and President of his class, Jere, a senior, President of the Student Council, Jamie, Student Council representative from his class, and Chris, 10, *and a very active busy boy, are back in school and love it. They still ride their horses, and find the weekend busy with many activities. Maureen who decided to come on the trip back with the family, has been the "Chief Culinary Artist", for a salary, and has been producing marvelous meals for the family. The boys are not looking forward to her return to college, for her Junior Year, in January, as it means going back to meals by a second-rate cook, or by a busy mother, both of which leave a lost to be desired.*

Denny and Sandee are in Los Angeles, and will be facing the world outside the service in January, as he will be discharged from the Marines at that time. Denny will be returning to college and Sandee will continue working. Mike is still in Vietnam, is no longer an active Airborne Ranger, as "water-on-the-knee" retired him this summer to a desk job. He is due home this spring, and will be out of the service and back in college come fall.

So another year with the Sullivans has almost come to an end; Gene likes his job very much, is finding it a challenge, Hope is probably more busy than ever, but life is treating us the very best, with much to be grateful for. In answer to the question which many asked this summer, yes, one day we will return to the States and lead a more normal, if less exciting life, but we are in no hurry.

Love to all of our friends, MERRY CHRISTMAS AND HAPPY NEW YEAR. Gene, Hope, Maureen, Jere, Pat, Jamie, Chris, Denny and Sandee in the USA, and Mike in Vietnam.

Christmas 1971
Tenastaling! December 16, 1971

In the year 1971, Christmas for the Sullivans Gene, Hope, Pat, Jamie and Chris, will again be celebrated in Addis Ababa, Ethiopia, and with plans of a move in June, 1972 will be their last Christmas here. The scientists are finding more evidence that "man originated here", as the Rift Valley extends from the Holy Land down through the Eastern part of Africa, and the belief is now that at one time the Red Sea did not exist. Many of the villages are a six to eight hour walk from a bus route (and this means, maybe a gravel surface road which is not passable during the three-month rainy season) and the villagers live much as the people of Biblical times. The people there resent tax collectors, for example, and as they only know of their "government", a village "headman", in one village this year when the tax collector from the Central Government came, he was warned not to return; of course he did, but they "skinned" him. Needless to say, a willing replacement has not been found.

The Ethiopian Government is concentrating of land reform, and large areas are being developed, cooperatives will be established, and farmers are being trained in methods which should increase their incomes, now an average of $8 – 20 per year, most of the money exchange is on a barter system, with salt being one of the most valuable items for exchange. Aid being given to Ethiopia is not only from the U.S., but also from the UN agencies, Sweden, Germany, Red China, Russia, England, Italy, Israel, Japan, and Holland – they all contribute large sums of money, equipment and personnel aimed at improving the Ethiopian standard of living.

Addis Ababa is the headquarters of the Organization of African Unity (OAU) and the UN Economic Commission for Africa (ECA) and has fifty-two foreign Embassies represented here. His Imperial Majesty Haile Selassie I is well liked and respected throughout the world and especially in Africa. Many of the African countries look to him for guidance and assistance when dealing in African affairs. We are all amazed at his vitality, as his schedule would exhaust a young man of 25.

The year 1971 brought changes as far as the US Embassy and USAID in Addis were concerned. An amalgamation was implemented and USAID was physically moved into Embassy quarters and many of the offices, especially supportive units, were integrated. Gene's office was moved into the Economic/Commercial Section where he now shares quarters with the Commercial Attaché and the liaison officer between Embassy and ECA. While the Commercial Officer was on leave this summer for six weeks, Gene served as the Commercial Attaché for the Embassy, as well as handling his own job as Private Enterprise Officer. During this year he was promoted to Class 2 in the Foreign Service Reserve. It was during this time that Vice President Agnew made his visit to Addis Ababa, and Gene and Hope were very much involved with this visit and had the good fortune of talking personally with the Vice President. He is an utterly charming man, and though some of his "off-the-cuff" remarks were hoped for, none were forthcoming.

Hope works full time, managing the AMCOM (American Commissary) and moved this facility to new quarters in August. She keeps four sets of books in this capacity as all non-appropriated funds have been moved from under Embassy sponsorship into her office; i.e., the duty-free gas coupons, the Commissary surcharge (paid by non-military persons for privileges of using the Commissary), and Snack Bars, and the AMCOM. She is also responsible for T&A Reports (Time & Attendance) and salary payments of all personnel working in these facilities. She orders and manages the Customs clearance for items sold, talks to salesmen, keeps appointments, chairs the Board meetings, etc., all in all, she is thriving and loving every minute of her job.

In January Maureen returned to college, after four months visiting in Addis. She soon found dorm living a "drag" and in April moved into her own apartment in Boston, just a block from the Boston University campus. Because of her transfer from the University of Montana, and the extended visit to Ethiopia, she will now graduate in December 1972.

In February, Gene and Hope were both in the Way-Off Broadway Players' production of "Harvey". Gene stole the show with her Orderly performance. He had the audience believing he not only did not believe, at first, in an invisible rabbit, but finally did believe and that it was right THERE. He now feels he is of professional standards (if USAID goes out of business he might try Broadway), and is rather hard to live with, you know the old "hand to the forehead—profile-nose in the air" bit!

In late March Hope was told she had to face a trip to the Military Hospital I Frankfurt, to correct a knee problem. So in April she packed a suitcase with writing paper, books, toothbrush, and nightie for a three-week hospital stay. Two days after the examination the doctors decided a physical therapy treatment should be tried first, hence she was released to outpatient status, with three hours of daily therapy, and twenty-one hours of freedom for sightseeing and fun. At this point a cable to Gene brought him, with a suitcase of clothes for Hope, for a ten-day unexpected vacation in Germany. Gene and Hope rented a VW and drove in all directions from Frankfurt on one-day trips. Spring in Germany is lovely, more so for those who have not had the job of experiencing four seasons in at least 16 years.

In June Jere graduated with honors from ACS (American Community School) and immediately starting planning to leave home – you know, fun in Europe enroute to Georgetown Foreign Service School in Washington, DC. His aim is to reach Peking before Dad. His parents did manage to keep him at home until the first part of July (they just withheld the airplane ticket) when he departed for the adult world and "life on his own".

To have maintained a family life with seven children – and suddenly realize you were now parents of only three teenagers (almost for Chris), was a big adjustment for Gene and Hope. They know they are finally joining the "normal", but reluctantly. To sit down to dinner at the large round table, which was originally built to accommodate all nine, has been difficult. To ease the transition, Gene and Hope, Jamie and Chris went to Greece for R&R vacation (Rest and Recuperation). Pat chose to forfeit his R&R at this time as he now attends Ground School (navigation, etc.) three nights a week.

On November 27 he left us as usual at 5:30 a.m., and returned to announce he had made his first solo flight. He will never be earthbound again. Now he is working on cross-country flights, lasting about four hours each. He is also required to work on the engines, make his flight checkouts, etc. At school he is a good student, but loves the extras too, photography, stage crewing for drama productions, and so forth. His schedule is probably heavier than his mother's!

But to return to Greece, the four of us rented a new Renault station wagon, which is a fantastic automobile in all ways, and started driving north along the east coast of Greece. The trip to Thassos, a northern island off of the city of Kavala, near the Greek-Turkish border, took us a week, but actual driving time is only about 13 hours. If we liked a place we stopped and stayed. Lunch on the beach with roaring surf, blue skies, sharing our bread, cheese, and salami with the sea gulls and fishermen is an experience not to be forgotten. Fortunately, Gene and his eight years of Greek background, could communicate with all, and this was our entry into many non-tourist areas. Of course we enjoyed the historical spots, enjoyed swimming in crystal clear water, joined the summer enthusiasm of the Greeks at their festivals and sitting outside eating late into the night. At Kavala, arrangements were made with a highly organized and very helpful Tourist Bureau for a few days on Thassos. We know now why starting with Shelly, persons wanted a Greek island on which to live. It is next to heaven. We chose one which had a summer population explosion, but these were mainly European and Greek visitors, as this area is off the American tourist track. The days were lazy, and lengthened into two weeks. Greece has now taken second to Hawaii among our favorite places.

Our return to Athens via the West Coast of Greece was marred only the fact we could not drive a rented car into Yugoslavia, but instead we discovered Delphi. Walking in the ruins of Apollo's temple was a fantastic spiritual experience. Though flooded with the summer tourists – all shuttering and snapping pictures, and grouped into bunches listening to their guides for a few minutes, then hopping on a tour bus for the next stop, one could find a corner to "listen" to the past. By comparison, Pompeii in Italy was a busy market village, Delphi was a temple, and the feeling of both exists to this day.

But all good things become memories, and our return to Addis, the busy routine of work and school bring us to September, October, November. The Way-off Broadway players presented "Dial M for Murder", with Hope and Gene working backstage. Because the Thanksgiving Luncheon for the American Women's Club was so successful last year, again Hope was asked to organize the affair. This event, given in the gardens of the Embassy Residence (we have 13 months of sunshine, according to Ethiopian Calendar, with mild 60 degree to 70 degree during the day with 30 degree to 45 degree in the evenings) had an overflow of 250 women this year, members and their non-American guests. Hope won't bore you with the logistical details, those who have done this know, and those who have not don't care, but let it suffice to say 260 pounds of turkey, 40 cans of cranberry sauce, 15 gallons of gravy, dressing, salad, 40 cans of sweet potatoes, 27 dozen rolls, 42 pumpkin and apple pies were demolished. The plans started in August with the ordering of the Turkeys. Various women were "helper" cooks but all to Hope's recipes and supervision.

But this only interrupted one day of the six weeks rehearsals of the "Sound of Music."

With a cast of 64, Hope and Gene directed and produced a favorite over the years. We were delighted when we sold out all performances, receiving raves. The last night we even had children sitting on the floor, Ethiopians bringing their own chairs, rather than miss the production. Addis does not have a theatre, and is starved for entertainment. Of course, we had many "tragedies" or at least, near tragedies. The first night at 6:45 with a curtain call for 7:30, all power in the area was turned off. We put makeup on by candlelight, dressed the stage of the Government-sponsored music school with candles, and planned a Shakespearean Theatre presentation. The director, Hope, ignored the pleas and moans of the sound man who said his tape recorder would not work with candlepower. But one minute before curtain, on the downbeat of the overture, the lights came on. Gene had called the Power Board at the Ministry, and managed to convince them to restore power. This happened two of the three nights, the third night the Royal Family was present.

Our Jamie at 14 was the second oldest child in the Von Trapp family, and though his boy soprano voice is starting to change, he did manage to maintain it during the "Sound of Music". He is busy taking piano lessons, needs to be punished to stop practicing, reads for hours, and has just discovered girls (other than mothers).

Many weekends during the year have been spent traveling around Ethiopia, and of course, camping in Langano (a lake about 4 hours drive south of Addis). Gene has finally joined the crowd, he does not complain loudly any more, and he did buy a tent when he found the new ones are so easy to erect. Camping for Gene, means driving the car to the location chosen, taking his porch chair out of the back of the car, and sitting in the sun to direct Boy Scout Chris in setting up of the camp. However, he almost sold it after the last trip to Langano as along about 11:00 p.m. on a dark, moonless night, a snorting, bubbling, half whinny, half roaring hippo emerged from the lake right in front of the tent. After we all returned from orbit, we followed the hippo (cowards that we are, with beams from the flashlight) until he disappeared into the underbrush. Needless to say, persons were rather hesitant to jump into the lake for a swim the next day. Probably our favorite place is Awash Game Park where there are many wild animals, also snakes, spiders, and crocodiles. This year after an absence of several years, lions have again been spotted. But to watch a herd of Oryx or gazelle leaping in what seems to be a choreographed dance through the high grass is an inspiring sight.

Though our family is flung worldwide, Mike re-upped in the Army in June after a discharge in March, asking again for Vietnam; Denny in Los Angeles, school daytime, working at night, Sandee, his wife also working; Maureen in Boston; Jere in Washington; Mom, Dad and three boys in Africa, we all wish you a happy, healthy, fruitful New Year.

The Sullivans

P.S. And a word about AID. Though we sit here in Africa, or Afghanistan, Chad, or Washington, waiting for Congress to recognize they have a right to eliminate Foreign Aid, but do they have a moral responsibility in the method and way of doing so?

Waiting means no salaries, no funds for even a pencil, though men are continuing to work. It does mean that we have the responsibility of answering the confused questions of host-country nationals who in their beginning struggles at establishment of free nations do not understand the American "democratic" process nor the fact we, the American Government, are not flat broke. Yes, we have confidence that our salaries will be forthcoming – we hope it won't be delayed until Mark or April or ? ; that Foreign Aid is needed, and good and will no doubt continue in some form; that some of us will not be part of the new Foreign Aid; but we are a dedicated people, or why would we have chosen to live in areas so underdeveloped by U.S. standards that it is hard to imagine the conditions until you experience them?

Christmas 1972

Nineteen Hundred and Seventy-two is running out, and in the lives of the Sullivan's it has been a year of sadness, joys, changes and rebuilding. The year started with a marvelous automobile trip with Gene when he went to Dira Dawa, in southeast Ethiopia near the Somali Border, on a business trip. This is a hot low altitude area near the Red Sea with a strong Indian-Arabic influence, and at one time was the thriving business center near the port to Ethiopia. Assab, is now replacing Djibouti as the seaport entry to Ethiopia with the building of a new paved road from the Red Sea to Addis Ababa. The boys, Pat, Jamie, Chris and I spent the days while Gene was working sightseeing and haunting the little shops. We made a stop at Kalubi, a church that Coptic Christians of Ethiopia consider with the same awe and religious fervor that Catholic Christians consider Lourdes in France. This church sits high on a mountain top, and each year in January they have a festival where the faithful walk from all over Ethiopia to the Church, a mass of humanity of about 20 to 30 thousand persons, where they ask God to grant favors. On receiving these favors during the year, the faithful return the following year to thank God for his goodness. Part of the superstition is that they must return by the same transportation as the previous year, if they walked they must return walking, by bus they must return by bus. There is the old story of the woman who received her wish, an upswing in her financial status, and returned in her new auto instead of on foot. When she was backing into a parking place at Kalubi, the brakes failed to work and her auto went down the side of the mountain.

It is an inspiring sensation, very colorful with the Priests in their elaborately gold and silver threaded embroidered robes and hats. All carry flywhisks, an object common in Ethiopia, made of the hairs from the tails of horses or monkeys on a handle. These are used to keep the "sticky" flies, of which there are millions, from your face. The flies in Ethiopia, seek any areas that is moist, since the climate is practically zero humidity, and this means they love your eyes, mouth and nose. The Ethiopian children in the rural areas are so accustomed to flies, or maybe they are so tired of chasing them, that you can always see a child with 100 to 200 flies glued to his face. Enroute back to Addis we made a stop in the Awash National Game Park, and were fortunate enough to see the last of the nineteen species of animals roaming the area, which we had not seen before, -- the zebra in a herd of about 200.

The year started out happy and gay, but a week after our return, Gene became very ill, and five days later died of Blackwater Fever Malaria.

Friends and residents of Addis Ababa came forth en masse to offer help and sympathy at this time, and in the week that it took for the clearance papers needed to ship Gene to the U.S., at least 1500 persons visited the house. Many of these were associated with Gene in connection with his job, and consequently I did not know them. Ethiopian tradition enforces at least five days mourning where friends come and sit and cry with the surviving members of the family. I mean really and truly cry. Though this is a bit foreign to our culture and customs, I provided the food and drink required and expressed my appreciation, as this was an expression of love and respect of Gene. At his funeral Memorial in Addis the Church was overflowing, and again the widow is required to stand at the door at the end of the service to receive condolences. I then proceeded to the States for services and temporary internment in Omaha for Gene.

I returned to Addis in the middle of February to continue with my job and with the school year for the boys. Though a bit unusual I requested that I be allowed to stay in Addis Ababa beyond the month allowed in the Foreign Service in a case of death of the employee, and this was granted on the grounds that I was employed by the American Embassy. At this time my contract expires in June 1973, but based on the past nine months of adjustment for both the children and I, I have just signed my contract for an additional year, June 1974. Adjustments this year have been many and in some cases great, but all of us are happy and busy in our new life. We miss Gene, but find that only the happy memories remain and we laugh many times knowing he would appreciate the current event. In July, I again traveled to Hawaii where Dennis and Jerry met me, and Gene was buried in his final resting place at the National Cemetery of the Pacific, with a Naval Ceremony.

The boys chose to return immediately to school, and each had their bad moments but have each matured and become more serious about school, all achieving the honor roll. Chris, now 12, is very active in sports, boy scouts and his social life. He loves to dance, and can't understand why mother won't let him attend the teenage parties with girls 14, 15, 16, since as he says, "Well, they like to dance with me because I'm such a good dancer". He won two trophies in the bowling league, for high bowler, and 1st place Team. He is personality plus, with all parents commenting on what a wonderful boy he is. Other friends ask both he and Jamie for camping weekends, and several of the father shave stepped in and are filling the 'dad' role, needless to say much appreciated on my part. Jamie, at 15, stands six feet tall, active on the baseball team, bowling, and loves theatre productions. Does he take after his mother? He participated in several shows this year, and was a lead dancer in the "Music Man". Pat, at 17, is now a man probably reaching maturity faster than he would have due to circumstances this past year. He is my 'man of the house', and willingly takes over many responsibilities which need to be done, with mom now both mother and dad and earning the living. He is very much involved with flying, his first love, now has about 75 hours in the air. He flew a plane to Nairobi three times this year as co-pilot for check-outs. He worked this summer with Axum Air, a charter company here in Addis Ababa, flying off to the south for a week or two at a time, flying crews to sites for Tenneco, an oil exploration company. We had one exciting time this fall, when he took off one morning on a trip to Dire Dawa. I think the Sullivans should avoid this area, and when he did not return at 7 p.m., I put in a call to find him. This is normally a round trip of about 4 ½ hours. By 8 p.m. the report was in that he had not reached Dira Dawa, and was lost. Nothing could be done during the night, except planning, so early in the morning, again the Addis community came to my rescue and 11 planes from the MAAG American Military took off on the search. My flyer friends donating their time, all together with the pilots and lookers, about 50 persons. I spent the day receiving visitors and answering the phone with the latest reports, but none were encouraging until about 2 p.m. when a report of an emergency signal received from the ground in the middle of the desert, was reported by one pilot. The happy word came in about 6 p.m. when the plane was sighted on the ground, and by 11 p.m. I had word he was fine, and would fly his own plane back the following day. He told his story upon his return, that he had filed his flight plan, had landed enroute on schedule for refueling; in Ethiopia you refuel your own plane from barrels left at certain dirt strips; had taken off again, but had taken the wrong check point and headed the wrong direction. This also is not unusual for Ethiopia, since until you are within a twenty-minute range of the five airports in Ethiopia there is no radio contact. Also there are no accurate maps in Ethiopia, it is not unusual for a pilot to be looking up with an altimeter reading of 9500 feet at a mountain which is marked 9000 feet on a map. This makes the flying interesting to say the least, but the pilots are aware of this and learn from flying experience, and memory.

By the time he had rectified his error, he was almost out of gas, knowing he could not reach Dira Dawa, he looked for a place to land his plane, which he did, on a 60-mile long dry salt river bed. He spent the night, guarding the plane, and fortunately he was in an area of friendly nomad tribesmen, who brought him food and water, and spent the night with him. The water, given to him in a goatskin bag, was dirty brown in color, the food mostly soupy goat milk yogurt type, but much appreciated. The fantastic thing about it was he had no after effects from this food or water. Other than he was worried about 'mom' he thought the whole thing a lark, and immediately took off again two days later. Mom, well, she is all for his flying, and knows that he is a good pilot. Jerry is in school in the second year at Georgetown Foreign Service School, Washington DC. Maureen graduates from Boston University next year. Mike is now out of the service and working in Honolulu, and Denny and Sandee are in school and working in Los Angeles.

In spite of the fact our lives have changed in routine, I am working harder but still love it, this year I added a couple of more responsibilities doing a research report of the HSIU, the university here in Ethiopia, on their staffing projections for the next 10 years, and supervising all the duty free imports for the American Government personnel via the Embassy. I am responsible for the non-appropriated *activities in the Embassy, gas coupons, Snack bars, Commissary, etc., managing, keeping the books, supervising the personnel. It keeps me hopping, but it is interesting. Life doesn't stop there; I still do my extra curricular affairs, such as Producing, directing "Music Man" this fall, with a cast of 84, singers, dancers and actors. Presenting it at the City Hall Theatre, to full houses, it was not only a financial success, (for charity) but an artistic success, plus a lot of fun. The annual Thanksgiving luncheon given for non-American guests of the American Women's community again served 250 persons under my direction. Only difference in all of these activities was the absence of Gene, who in the past donated much advice, comfort and physical help, of which I was not completely aware until this year.*

And why do we all choose to stay in Ethiopia, instead of coming home to American? The obvious answer is that we have lived all these years overseas since leaving Maryland in 1956, and we enjoy the life. The three boys still at home with me have been born and reared overseas, and love the life, they like the contact with people, the culture which is so different than America, and currently, Ethiopia is home for us. We have accepted and made our new life in familiar surroundings, growing rather than changing. The Ethiopian people have been kind and helpful, and are very flattered that we have chosen to stay. It is really easier for us to slow down the car and go around a donkey in the road, or a herd of cows going home from the field for the night, than to dodge rush hour traffic in the U.S. We find that reading in the evening is marvelous, and that we don't miss the latest TV show. That boiling our water, filtering it, really makes better tasting water than tap water from the sink. That you are never bored learning a new people and culture. That the reason why the insurance company cannot include a missing box in a survey report is that the man making the survey can't see it. That the reason why it takes six hours on three different days to renew a driver's license is because 10 people need employment and it takes that long to contact all of them. That you have to buy tubeless tires, and put a tube in them after all tubeless tires are the latest tires (here), but if you hit one hole or rock on the underdeveloped, badly maintained rocky roads, the tubeless tire doesn't work. You laugh when your phone doesn't work, or the electricity is off, or the pipes became stuffed with dirt and you have no water for a couple of weeks, while they dig the whole yard up looking for the pipes. You smile and make your report to the police when the horses disappear, after all it is the season when all the horses are stolen so they can be used for transport of the coffee beans from Jimma to Addis, and if one wants to make a bit of money he must have a horse. Chances are that you will find your horse when the season is over. You ponder when the night zabanya (guard) rushes in and is practically hysterical because the day zabanya said a bad word to him, especially when he usually fades into the woodwork. It is our way of life to deal and trade in two or three currencies at the same time, converting in your head, to speak and converse in two languages, sometimes three at the same time. Dinner is always on the table when you come home, no worries about when to find time to iron, to leave the dishes on the table, knowing they will be on the table clean the next day, to have a marvelous day after day of sunshine with no sidewalks to shovel or grass to cut, to have a good school with only 325 students in grades 1 – 12, virtually free of any problems of the American community, to have activities for the children, like bowling league, horses to ride, gymkhana's, Saturday baseball competitions, Family picnics, square dancing on Friday nights, community activities which involve doing charity works for the desperately needy Ethiopians, teen club outings, touring Ethiopian cultural spots, camping and fishing where you can catch Blue Nile Perch which weigh up to 300 – 350 pounds. All these things make us love Ethiopia and our life overseas, and have helped us decide, "Life is again gay and Happy".

Merry Christmas from Addis Ababa, Ethiopia, from the Sullivans: Hope, Pat, Jamie and Chris. We wish to thank all of you for your kind thoughts and wishes this year especially. This letter brings you up to date on us, and we pray that your coming year will be as good to you as God has been to us this past year – He took Gene from us, but gave us so much in return.

About the Author: M.H. Sullivan

Prior to moving to New Hampshire in 1977, the author spent most of the previous 20+ years living overseas. As the daughter of a U.S. State Department diplomat, she lived in Korea, Taiwan, the Philippines, Thailand, and Ethiopia.

After graduating from Boston University, Maureen worked in Washington, D.C. as a travel agent and then as a staff aide on Capitol Hill. After getting her Master's degree from Simmons College Graduate Program in Management, Maureen worked as a technical writer in the software industry and later in the medical devices industry. She moved to NH in 1977, married in 1978, and has lived in NH ever since. She has two daughters and a granddaughter.

Maureen was the publisher of the *Southern NH Children's Directory* and related publications from 1994 to 1999. She is the author of three novels and a memoir.

Books by M.H. Sullivan:

Trail Magic: Lost in Crawford Notch

The Sullivan Saga: Memories of an Overseas Childhood

Jet Trails: Looking for Blue Skies

Goodbye Woodstock: The Last Reunion

For more information, go to www.romagnoli-publications.com.

Printed in Poland
by Amazon Fulfillment
Poland Sp. z o.o., Wrocław
27 September 2023

6e03b7f2-83b8-474c-b741-f4423601ddfcR01